William Daunt

Eighty-five years of Irish history

1800-1885. Vol. 1

William Daunt

Eighty-five years of Irish history
1800-1885. Vol. 1

ISBN/EAN: 9783337124908

Printed in Europe, USA, Canada, Australia, Japan

Cover: Foto ©ninafisch / pixelio.de

More available books at **www.hansebooks.com**

EIGHTY-FIVE YEARS OF IRISH HISTORY
1800—1885.

"We know our duty to our Sovereign, and are loyal: we also know our duty to ourselves, and are resolved to be free."—*Declaration of Dungannon Volunteers*, 1782.

"You may make the Union binding as a law, but you can never make it obligatory on conscience. It will be obeyed as long as England is strong; but resistance to it will be in the abstract a duty, and the exhibition of that resistance will be merely a question of prudence."—RIGHT HON. WILLIAM SAURIN.

"Union is Irish alienation."—RIGHT HON. HENRY GRATTAN.

"Union is not unity. Heterogeneous and repugnant things may be arbitrarily tied together, but this is not unity. Closer contact elicits the repugnances which rend all external bonds asunder."—CARDINAL MANNING.

"Independence sends life through all the veins of a nation."—GOLDWIN SMITH.

EIGHTY-FIVE YEARS

OF

IRISH HISTORY.

1800—1885.

BY

WILLIAM JOSEPH O'NEILL DAUNT.

IN TWO VOLUMES.
VOL. I.

LONDON:
WARD AND DOWNEY,
12, YORK STREET, COVENT GARDEN, W.C.
1886.

PREFACE.

The enactment of the Legislative Union in 1800 has been followed by almost incessant agitation to obtain its repeal. The desire of the Irish people to recover their right of domestic legislation is as natural as a sick man's desire for restoration to health. Ireland's vital need is Self-Government; the exclusive control and development of her own resources. "Placed," says the late Robert Holmes, "on the western skirt of Europe, with three-fourths of her shores washed by the Atlantic, after the discovery of a new world had opened to European enterprise new objects of adventure and new sources of aggrandisement, Ireland seemed destined to be an important connecting link in the intercourse between the Eastern and Western Hemispheres. Independent of the discovery of America, and the new field thereby opened for commercial enterprise, the situation of Ireland seemed peculiarly fitted for maritime pre-eminence. . . . Ireland, too, had before her many glorious examples of what free States, very inferior to her in extent of territory and other natural advantages, could achieve by commercial daring. The powers of independent existence seemed to be marked in her structure in such bold characters by nature, that it required the unceasing efforts of an active and malignant policy to defeat the obvious purposes of Creation." *

That active and malignant policy was never more perniciously exercised than in its efforts, first to corrupt, and then to suppress, the Irish Legislature. To emancipate our country from its deadly influence is the purpose which has never been absent from the Irish mind for eighty-five years. It is a purpose consistent with the most devoted loyalty to the Crown. Its achievement would give strength and stability to Irish Constitutional loyalty by removing that fruitful source of discontent—the denial to Ireland of her indefeasible right of Self-Government.

In the following pages I have traced our exertions to recover that right—exertions in which I have been an humble but zealous participator.

During the recent debates that have followed Mr. Gladstone's introduction of the Government of Ireland Bill, an effervescent Orange member referred to the rebellion of 1798 as the result of Grattan's Constitution. "It was Pitt who did it," exclaimed Mr. Gladstone. This utterance of the Premier is extremely valuable. There is in England a nearly universal unacquaintance with the real character of the Union, as well as of the

---

* "The Case of Ireland Stated." By Robert Holmes, Esq. 1847.

sanguinary means employed to achieve it. Therefore it is important that the English people should learn, on the high authority of the Premier, that the Act of Union is not only leprous with corruption but encrusted with blood—with the blood of the multitudes who, on both sides, fell in the rebellion which was deliberately provoked and fomented by Pitt and his agents as an indispensable preliminary to the destruction of the Irish Parliament. It was indeed Pitt who did it.

It is inspiriting to hear Mr. Gladstone sympathetically quoting from Grattan such a sentence as this: "I demand the continued severance of the Parliaments with a view to the continued and everlasting unity of the Empire."

"Was that," continued Mr. Gladstone, "a flight of rhetoric, an audacious paradox? No, it was the statement of a problem which other countries have solved, and under circumstances much more difficult than ours."

Mr. Stansfeld is equally explicit in his recognition of the just claim of Ireland to autonomy. "Ireland," says the right hon. gentleman, "is a nation, and the denial of her nationality is an insult to her people." And again: "I believe in nationality—I believe in Irish nationality."

Such a declaration from a Cabinet Minister shows a vast change from the time when Lord John Russell coldly spoke of substituting what he called "Imperial nationality" for Irish nationality; or when Sir Robert Peel styled the legislative Union a "compact" too deeply rooted in the Constitution to suffer disturbance.

Our cause has many elements of strength. The first is its plain justice. The second is the great and rapid progress of English opinion in our favour, which progress has been accelerated by the Parnellite organisation in and out of the House of Commons. A third omen of our strength is, I think, the hostility of the Orange party; for it is a simple fact that their hostility has been usually followed by the triumph of whatever measure they opposed. They tried to prevent Her Majesty's accession to the Throne, and to make the Duke of Cumberland King. The traitorous plot fell through, and Her Majesty reigns. They declared that they never would permit the Emancipation of the Catholics—the Catholics were, of course, emancipated. They would not tolerate Municipal Reform. Orange opposition had its usual result—Municipal Reform was triumphantly carried. Then came Disestablishment of the State Church—Orange thunder shook the firmament. "No surrender" was shouted from every Orange platform. As on all previous occasions, Orange hostility was followed by the exhibition of Orange impotence—the State Church was disestablished. They now assail Home Rule with the menaces to which we are accustomed; they are to shake the torch of civil war all over Ireland with terrific glare; ditches are to be lined with heroes bearing rifles and Bibles—in short, Orange opposition is to be as formidable to Home Rule as it has been to the Queen's accession, and to all the other measures unpalatable to Orange prejudice. Mr. Gladstone accurately appreciates the value of their threats. "If," he says, "upon any occasion, by any individual or section, violent measures have been threatened in certain emergencies, I think the best compliment I can pay to those who have threatened us is to take no notice whatever of the threats, but to treat them as momentary ebullitions."

It is especially interesting at the present juncture to look back at the time of the Union, at the acts and objects of its promoters and of their opponents, and at the successive agitations to shake off an unnatural and irritating yoke—a yoke as repulsive to the feelings of the great majority of the Irish nation as it is injurious to their material interests.

W. J. O'NEILL DAUNT.

KILCASCAN, CO. CORK.
    June, 1886.

CONTENTS.

CHAPTER I.
RECORDS OF THE UNION PERIOD 1

CHAPTER II.
HOW THE REBELLION OF 1798 WAS PROVOKED . . 14

CHAPTER III.
PARLIAMENTARY CORRUPTION IN ENGLAND AND IRELAND 49

CHAPTER IV.
HOW IRISH DISCONTENT IS VIEWED BY SOME ENGLISH WRITERS 67

CHAPTER V.
THE DIPLOMACY OF MARQUIS CORNWALLIS . . . 76

CHAPTER VI.
REPEAL AGITATION—SECTARIAN OBSTRUCTION . . 91

CHAPTER VII.
THE EMANCIPATION STRUGGLE 113

CHAPTER VIII.
THE ZEAL OF A PACIFICATOR 139

CHAPTER IX.
ANTI-TITHE AGITATION OF 1831-2 154

CHAPTER X.
THE DISESTABLISHMENT CAMPAIGN 168

CHAPTER XI.
STATE CHURCH ARGUMENTS EXAMINED . . . 175

CHAPTER XII.
PROGRESS OF THE ANTI-TITHE MOVEMENT . 205

CHAPTER XIII.
THE REPEAL CAMPAIGN OF 1832 223

CHAPTER XIV.
ELECTIONEERING AGITATION IN 1832 . . . 247

CHAPTER XV.
NATIONAL COUNCIL CONVENED BY O'CONNELL IN 1833   263

CHAPTER XVI.
IRISH POLICY OF THE FIRST REFORMED PARLIAMENT   278

CHAPTER XVII.
RESULTS OF THE COERCION ACT OF 1833 . . . 285

CHAPTER XVIII.
THE REPEAL DEBATE OF 1834 303

EIGHTY-FIVE YEARS

OF

IRISH HISTORY, 1800—1885.

CHAPTER I.

MR. GLADSTONE'S TESTIMONY.

AMONG the traditionary anecdotes of the Union struggle, it is told that when Lord Castlereagh visited Mr. Shapland Carew, the Member for the County Wexford, in order to offer him a peerage and some other more substantial advantages, as inducements to vote for the Legislative Union, Mr. Carew indignantly exclaimed: "I will expose your insolent offer in the House of Commons to-night; I will get up in my place and charge you with the barefaced attempt to corrupt a legislator."

Castlereagh coolly replied: "Do so, if you will. But if you do, I will immediately get up and contradict you in presence of the House. I will declare, upon my honour, that you have uttered a falsehood; and I shall follow up that declaration by demanding satisfaction as soon as we are beyond the reach of the Serjeant-at-Arms."

Mr. Carew, it is said, desired the noble Secretary of State to get out of his house with all possible expedition, on pain of being kicked down the hall-door steps by his footman. Castlereagh accordingly withdrew; but Carew did not execute his threat of exposing the transaction to the House. It were idle to speculate on the motives which induced him to practise that forbearance. The incident vividly illustrates the desperate and unprincipled determination with which the Government and its tool pursued their object.

The Irish aristocracy and gentry of that period were a race of men who lived high, drank hard, fought duels, and often pursued a career of reckless extravagance. These habits were generated by their situation, which rendered them, to a very considerable extent, the irresponsible monopolists of local power. They largely partook of the national taste for splendour and magnificence—a taste which, duly regulated, tends to adorn the land and to refine and civilise the people; but which, in the circumstances then affecting the upper classes in Ireland, ensnared its votaries into that wasteful and ruinous expenditure which threw so many of their number upon the worst expedients of political corruption to retrieve their shattered fortunes.

The penal laws had wrought a most disastrous

separation of the people from the gentry. The dominant Protestant party—the jovial, fox-hunting, claret-drinking squirearchy—all looked down on their Catholic countrymen as a totally inferior race of beings, intended by God Almighty for the inheritance of serfdom, and with whom it would be a degradation to suppose they could have the least community of interest. They were trained from the cradle to look thus scornfully on the Catholics. Contempt was a doctrine of their political Bible.

On the part of the Catholics, the moral consequences of the penal gulf that divided them from their more favoured countrymen were various, according to the varying dispositions of men. There was, amongst some, the reaction of deep and deadly hate. Others were awed into a social idolatry of Protestants. I knew one most respectable and very wealthy Catholic merchant who declared that when a boy at school, about the year 1780, he felt overwhelmed and bewildered at the honour of being permitted to play marbles with a Protestant schoolfellow. Every Protestant cobbler and tinker conceived himself superior to the Catholic of ancient lineage and ample inheritance. No wonder that there should have been offensive assumption on the one side, and rankling animosity as well as degrading servility on the other, when the law placed all the good things of the State in the hands of the few, and excluded the many from all participation in place, power, and emolument.

The Protestant aristocracy of Ireland wanted

that wholesome check, that strong guarantee of political honesty, which would have arisen from contact with and representative dependence on the people. A whole people never can be bribed. But the people—the Catholic masses of Ireland—were a political nonentity for nearly the whole century. They formed no element of power, no ingredient in the speculating politician's calculations; a Lord Chancellor announced that the law of the land assumed their non-existence. And even after some of the restrictions on Catholics had been removed, the sentiment of Protestant contempt survived in full force, preventing that cordial coalition, that thorough mutual understanding between the two classes, which alone could have availed to defeat the ministerial assault on Irish legislative independence.

The Protestant nobility and squirearchy, half fearing and entirely despising their disfranchised countrymen, had for a long time looked upon themselves rather in the light of an English garrison occupying the country than as the legitimate aristocracy of Ireland. The notorious Doctor Patrick Duigenan, in a speech against the Catholic claims delivered in the House of Commons, 4th February, 1793, said: "In truth the Protestants in Ireland are but a British garrison in an enemy's country."* Yet, despite the colossal power of corruption, and the pernicious influence of religious

---

* Speech, page 51. I possess the Doctor's oration in the shape of a pamphlet published at the time.

bigotry, the very circumstance of their residing in, and making laws for, Ireland, had begun to produce its natural results on the minds of her domestic rulers about the time of the American war. The spark of patriotism had ignited the Protestant heart, and blazed up with dazzling brilliancy in the memorable and successful struggle of the Irish volunteers for Free Trade in 1779, and for constitutional independence in 1782.

But—fatal error!—the Catholics were not incorporated into the Constitution. Glorious and imposing was the superstructure; but it was fated to perish, because its foundations were too narrow to sustain its weight. It did not rest on the broad basis of the people. Yet the Catholics had done their best to assist in achieving the triumph of that period. Doctor Duigenan, in the speech already cited,* bears the following testimony: "The Catholics," he says, "not only mixed with Protestants in most of the volunteer corps throughout the kingdom, were regimented, carried arms publicly, and learned military tactics, but they formed themselves into large and numerous corps, well armed, accoutred, and instructed in military exercise, and marched, and appeared in military array on all occasions as other volunteers. I saw myself a corps of Dublin volunteers, called the Irish Brigade, nineteen in twenty of which were Catholics, march through the city of Dublin, and

---

* Pages 23, 24.

close to the gates of the Castle, the residence of His Majesty's Lieutenant, along with other volunteers, to be reviewed in His Majesty's Phœnix Park."

Elsewhere, in the same speech, the Doctor says: "Thousands of Irish Catholics carried arms during the season of volunteering without having procured any license whatever." *

This evidence of the active part borne by the Catholics in the national struggle to recover the Irish Constitution occurs in a speech directed against the admission of the Catholics to any of the privileges of the Constitution they had helped to establish. Sir Jonah Barrington, in recording the activity of the Catholics in the volunteer organisation, adds that they placed themselves under the command of Protestant officers.†

The Protestant patriotism of 1782 was a gallant and a goodly display; yet it presented some anomalous features. There was in it a great deal real, and something illusory. It was a curious sight, that of men in arms to enfranchise their country, yet resolved to perpetuate the disfranchisement of the great body of its inhabitants; men in arms to assert the honour and dignity of Ireland, yet entertaining a cordial contempt for five out of every six of its people. In truth, the Protestants had been so long accustomed to omit the Catholics from their political arithmetic that they had learned to look upon themselves—being then about one-

---

* Page 49.   † "Rise and Fall of the Irish Nation," chap. xvi.

sixth—as forming the sum total of the Irish nation. The thunder of Grattan had not yet shaken the strongholds of their bigotry. Their ambition culminated in the establishment of a free constitution, of whose political benefits they were to be the monopolists.

Another anomaly was to be found in the fact that the bitterest enemies of Catholic Emancipation were sometimes the most strenuous champions of theoretic Irish independence. At a meeting of some of the friends of the volunteer movement, held in their house in Grafton Street, which Flood, Grattan, and Bartholomew Hoare attended, Flood, whose hostility to the Catholic claims was inflexible, proposed to his *confrères* a plan of total separation from England. Grattan said: "If you persevere in your proposition I certainly shall not oppose it here; but I shall quit this room, and proceed at once to the Castle—to my Sovereign's Castle—and there disclose the treason, and denounce the traitor."

Yet Flood, the separatist, could not tolerate the notion of emancipating the Catholics; whilst Grattan, the zealous friend of the Catholics, and the champion of a free Irish Parliament in connection with the British Crown, denounced the ultra patriotism of the Protestant ascendency statesman, as treason. Flood, I need not add, withdrew his proposition.*

---

* This anecdote was told me by O'Connell, to whom it had

Emancipation, under an Irish Parliament, would have speedily blended all classes of religionists in one political mass. But the Catholics continued unemancipated; the Protestants remained a separate and exclusive band, distinct from, and rarely sympathising with, their fellow-countrymen. Thus placed far aloof from the people, there was little to countervail the corrupting influence of a profligate Court with which they were brought into close contact, and which derived immense facilities of corruption from the number of pocket boroughs in the Irish House of Commons. With an unreformed Parliament and an unemancipated people, the distributors of place and pension enjoyed an easy sway. The pension list was swollen to an enormous magnitude; the number of sinecures incessantly augmented; and parliamentary profligacy came at last to be so general, that men lost all sense of its shame through the force of its prevalence.

Whilst the Government thus practised corruption on the largest scale, there were social vices peculiar to the period which extensively prevailed among the upper ranks. Of these practices the principal were duelling and drinking, which were carried to an excess happily now almost incredible. Take, for a specimen, Mr. Bagenal of Dunleckny, in the County Carlow—*King* Bagenal, as he was called throughout his extensive territories; and within

---

been narrated by Bartholomew Hoare, one of the persons present on the occasion referred to.

their bounds no monarch was ever more absolute. Of high Norman lineage, of manners elegant, fascinating, polished by extensive intercourse with the great world, of princely income and of boundless hospitality, Mr. Bagenal possessed all the qualities and attributes calculated to procure for him popularity with every class. A terrestrial paradise was Dunleckny for all lovers of good wine, good horses, good dogs, and good society. His stud was magnificent, and he had a large number of capital hunters at the service of visitors who were not provided with steeds of their own. He derived great delight from encouraging the young men who frequented his house to hunt, drink, and solve points of honour at twelve paces. His politics were popular; he was mover of the grant of £50,000 to Grattan in 1782. He was at that time member for the County Carlow.

Enthroned at Dunleckny, he gathered round him a host of spirits congenial to his own. He had a tender affection for pistols; a brace of which implements, loaded, were often laid before him on the dinner-table. After dinner the claret was produced in an unbroached cask; Bagenal's practice was to tap the cask with a bullet from one of his pistols, whilst he kept the other pistol *in terrorem* for any of the *convives* who should fail in doing ample justice to the wine.

Nothing could be more impressive than the bland, fatherly, affectionate air with which the old gentleman used to impart to his junior guests the results of his own experience, and the moral lessons which should regulate their conduct through life.

"In truth, my young friends, it behoves a youth entering the world to make a character for himself. Respect will only be accorded to character. A young man must show his proofs. I am not a quarrelsome person—I never was—I hate your mere duellist; but experience of the world tells me there are knotty points of which the only solution is the saw-handle. Rest upon your pistols, my boys! Occasions will arise in which the use of them is absolutely indispensable to character. A man, I repeat, must show his proofs—in this world courage will never be taken upon trust. I protest to heaven, my dear young friends, that I advise you exactly as I should advise my own son."

And having thus discharged his conscience, he would look blandly round upon his guests with the most patriarchal air imaginable.

His practice accorded with his precept. Some pigs, the property of a gentleman who had recently settled near Dunleckny, strayed into an enclosure of King Bagenal's and rooted up a flower-knot. The incensed monarch ordered that the porcine trespassers should be shorn of their ears and tails; and he transmitted the severed appendages to the owner of the swine with an intimation that he, too, deserved to have his ears docked; and that only that he had not got a tail, he (King Bagenal) would sever the caudal member from his dorsal extremity.

"Now," quoth Bagenal, "if he's a gentleman he must burn powder after such a message as that."

Nor was he disappointed. A challenge was given by the owner of the pigs. Bagenal accepted it with alacrity, only stipulating that as he was old and feeble, being then in his seventy-ninth year, he should fight sitting in his arm-chair; and that as his infirmities prevented early rising the meeting should take place in the afternoon. "Time was," said the old man with a sigh, "that I would have risen before daylight to fight at sunrise, but we cannot do these things at seventy-eight. Well, heaven's will be done."

They fought at twelve paces. Bagenal wounded his antagonist severely; the arm of the chair in which he sat was shattered, but he escaped unhurt; and he ended the day with a glorious carouse, tapping the claret, we may presume, as usual, by firing a pistol at the cask.

The traditions of Dunleckny allege that when Bagenal, in the course of his tour through Europe, visited the petty Court of Mecklenburg Strelitz, the Grand Duke, charmed with his magnificence and the reputation of his wealth, made him an offer of the hand of the fair Charlotte, who, being politely rejected by King Bagenal, was afterwards accepted by King George III.

Such was the lord of Dunleckny, and such was many an Irish squire of the day. Recklessness characterised the time. And yet there was a polished courtesy, a high-bred grace in the manners of men who imagined that to shoot, or to be shot at, on "the sod," was an indispensable ingredient in the character of a gentleman. Look at Bagenal, nearly fourscore, seated at the head of his table. You observe the refined urbanity of his manner, and the dignified air which is enhanced, not impaired, by the weight of years. You draw near to participate in the instructions of this ancient moralist. What a shock—half ludicrous, half horrible—to find that he inculcates the necessity of practice with the hair-triggers as the grand primary virtue which forms the gentleman!

At a somewhat later period the same extravagant ideas prevailed. At a contested election for the County of Cork, the well-known "Bully Egan" fought fourteen duels. Pugnacious barristers, whose knowledge of law was not very profound, sometimes made large sums of money at elections where fighting counsel were required. Elections in those days often lasted a fortnight or three weeks. Indeed they occasionally lasted longer. It is stated that Lord Castlereagh's first elections for the County Down lasted for forty-two days, and cost £60,000. Contests thus protracted might average, if party or personal animosity ran high, from one to two duels a day. It accordingly was the policy of the candidates to select good shots for their counsel. Within the present century Mr. Thomas O'Meara was agent at a Clare election, where he conducted the business of his client in a style so pacific as to excite the astonishment of a friend who was aware of his fire-eating propensities. "Why, Tom," said his friend, "you are marvellously quiet. How does it happen that you haven't got into any rumpus?" "Because my client does not pay me fighting price," replied Tom, with the most business-like air in the world. The tariff included two scales of payment for election counsel, the talking price and the fighting price.

These delirious notions were undoubtedly the indirect results of the anomalous position of the "Protestant garrison" in Ireland; of their immense and irresponsible social power, and of the lax, devil-may-care morality systematically acted on in the government of the country by successive administrations.

At an election for the County of Wexford in 1810, when Messrs. Alcock and Colclough were rival candidates, some tenants of a friend of Alcock declared their intention of voting for Colclough. "Receive their votes at your peril!" exclaimed Alcock. Colclough replied that he had not asked their votes, and that he certainly would not be bullied into rejecting them. Alcock thereupon challenged Colclough to fight. They met on the next day; the crowd who assembled on the ground included many magistrates; Colclough was shot through the heart, and Alcock, having thus got rid of his opponent, was duly returned for the county. He was tried at the next assizes for the murder of Colclough. Baron Smith publicly protested against finding him guilty, and the jury unanimously acquitted him.

CHAPTER II.

HOW THE REBELLION OF 1798 WAS PROVOKED.

"Of that system of coercion which preceded the late insurrection in Ireland, of the burning of villages, hanging their inhabitants, transporting persons suspected without trial, strangling and whipping to extort confession, and billeting the military at free quarters in districts in which individuals had been disorderly, his lordship (Charlemont) has been uniformly the declared enemy."—*Memoir of Lord Charlemont in "Public Characters of* 1798." Dublin, 1799.

THE motto I have prefixed to this chapter describes the mode taken by the agents of Pitt's government to lash Ireland into that rebellion which was used as one of the arguments against our legislative independence. The rebellion, which the authorities "made to explode" (the words are Lord Castlereagh's), was deliberately provoked, in order to give England a pretext for filling Ireland with troops to crush out popular opposition to the Union. While military force was thus employed to destroy our Constitution, bribery on a scale of unprecedented magnitude was employed to purchase votes for the Union in the Houses of Parliament.

It is sometimes weakly urged that the venality

of the last Irish Parliament is a perpetual disqualifier of the Irish people from the right of self-legislation. It might as well be said that the owner of an estate was disqualified from the rights of possession by the rascality of his agent. The Irish people had nothing to do with the venality of their legislators. The sin was not theirs, nor should its punishment be visited on them. And in the last grand struggle, the men who really were their representatives—the men who were returned for open, popular constituencies—nearly all voted against the ministerial project, and for the preservation of the Irish Parliament.

In glancing, however rapidly, at the Repeal agitation, we should not lose sight of that which is ever uppermost in the mind of every Irish Repealer—namely, that the Union is the offspring of conjoined fraud and force; that the means by which it was achieved were such as would inevitably vitiate any private transaction between two individuals. That Lord Castlereagh found many nominees for pocket-boroughs, many placemen, and every staff officer * in a Parliament which had been dexterously packed for the question, who were not so impracticable as Mr. Shapland Carew, was by no means the worst feature in the case. The machinery of crime which was to effectuate the Union had been long in preparation. With respect to the turbulent condition of Ireland for some years prior

---

* Except Colonel O'Donnell.

to the Union—with respect to the share the Government had in producing that turbulence, I shall not enter into lengthened details.

The following brief statements must suffice:

The Government goaded the people to rebellion, in order that the popular strength might be paralysed by civil war and its attendant horrors, so as to enable Mr. Pitt to force the Legislative Union on a prostrate and divided people. So far back as 1792, Edmund Burke had used these remarkable words: " By what I learn, the Castle considers the outlawry (or at least what I look upon as such) of the great mass of the people of Ireland as an unalterable maxim in the government of Ireland."

The Presbyterian population, principally fixed in Ulster, demanded a Reform of the House of Commons. The Catholics, outnumbering all the other bodies of religionists, demanded the full rights of citizenship. The Nationalists of all creeds who composed the confederation of United Irishmen would at the outset have been perfectly satisfied by the concession of these just demands. It appears from Tone's autobiography that the Irish public did not ask for separation from England; for he tells us that when he published a pamphlet in which separation was propounded, he found that the public mind had not advanced to that point; "and my pamphlet," he adds, "made not the smallest impression."*

---

* "Life and Writings of Theobald Wolfe Tone," p. 33. McCormick's edition.

The efficacy of a thorough reform in allaying discontent is stated also by Arthur O'Connor to the secret committees of the Lords and Commons by whom he was examined in 1798. His words are these:

"Restore the vital principle of the Constitution which you have destroyed, by restoring to the people the choice of representatives who shall control the executive by frugal grants of the public money, and by exacting a rigid account of the expenditure. Let the people have representatives they can call friends—men in whom they can place confidence—men they have really chosen—men chosen for such a time that if they should attempt to betray them they may speedily have an opportunity of discarding them. Give them such a House of Commons, and I will answer for the tranquillity of the country."

But the tranquillity of the country just then would not have suited Pitt's designs against Ireland.

"Pitt," says Thorold Rogers, "permitted in Ireland a reign of terror hardly less atrocious, though better concerted, than the massacres of September, and the fusillade at Lyons."

The reign of terror, the intolerable persecution of the people, was indispensable to create and intensify the mutual district of the Catholic and Protestant communities, whose combination was essentially necessary to defeat the machinations of their common enemy. For in the confusion of a popular outbreak, nothing could be easier than to give the appearance of a war of religion to the inevitable outrages on either side. England could then take advantage of the dissensions her manœuvres had inflamed. She could assume the position of a coercive mediator, and say, "As you Irish are maddened by your religious hatreds, we must take you in hand and protect you from each other."

To extinguish sectarian animosity was one of the leading objects of "The United Irishmen." "All we wanted," says Arthur O'Connor, "was to create a House of Commons which should represent the whole people of Ireland; and for that purpose we strove to dispel all religious distinctions from our political union." *

To exasperate the friends of Reform, not only by an insolent rejection of their claims, but also by a shameless perseverance in the practice of parliamentary corruption, became a settled part of the policy of the Government. It was likewise resolved to exasperate the Catholics, who, according to Tone, required nothing more than equal justice to render them thoroughly peaceable and loyal. I quote the words of Tone, who, the reader will remember, was a Protestant:

"The Dissenters," he says, "from the early

---

* "Memoir: being a Report of the Examinations of Messrs. Emmett, O'Connor, and MacNevin, before the Secret Committees of the Lords and Commons." Published by themselves; p. 62.

character of their sect, were mostly Republicans from principle. The great mass of the Catholics only became so from oppression and persecution. Had they not been goaded by tyranny in every hour and in every act of their lives, had they been freely admitted to an equal share in the benefits of the Irish Constitution, they would have become, by the very spirit of their religion, the most peaceable, obedient, orderly, and well-affectioned subjects of the empire. Their proud and old gentry, and their clergy, inclined even rather to feudal and chivalrous, and somewhat to Tory principles, than to Democracy. But common sufferings now united them in a common hatred of the Government, and desire for its subversion."*

Opposed to the just demands of Reform and Catholic Emancipation were the powerful parties who enjoyed the great pecuniary profits of parliamentary corruption, and the monopoly of office and of political influence which Reform and Emancipation would necessarily terminate. The monopolists and bigots were supported by the whole power of the English Government against the great majority of their fellow-countrymen. In such a state of things it was not difficult for an able and unscrupulous Minister to embroil this kingdom in a civil war, the results of which might facilitate his favourite scheme of a Union. By encouraging

---

* "Life of Tone," *ut supra*, p. 90.

political profligacy in the Irish Parliament, he might hope to render that body unpopular with the Irish nation. By playing off contending parties against each other, and inflaming their mutual hostility, he might make the Catholics look upon the rule of an English Parliament as a smaller evil than the Orange brutality to which he took good care they should be subjected at home.

The Report of the Secret Committee of the Irish House of Commons, printed "by authority" in 1798, affirms that by the original papers seized at Belfast in the month of April, 1797, the numbers of United Irishmen in the province of Ulster alone were stated to amount to nearly 100,000. Throughout the writings of Wolfe Tone we find Ulster invariably named as the first and best-prepared province in the revolutionary movement, of which the nucleus was in Belfast. It seems to have been considered by the English Cabinet that the Catholics would be more effectually stimulated to unite with the Northern conspirators, by alternating their "outlawry" with promises of speedy and complete emancipation; by then suddenly dispelling the hopes thus excited, and recurring to a system of barbarous persecution.

This game was adroitly played. On the 15th of October, 1794, the illustrious Grattan had an interview with Pitt on Irish affairs. "Mr. Grattan," says his son, "stated to him what his party desired, and mentioned the measures that he thought Ireland required. The essential one was the Catholic question." With regard to the Catholic question, Mr. Pitt used these words: "Not to bring it forward as a Government measure; but if Government were pressed, to yield it."* Mr. Grattan observes that this was unquestionably a concession of the Catholic question, for Pitt well knew the question would be pressed. We have Earl Fitzwilliam's authority for the fact that Pitt and his Cabinet empowered his lordship, when accepting the Viceroyalty of Ireland, to support the claims of the Catholics. In his letter to the Earl of Carlisle he says: "It was at the same time resolved that if the Catholics should appear determined to stir the business, and to bring it before Parliament, I was to give it a handsome support on the part of the G[overnmen]t."† Pitt, in fact, included the full emancipation of the Catholics in the programme settled between the King's Ministry and Earl Fitzwilliam, previously to that nobleman's departure from London to assume the reins of government in Ireland. And Earl Fitzwilliam tells us that on no other terms would he have accepted the office of Viceroy. How completely he fell into the trap laid by Pitt, how thoroughly he credited the sincerity of Pitt's insincere declarations in favour of the Catholics, can best be learned from his lordship's own words. He says: "From a full consideration of the real merits of the case, as well as from every

* "Life of Grattan," by his Son, vol. iv. p. 177.
† Earl Fitzwilliam's "Letter to the Earl of Carlisle," p. 4. Dublin, 1795.

information I had been able to collect of the state and temper of Ireland from the year 1793, I was decidedly of opinion that not only sound policy, but justice, required on the part of Great Britain, that the work which was left imperfect at that period ought to be completed, and the Catholics relieved from every remaining disqualification. In this opinion the Duke of P[ortlan]d uniformly concurred with me; and when this question came under discussion previous to my departure for Ireland, I found the Cabinet, with Mr. P[itt] at their head, strongly impressed with the same conviction. Had I found it otherwise, I never would have undertaken the g[overnmen]t."*

It is quite clear that Earl Fitzwilliam considered himself the authorised herald of emancipation to the Irish Catholics. But Pitt had no other intention than driving the Catholics to desperation by disappointing the hopes thus treacherously excited. On the 8th of February, 1795, the Duke of Portland wrote to the Viceroy that Emancipation was to be postponed, and that its postponement would be "the means of doing a greater service to the British Empire than it has been capable of receiving since the Revolution, or, at least, since the [Scotch] Union."† The "greater service" thus indicated was the destruction of the Irish Parliament.

---

* Letter, pp. 2, 3. The Duke of Portland was then principal Secretary of State for the Home Department; Mr. Pitt was Chancellor of the Exchequer.

† "Letter to the Earl of Carlisle," p. 14.

The reader will remember that, in 1792, Mr. Burke said that the treatment received by the Catholics amounted, in his judgment, to outlawry. In 1795 Lord Fitzwilliam, during his short Vice-royalty, warned Pitt's Cabinet, in a letter to the Duke of Portland, that the course pursued by Pitt would, if persevered in, "raise a flame in the country that nothing short of arms would be able to keep down;"* and in his Letter, already cited, to the Earl of Carlisle, he asks, in reference to the ministerial policy, "must the Minister of England boldly face, I had almost said the *certainty* of driving this kingdom into a rebellion, and open another breach for ruin and destruction to break in upon us?" †

Lord Fitzwilliam's remonstrances do honour to his heart and to his statesmanship. He might, however, have spared them. A rebellion was just what Pitt wanted. The mutual atrocities it would produce were certain to inflame the reciprocal animosities of the belligerents to a pitch of fury, and furnish a convenient pretext for introducing martial law, and overwhelming the kingdom with troops. Under the reign of terror thus established the task of destroying the Irish Parliament would be comparatively easy.

Pitt calculated that if Emancipation were per-

---

* In Earl Fitzwilliam's Letter to Lord Carlisle, he states that he addressed that warning to the Duke of Portland.

† "Letter to the Earl of Carlisle," p. 24. The word "*certainty*" is italicised by his lordship.

sistently denied to the Catholics in the Irish Legislature, their support of a Union might be purchased by holding out a hope that the Imperial Parliament would enfranchise them. Reports of this project having got into circulation, an aggregate meeting of Catholics, held in Dublin on the 9th of April, 1795, passed the following resolution :

"Resolved unanimously, That we are sincerely and unalterably attached to the rights, liberties, and independence of our native country; and we pledge ourselves, collectively and individually, *to resist even our own emancipation*, if proposed to be conceded on the ignominious terms of acquiescence in the fatal measure of an Union with the sister kingdom."

Of the pretended assent of the English Cabinet to Catholic Emancipation, and the disastrous result of retracting that assent, Sir Laurence Parsons thus expressed himself in the Irish House of Commons on the 2nd of March, 1795 :

"If the British Cabinet had held out an assent and had afterwards retracted, if the demon of darkness should come from the infernal regions upon earth and throw a firebrand among the people, he could not do more to promote mischief. The hopes of the public were raised, and in one instant they were blasted. . . . . He protested to God that in all the history he had read, he had never met with a parallel of such infatuation as that by which he (Mr. Pitt) appeared to be led.

Let him persevere, and you must increase your army to myriads ; every man must have five or six dragoons in his house."

It was not infatuation, except so far as infatuation consists in deliberate and systematic wickedness. To provoke rebellion was the object of Pitt's policy ; and the exasperation of the Catholics, excited by political disappointment, contributed to the success of that policy.

On the 29th of January, 1799, when the ministerial scheme of Union had sufficiently ripened, the Duke of Portland wrote to Lord Castlereagh: "Catholic Emancipation must not be granted but through the medium of an Union, and by means of an united Parliament."* Next day (30th) the Duke wrote more strongly to the same effect. The Viceroy (Marquis Cornwallis) had previously written to the Duke of Portland, "Were the Catholic question to be now carried the great argument for an Union would be lost, at least so far as the Catholics are concerned."†

Here we have the key to the "service" which Pitt's Cabinet expected to derive from postponing the concession of the Catholic claims which Lord Fitzwilliam was instructed to support in 1795, and which Pitt, in 1794, had directly led Grattan to expect.

A rebellion was deemed a useful means of laying waste the strength of this kingdom. But

---

* "Cornwallis Correspondence," vol. iii. p. 59. † *Ibid.*

the desired outbreak was not to be left to the chance of mere political exasperation. Stronger provocatives than the breach of ministerial promises were to be applied to the Catholics.

Lord Fitzwilliam, a man of high honour, could not act on Pitt's infernal policy. He was of course recalled. Of the effects of that recall upon the public mind a contemporary writer says:

"The nation again seemed to sink into despondency. The houses, shops, etc., in every street through which he passed, were all shut upon the memorable day on which he sailed for England; and at noonday a solemn silence and melancholy mourning marked the metropolis, and seemed to indicate the sad catastrophe which has since befallen that ill-fated country."*

Discontent was fearfully increased by the system of torture put in practice against the people in various districts. The following evidence, given by Lord Gosford, describes that system as it existed in 1795 and 1796.:

"A persecution," says his lordship,† "accompanied with all the circumstances of ferocious cruelty, is now raging in this country. Neither age, nor sex, nor even acknowledged innocence can excite mercy. The only crime which the wretched objects are charged with is the profes-

---

* Memoir of Earl Fitzwilliam in "Public Characters of 1799 and 1800," p. 272.

† Address of Lord Gosford to the Magistracy of Armagh, printed in the *Dublin Journal*, 5th January, 1796.

sion of the Roman Catholic faith. A lawless banditti have constituted themselves judges of this new delinquency, and the sentence they pronounce is equally concise and terrible; it is nothing less than confiscation of property and immediate banishment. It would be painful to detail the horrors of this proscription—a proscription that exceeds, in the number of its victims, every example of ancient and modern history. For, when have we heard or read of more than half the inhabitants of a populous country being deprived of the fruits of their industry, and driven to seek shelter for themselves and their families where chance may guide them? *These horrors are now acting with impunity.* The spirit of justice, without which law is tyranny, has disappeared in this country."

The persecution Lord Gosford describes took place in 1795.

So far Pitt's policy had borne its intended fruit.

The late Lord Holland, speaking of the recall of Earl Fitzwilliam from the Viceroyalty, says :

"His recall was hailed as a triumph by the Orange faction, and they contrived about the same time to get rid of Mr. Secretary Pelham, who, though somewhat time-serving, was a good-natured and a prudent man. Indeed, surrounded as they were with burning cottages, tortured backs, and frequent executions, they were yet full of their sneers at what they whimsically termed 'the clemency' of the Government, and the weak character of their Viceroy, Lord Camden. . . . The fact is incontrovertible that the people of Ireland were driven to resistance, which possibly they meditated before, by the free quarters and excesses of the soldiery, which were such as are not permitted in civilised warfare, even in an enemy's country." *

The evidence of the Protestant Bishop of Down (Right Rev. Doctor Dickson) illustrative of some of the particular features of the system, is thus given by Lord Holland in the work now quoted:

"Dr. Dickson assured me that he had seen families, returning peaceably from mass, assailed without provocation by drunken troops and yeomanry, and the wives and daughters exposed to every species of indignity, brutality, and outrage, from which neither his remonstrances, nor those of other Protestant gentlemen, could rescue them. The subsequent Indemnity Acts deprived of redress the victims of this wide-spread cruelty."

Of particular outrages committed on the people by the armed agents of power, the following quotation from Lord Moira will furnish illustrative specimens:

"I have," says Lord Moira, "known a man, in order to extort confession of a supposed crime, or of that of some neighbour, picketed till he actually fainted; picketed a second time till he fainted

---

* "Memoirs of the Whig Party during my Time," by Lord Holland, edited by his Son. Longmans, 1852.

again; and when he came to himself, picketed a third time till he once more fainted; and all this upon mere suspicion. Men had been taken and hung up till they were half dead, and afterwards threatened with a repetition of this treatment unless they made a confession of their imputed guilt." *

The picketing mode of torture consisted in suspending the victim by his arms, while his foot had nothing to rest on but the point of a sharpened stake. Horrible as was the tyranny described by Lord Moira, yet it seems that he did not tell the worst cases, for on the 2nd of December, 1797, he wrote as follows to the Hon. Valentine Lawless: †

"You have truly observed that in my recital I suppressed many of the grossest instances of outrage, with the details of which I could not but be acquainted."

Lord Moira took care to state that the crimes he described were not isolated outrages. "These," said he, "were not particular acts of cruelty, but formed part of the new system."

The object of that system was to carry the Union.

The late General Cockburn gives, in his "Letters" (p. 47), an account of the documents prepared to enable Lord Moira to substantiate

---

* Speech of Lord Moira in the British House of Lords, 22nd November, 1797.

† Fitzpatrick's "Life of Lord Cloncurry," p. 150.

his statements, and he adds: "They (the documents) contained details of the most horrible outrages on the people, of cruelty and foul deeds, that perhaps, after all, it may be as well to have now effaced from Irish records of violence; and though the people in many cases were driven to retaliation, it was not before murder, burning, destruction of property (often on suspicion of being suspected) and flogging, drove them to desperation."

I add the testimony of Henry Grattan. On the 26th of February, 1796, he said in the Irish House of Commons that it was "a persecution conceived in the bitterness of bigotry, carried on with the most ferocious barbarity by a banditti, who, being of the religion of the State, had committed with greater audacity and confidence the most horrid murders, and had proceeded from robbery and massacre to extermination."

The outrages referred to in the above passage were chiefly committed in the County Armagh. Grattan, in an address to his fellow-citizens in 1797, enumerates among the crimes with which he charges Government, "the order to the military to act without waiting for the civil power; the imprisonment of the middle orders without law; the detaining them in prison without bringing them to trial; the transporting them without law; burning their houses; burning their villages; murdering them; crimes many of which are public, and many are committed which are concealed by the suppression of a free press by military force . . . finally, the introduction of practices not only unknown to law, but unknown to civilised and Christian countries."

Plowden tells us in his "History of Ireland," that in the beginning of 1796, "it was generally believed that 7,000 Catholics had been forced or burned out of the county of Armagh, and that the ferocious banditti who had expelled them had been encouraged, connived at, and protected by the Government."*

In the examination of the United Irishmen by the Secret Committees of the Lords and Commons the Lord Chancellor asks Emmett, "What caused the late rebellion?" To which question Emmett answers, "The free quarters, the house-burnings, the tortures, and the military executions, in the counties of Kildare, Carlow, and Wicklow." †

Arthur O'Connor, in his examination before the Secret Committees of the Lords and Commons in 1798, complains of "the uniform system of coercion and opposition which had been pursued from 1793 by the Irish Government against the Irish people;" and on being asked to state the object contemplated by the United Irishmen in organising their society, he answers in the following words: "We saw with sorrow that the cruelties practised by the Irish Government had raised a dreadful spirit of revenge in the hearts of the people; we saw with horror that to answer their immediate views, the Irish

---

* Plowden's "History of Ireland," vol. ii. p. 377.
† See Madden's "United Irishmen," First Series, p. 111.

Government had revived the old religious feuds; we were most anxious to have such authority as the organisation afforded, constituted to prevent the dreadful transports of popular fury."

A member of the Committee (apparently Lord Castlereagh) remarks that "Government had nothing to do with the Orange system, or their oath of extermination." To which O'Connor thus replies: "You, my lord (Castlereagh), from the station you fill, must be sensible that the executive of any country has it in its power to collect a vast mass of information, and you must know from the secret nature, and the zeal of the Union, that its executive must have had the most minute information of every act of the Irish Government. As one of the executive, it came to my knowledge that considerable sums of money were expended throughout the nation in endeavouring to extend the Orange system, and that the Orange oath of extermination was administered. When these facts are coupled, not only with the general impunity that has been uniformly extended towards all the acts of this infernal association, but [with] the marked encouragement its members have received from Government, I find it impossible to exculpate the Government from being the parent and protector of these sworn extirpators." *

O'Connor's reasoning on this point is irresistible. The Government were merely carrying

---

* Madden's "United Irishmen," Second Series, 8vo, pp. 318, 319.

out Pitt's policy. Of that policy Lord Holland's opinion may be learned from the following passage in the work already quoted: "My approbation," says his lordship, "of Lord Edward Fitzgerald's actions remains unaltered and unshaken. His country was bleeding under one of the hardest tyrannies that our times have witnessed."

As to the administration of the law, it was not very easy for the people to repose confidence in its justice when such an incident as the following could occur. In the spring of 1797, Solicitor-General Toler, afterwards Lord Norbury, presided during the illness of one of the judges in the criminal court at the assizes for the County Kildare. Captain Frazer, a Scotchman, was prosecuted for the murder of a peasant named Christopher Dixon, under the following circumstances: Part of the County of Kildare, near Carberry, was at that time proclaimed. Other parts were exempt from proclamation. There was a flying camp in the proclaimed part, consisting of the Frazer Fencibles, under the command of Captain Frazer. One night, on his return through Cloncurry to the camp from a jovial dinner-party at Maynooth, Frazer saw Dixon repairing a cart by the roadside. Thinking that he was in his own proclaimed district, he seized Dixon for being out after sunset, and made him mount behind the orderly dragoon in attendance, with the purpose of taking him to the camp to flog. Passing a turnpike-gate, Dixon asserted that the proclamation did not extend to the district in which he had been found, at the same time appealing to the gatekeeper to confirm his assertion. The gatekeeper said that the district in question had not been proclaimed; upon which Dixon descended from the crupper of the orderly's horse and went towards home. Frazer and the dragoon furiously pursued him, and gave him sixteen wounds, of which seven or eight were mortal. A coroner's jury returned a verdict of "Wilful Murder" against the homicides. A neighbouring magistrate, Mr. Thomas Ryan, endeavoured to take Frazer, but his soldiers resisted. Mr. Ryan reported the facts to Lord Cloncurry, who was then in Dublin, and who directed his son, the Hon. Valentine Lawless, to visit the Commander of the Forces, Lord Carhampton, in order to demand the body of Frazer in pursuance of the provisions of the Mutiny Act. Mr. Lawless made the demand in presence of Mr. Ryan, and of Colonel (afterwards General Sir George) Cockburn. Lord Carhampton refused to give up Frazer. Mr. Lawless thereupon told his lordship that Frazer was *ipso facto* cashiered.

At the assizes Frazer went voluntarily to be tried. His approach to the Court House was a sort of ovation, for he was attended by a military band playing "Croppies, lie down."

Mr. Toler presided. On the bench beside him sat the Duke of Leinster and the unfortunate Lord Edward Fitzgerald. The facts of the case were distinctly proved by unexceptionable witnesses.

There were many persons examined who deposed to the good and peaceful character of the deceased, his exemption from all "treasonable" machinations, and his general habits of morality and industry. There were also witnesses upon the other side who testified to the admirable character of Captain Frazer and the orderly dragoon, investing them especially with the military virtues.

Mr. Toler charged home for an acquittal. He regretted the homicide—it was very unfortunate—good, respectable man—worthy character, and so forth—witnesses of unimpeachable credit had said so. "There had, however, been witnesses who gave a most admirable character to the gallant captain in the dock, which the jury could by no means overlook—he was a brave and faithful soldier to his King—loyal—devoted—in a word, the sort of person needed in this unhappy country at the present time. The occurrence for which he was tried was most deeply to be deplored; he would not disparage the deceased; he would only say that if he had been as good as the witnesses for the prosecution had represented him, he was well out of a wicked world. If, on the contrary, he were a firebrand" (here Toler looked significantly at Mr. Lawless), "the world was well rid of him."

A judicial dilemma well worthy of record. The jury acquitted Captain Frazer.*

I shall add a few incidents—the results of the

---

* I possess the above narrative in the handwriting of Valentine, second Lord Cloncurry, by whom it was kindly given

Governmental policy of the period—recorded in the narrative of Miles Byrne, a native of the County Wexford; one of those men who were goaded by intolerable persecution to join the insurgents. He subsequently went to France, and ended his days as *chef-de-bataillon* in the French service. I give the title of Miles Byrne's work below.*

"Flogging, half-hanging, picketing," says Colonel Byrne, "were mild tortures in comparison of the pitch-caps that were applied to those who happened to wear their hair short, called croppies. The head being completely singed, a cap made of strong linen well imbued with boiling pitch was so closely put on that it could not be taken off without bringing off a part of the skin and flesh from the head. In many instances the tortured victim had one of his ears cut off." †

"In short, the state of the country previous to the insurrection is not to be imagined, except by those who witnessed the atrocities of every description committed by the military and the Orangemen who were let loose on the unfortunate, defenceless, and unarmed population." ‡

---

to me with the purpose of being used in the first edition of "Ireland and her Agitators." For the infamous character of Lord Carhampton, see Fitzgerald's "Sham Squire," and the sequel to that work.

* "Memoirs of Miles Byrne," *Chef-de-bataillon* in the service of France, Officer of the Legion of Honour, Knight of St. Louis, etc. Edited by his Widow. Paris: Gustave Bossange et Compagnie, 25, Quai Voltaire, 1863. The work is in three volumes.

† *Ibid.*, vol. i. p. 32. ‡ *Ibid.*, p. 34.

Byrne mentions that among the "Loyalists" most active in applying the pitch-cap was a clergyman named Owens. This reverend gentleman was afterwards seized at Govey by the rebels, who applied the pitch-cap to himself.

Among the more zealous and prominent Orangemen whose deeds are recorded by Byrne, Mr. Hunter Gowan of Mount Nebo, and Captain Beaumont of Hyde Park, hold a principal place. Of the former Byrne gives the following anecdote: "Hunter Gowan, Justice of the Peace, captain of a corps of yeoman cavalry, knowing that Patrick Bruslaun, a near neighbour of his, and with whom he had always lived on the most friendly terms, was confined to bed with a wound, rode to Bruslaun's house, knocked at the door, and asked Mrs. Bruslaun in the kindest manner respecting her husband's health. 'You see,' said he, pointing to his troops drawn up at a distance from the house, 'I would not let my men approach lest they might do any mischief. Conduct me to your husband's room; I want to have a chat with poor Pat.' She, not having the least suspicion of what was to follow, ushered Gowan to her husband's bedside. He put out his hand, and after exchanging some words with poor Bruslaun, deliberately took out his pistol and shot him through the heart. Turning round on his heel, he said to the unfortunate woman, 'You will now be saved the trouble of nursing your damned rebel Popish husband.' These details I had from Mrs. Bruslaun's lips; and how many more of the same kind could I not add to them, were it of any use now to look back to that awful epoch of English tyranny and slaughter in Ireland." *

Of Captain Beaumont's loyal zeal we are given the following instance; the victims upon this occasion were the writer's uncle and cousin, Mr. Breen of Castletown and his son. "Captain Beaumont of Hyde Park had both him and his son murdered in the presence of my aunt Breen and her four daughters, on the lawn before the hall door. Beaumont, who was escorted by a detachment of cavalry, knocked at the door and asked to see my uncle, with whom he was on the most friendly terms. As soon as Mr. Breen came out, Beaumont's first question was: 'Are your sons Pat and Miles at home?' 'Certainly; where should they be?' was the answer of the poor father. 'Well, let them appear, or those men who accompany me won't believe it.' When they came out, the father, and the eldest son Pat, were placed on their knees and immediately shot. Miles, who was only sixteen years of age, was sent prisoner to Arklow, and from thence aboard a guard-ship in the Bay of Dublin. No pen can describe the state of my unfortunate aunt and her four daughters at this awful moment. To add to their misery, one of the assassins had the brutality to tell the eldest daughter, Mrs. Kinsla, who had been married but a year or two before, that she would find something

---

* "Memoirs of Miles Byrne," vol. i. pp. 236, 237.

else to weep over when she returned home. She had come but half-an-hour before to visit her family, her own place being but a short mile from her father's house. As the monster told her, when she went home she found her husband lying dead in the courtyard, and a young child of a few months old in his arms. The unfortunate man had taken it out of its cradle, thinking that the sight of the poor infant might soften Beaumont's heart and incline him to mercy. But this stanch supporter of the Protestant ascendency could not let so good an opportunity pass of proving his loyalty to his king by thus exterminating a Catholic neighbour."*

Most persons who know anything of the rebellion of 1798 have heard of Father John Murphy, parish priest of Monageer and Boulevogue, who held a command among the Wexford insurgents.†

Colonel Byrne tells us that Father Murphy, like many other priests, had seriously advised the people to surrender their weapons to the Government. But on the 26th of May, 1798, a party of yeomanry scoured the parish, burning and destroying all before them. When Father Murphy saw his chapel and his house in flames, as well as many other houses in the parish, his patience was exhausted,

---

* "Memoirs of Miles Byrne," vol. i. p. 254, *et seq.*

* This is the Father Murphy of whom the editor of the "Cornwallis Correspondence" gives the following character: "A thorough ruffian—the worst possible specimen of a reckless demagogue. He persuaded his infuriated followers that he was invulnerable, and used to show them bullets which he said he had caught in his hands."

and in reply to the crowd who gathered round him for advice, "he answered abruptly that they had better die courageously in the field than be butchered in their houses; that for his own part, if he had any brave men to join him, he was resolved to sell his life dearly." *

In addition to these testimonies, we have the Marquis Cornwallis's direct and positive assertion (which I shall quote at length in a future chapter of this work) that the country had been driven into rebellion by violence and cruelty.† His Excellency had previously described the violence as displaying itself in the burning of houses, the murder of the inhabitants, the infliction of torture by flogging, and universal rape and robbery.‡

Those who brand with every epithet of ignominy the names and principles of the insurgents of 1798, should ask themselves whether such elaborate pains had ever been taken in any other country to goad a reluctant people into insurrection? With the cup of hope held brimful to the lips, to be rudely dashed aside next moment; with a regularly organised system of torture; with a social condition of frightful insecurity; without any protection from the established tribunals of the law—whither were the people to turn for succour? To the so-called tribunals of justice? A sanguinary buffoon upon

---

* "Cornwallis Correspondence," vol. i. p. 46.

† His Excellency wrote this on the 16th November, 1799. "Correspondence," vol. iii. pp. 144, 145.

‡ *Ibid.*, iii. 89.

the Bench might openly recommend the impunity of their murderers in a harangue of solemn banter. Should they turn to the Government for help? The Government had a direct interest in their sufferings and turbulence. Where, then, were the people to look for the removal of their grievances? They were absolutely driven to their own rude, undisciplined, and inefficient warfare. The blazing cottage—the tortured peasant—the violated wife or daughter—the familiar outrages on property and life—the demoniac license of which they were the victims, literally left them no alternative but rebellion. Instead of their outbreak in 1798 being a subject of astonishment, the real wonder would have been, if, with such intolerable provocation, they had not resorted to arms. Good men may now regard their struggle with the feeling expressed in the celebrated lines of a Protestant Fellow of Trinity College:

> Who fears to speak of ninety-eight?
> Who blushes at the name?
> When cowards mock the patriot's fate,
> Who hangs his head for shame?

No. The true shame and sin were with the Government, whose oppressive crimes compelled a peace-loving people to take the field in their own defence.

The country at length became embroiled enough to satisfy the most ardent aspirations of Pitt, Clare, and Castlereagh. Troops were poured in, to the number of 137,590.* Among other proofs of the complicity of the Government is the damning fact that they might have prevented the rebellion by arresting its leaders at any moment during thirteen months immediately preceding the outbreak. The Appendix marked No. XIV. of the Report of the Secret Committee of the House of Commons, printed by the authority of Government in 1798, is prefaced with the following words:

"The information contained in this number of the Appendix was received from Nicholas Maguan, of Saintfield, in the county of Down, who was himself a member of the Provincial and County Committees, and also a colonel in the military system of United Irishmen. He was present at each of the meetings of which an account is here given; and from time to time, immediately after each meeting, communicated what passed thereat to the Rev. John Clelland, a magistrate of said county." †

Mr. Clelland was land-agent to Lord Castlereagh's family, and through him the Government received the fullest information respecting the machinery of the impending insurrection, the names

---

* These figures are taken from a speech delivered by Lord Castlereagh on the 18th of February, 1799, prefacing a motion on military Estimates.

† "Report of the Secret Committees," printed by authority. It should be observed that the examinations of Arthur O'Connor, Samuel Neilson, and Thomas Addis Emmett were so greatly abridged in the Government publication, that those gentlemen took means to publish them in full. I possess both their publication and that of the Government.

of its leaders, and their plans and movements. He is shown to have received communications from Magnan immediately after each meeting. Now, the meeting, of which an account is first given in Appendix No. XIV., was held on the 14th of April, 1797, or about thirteen months before the Rebellion broke out. It is clear that at any time during that period the Government could have prevented the explosion by the simple act of taking the leaders into custody. But the reader has seen that the quiet prevention of an outbreak was inconsistent with their guilty policy. Their plan was to convulse the frame of society to its centre; to create mutual hatred and terror between the Protestant and Catholic inhabitants of the land; to paralyse both into a total incapacity to resist the Union; to promote the burnings, the murders, the unspeakable atrocities which forced the people to rebel; to coerce both Protestants and Catholics with an irresistible army of occupation; and then, by means of gigantic and unprecedented bribery, to corrupt the Parliament (which had been dexterously packed for the occasion) to vote its own extinction.

They must have been short-sighted statesmen who calculated that an Union thus produced by force and bribery could ever be maintained by any other means than force and bribery. They must have known but little of human nature if they imagined that a people whose legislature had been made the subject of a regular purchase and sale could ever acquiesce in that traffic. They must have known nothing of the Irish nature if they expected that the series of demoniac crimes which culminated in the destruction of the Irish Parliament could ever be effaced from the national memory; or that the recollection would ever be unaccompanied with the resolve to recover, whenever God should send us the means, the Constitution of which we were wickedly plundered.

And it was an Union thus achieved that Mr. Pitt described as a compact voluntarily entered into on the part of Ireland. Mr. Under-Secretary Cooke did not venture to deny that Ireland was dissatisfied with the hateful measure; but then he predicted that when once fast clutched in the embraces of England, "dissatisfaction would sink into acquiescence, and acquiescence soften into content."

The fallacy of this prediction has been shown by the incessant agitation for Home Government from 1800 to the present day.

Amongst the Irish Parliamentary Unionists the most prominent leader was Lord Chancellor Clare. His only motive was the hope of personal aggrandisement. He had, by his commanding talents and great strength of character, acquired a dictatorship in the Irish House of Lords. Over the imbecile puppets who formed the majority of that assembly he domineered with the most insolent tyranny; and he indulged in visions of the vastly enlarged power with which a dictatorship in the British Parliament would invest him. It never occurred to him that he should not be equally dominant there as he was in the Upper House of the Irish Legislature.

Clare had a species of intellect not uncommon amongst the leaders of the French Revolution, of which the leading trait was its strong but ill-directed energy. His bigotry against the Catholics was intense. In private society he seldom named them without some contemptuous epithet. He threw all his abilities into the struggle for the Union. In order to give the reader some idea of the habitual insolence with which he bullied the Irish peers, I shall quote the following audacious attack made by him on the Earl of Charlemont, the Marquis of Downshire, and some other lords, who ventured to oppose the Union:

"If loud and confident report," said Lord Clare, "is to have credit, a consular exchequer has been opened for foul and undisguised bribery. I know that subscriptions are openly solicited in the streets of the metropolis to a fund for defeating the measure of Union. I will not believe that the persons to whom I have been obliged to allude can be parties to it. One of them, a noble earl" (Charlemont) "I see in his place; he is a very young man, and I call upon him as he fears to have his entry into public life marked with dishonour; I call upon him as he fears to live with the broad mark of infamy on his forehead and to transmit it indelibly to his posterity, to stand up in his place and acquit himself before his peers of this foul imputation. I call upon him publicly to disavow all knowledge of the existence of such a fund; or if he cannot disavow it, to state explicitly any honest purpose to which it can be applied. If it can exist, I trust there are sufficient remains of sense and honour in the Irish nation to cut off the corrupted sources of these vile abominations."

Here, indeed, was "Satan lecturing against sin." In order properly to appreciate the brazen audacity of this insolent attack, it must be remembered that he who thus denounced the imputed iniquities of the patriotic party, was himself the *employé* of a Government who were openly and shamelessly practising every art of corruption in favour of their measure.

The work entitled "Public Characters of 1799-1800," thus speaks of Lord Clare's parliamentary tactics: "His firmness, his confidence in his own powers, and the bold tone in which he hurled defiance at his parliamentary opponents on every question connected with legal or constitutional knowledge, often appalled the minor members of opposition, and sometimes kept even their chiefs at bay. These qualities, however, did not always constitute a sure defence. The repulse, which on one memorable evening of debate he experienced on the part of the present Lord, then Mr. O'Neill of Shane's Castle, whose manly and honest mind caught fire at the haughty and dictatorial language with which the Attorney-General had dared to address him, is remembered by those who were then conversant in the politics of the day, and probably will not soon be forgotten."

Although Pitt had used Lord Clare in effecting the Union, yet, when the nefarious work was done, he heartily despised his Irish utensil. Clare fancied that attacks on his own country would receive the applause of the English House of Lords. In the "Life of Grattan" it is recorded that when Clare, in that assembly, dealt out his sweeping censures upon Ireland, "uttering very violent principles in a very violent and intemperate manner," Pitt, who had been listening for some time, at length turned to Wilberforce, who stood next him, and exclaimed: "Good God! did you ever, in all your life, hear so great a rascal as that?"

Clare, whose ambitious spirit was inflated with arrogance and success, soon tried the experiment of insulting the peers of England. He called the Whig lords Jacobins. The Duke of Bedford flung back the insult with the spirit that beseemed a British peer. "We would not," said he, "bear such language from our equals; far less will we endure it from the upstart pride of chance nobility."

The feeling of the whole House was with the Duke. Clare had not the poor consolation of sympathy or pity from any man, even of his own political party. His influence, once almost omnipotent, was now extinct. He returned, mortified and broken-hearted, to the country he had betrayed and ruined, cursing the part he had taken in promoting the Union. "There was a time," he said, with great bitterness, "when no appointment could be made without my sanction; now I am unable to make so much as a clerk in the Excise."

He tried to dissipate his chagrin by violent equestrian exercise. His death was hastened by a severe hurt he received while riding in the Phœnix Park. He died in January, 1802, expressing in his last hours deep though unavailing remorse for his criminal co-operation with Pitt against the Irish Constitution. His fall may be regarded as a signal instance of the retributive justice of Providence.

Of his lineage the following account is given in the publication already quoted: "He is removed but two degrees from a man in the humblest walk of society—a Catholic peasant—whose life was distinguished only by a gradual transition from extreme poverty to an honourable competency; and that, too, acquired by useful industry."

By his criminal political career he gained a peerage, which is now extinct. The so-called honours, for which he bartered the vital interests of his country, have passed away.

CHAPTER III.

PARLIAMENTARY CORRUPTION IN ENGLAND AND IRELAND.

> How did they pass this Union?
> By perjury and fraud.
> By slaves who sold, for place or gold,
> Their country and their God;
> By all the savage acts that yet
> Have followed England's track,
> The pitch-cap and the bayonet,
> The gibbet and the rack.
> And thus was passed the Union
> By Pitt and Castlereagh;
> Could Satan send for such an end
> More worthy souls than they?
>
> *Spirit of the Nation.*

A SCOTCH essayist on Irish politics once expressed his curiosity to know by what magic William Pitt induced the minor members of the Irish peerage to consent to the Union. The great lords who had influence in the House of Commons were bought over on intelligible principles. The Earl of Shannon, for example, was paid £45,000 for his adhesion. Besides, the chiefs of the peerage could look forward to seats in the Imperial Parliament as

Irish representative peers; whereas the smaller lords, in losing their Irish privilege of hereditary legislation, lost all that made their titles anything better than nicknames; whilst they had little or no chance of election to the central Legislature.

It certainly seems, at first sight, surprising that a considerable body of hereditary legislators should slavishly surrender the proudest privilege of the citizen, and receive for it no equivalent. Their act was an abandonment, apparently, of personal and national dignity. In 1785 Lord Lansdowne, in the British House of Lords, expressed his belief that an act of such degrading self-disfranchisement was impossible. An Union having been then casually mentioned, his lordship spoke of "the idea of an Union as a thing that was impracticable. High-minded and jealous," he said, "as were the people of Ireland, we must first learn whether they will consent to give up their distinct Empire, their Parliament, and all the honours which belonged to them." In point of fact the people of Ireland not only never did consent to the scandalous surrender, but opposed it to the utmost of their power. Nearly all the unbribed intellect of Ireland was against it. Our surprise at the share of the Irish House of Lords in enacting the Union is, however, diminished when we analyse the composition of the peers and examine their habits.

Let us first do all honour to the gallant band who, headed by the Duke of Leinster and the Earl of Charlemont, resisted the Union to the last. The

Lords' Protest against the Union is a noble document, full of sagacity and patriotism. Alas! those who signed it were in a minority.

With respect to the rest of the peers, if we look into the Irish peerage list, we shall find that more than half of those existing in 1800 had received their creations from the then reigning monarch, George III. Of these men, thus personally bound to the Court, a considerable number were indebted for their elevation to the grossest political dishonesty. They cared nothing for their country, except for the purpose of trafficking upon it. Corruption had been carried to such an extent as to justify Grattan's indignant complaint that the Minister's familiar practice was to purchase the members of one House with the money obtained by selling seats in the other.

Again, a great portion of the Irish peers had nothing Irish about them but their titles. They had not a foot of property in the kingdom. They never entered it. They had no more compunction in voting for the extinction of the Irish Parliament than they would have had in voting away an Otaheitan Legislature. Take up a Dublin almanack for the year 1800, and run your eye over the peerage list; you will find many of the peers possessing also English titles and English residences. Exclusively of these, you will find that out of fifty-seven viscounts, there were no less than eighteen who had got no Irish residence at all. Run your eye over the barons, and you will find that out of

sixty-five, there were in that year no less than
thirty-four whose connexions, residences, and
property were altogether English.

Again, some of the most bustling and prominent
peers then residing in Ireland were either English
lawyers, or the sons of Englishmen who had been
thrust upon the Irish Bench, and thence into the
Irish peerage. These men had not yet acquired
Irish sentiments or feelings; they were still
essentially foreigners; they rejoiced at an opportunity to strike a blow at Ireland.

Amongst those whom a descent of some half-
dozen generations entitled to call themselves Irish,
the greater number had so habitually looked on
politics as a game to be played for the purpose of
personal aggrandisement, that they had no conception of anything like political principle. There
was a thorough moral recklessness about them
which rendered them quite ready for any act of
political desperation, provided it did not tend to
enlarge the power of the people. Their personal
habits necessarily fostered this recklessness. Their
profusion and extravagance were great; and some
of them—not a few—resorted to modes of raising
the wind which showed that they mingled few
scruples with their system of financial pneumatics.
There was, withal, a strong dash of odd drollery in
the brazen shamelessness of their expedients.

A curious specimen of this order of men was
Lord M——y. His title was the result of some
dexterous traffic in Parliamentary votes. His

manners were eminently fascinating, and his habits social. He had a favourite saying that a gentleman could never live upon his rents; a man who depended on his rents had money only upon two days in the year, the 25th of March and the 29th of September. He accordingly left no expedient untried to furnish himself with money every other day too.

It chanced that when Lord Kerry's house in St. Stephen's Green was for sale, a lady named Keating was desirous to purchase a pew in St. Anne's Church appertaining to that mansion. Mrs. Keating erroneously took it into her head that the pew belonged to Lord M——y; she accordingly visited his lordship to propose herself as a purchaser.

"My dear madam," said he, "I have not got any pew, that I know of, in St. Anne's Church."

"Oh, my lord, I assure you that you have; and if you have got no objection, I am desirous to purchase it."

Lord M——y started no farther difficulty. A large sum was accordingly fixed on, and in order to make her bargain as secure as possible, Mrs. Keating got the agreement of sale drawn out in the most stringent form by an attorney. She paid the money to Lord M——y; and on the following Sunday she marched up to the pew to take possession, rustling in the stateliness of brocades and silks. The beadle refused to let her into the pew.

"Sir," said the lady, "this pew is mine."

"Yours, madam?"

"Yes; I have bought it from Lord M——y."

"Madam, this is the Kerry pew; I do assure you Lord M——y never had a pew in this church."

Mrs. Keating saw at once she had been cheated, and on the following day she went to his lordship to try if she could get back her money.

"My lord, I have come to you to say that the pew in St. Anne's——"

"My dear madam, I'll sell you twenty more pews if you have any fancy for them."

"Oh, my lord, you are facetious. I have come to acquaint you it was all a mistake; you never had a pew in that church."

"Hah! so I think I told you at first."

"And I trust, my lord," pursued Mrs. Keating, "you will refund me the money I paid you for it."

"The money? Really, my dear madam, I am sorry to say that is quite impossible—the money's gone long ago."

"But—my lord—your lordship's character——"

"That's gone too!" said Lord M——y, laughing with good-humoured nonchalance.

I have already said that this nobleman's financial operations were systematically extended to every opportunity of gain that could possibly be grasped at. He was colonel of a militia regiment; and, contrary to all precedent, he regularly sold the commissions, and pocketed the money. The Lord Lieutenant resolved to call him to an account for his malpractices, and for that purpose invited him to dine at the Castle, where all the other colonels of militia regiments then in Dublin had also been invited to meet him. After dinner the Viceroy stated that he had heard with great pain an accusation—indeed, he could hardly believe it—but it had been positively said that the colonel of a militia regiment actually sold the commissions.

The company looked aghast at this atrocity, and the innocent colonels forthwith began to exculpate themselves. "I have never done so." "I have never sold any." "Nor I." The disclaimers were general. Lord M——y resolved to put a bold face on the matter.

"I always sell the commissions in my regiment," said he, with the air of a man who announced a practice rather meritorious. All present seemed astonished at this frank avowal.

"How can you defend such a practice?" asked the Lord Lieutenant.

"Very easily, my lord. Has not your Excellency always told us to assimilate our regiments as much as possible to the troops of the Line?"

"Yes, undoubtedly."

"Well, they sell the commissions in the Line, and I thought that the best point at which to begin the assimilation."

It is told of this nobleman, that when he was dying he was attended by a clergyman, who remonstrated with him on the scandalous exploits of his past life, and strongly urged him to repent.

"Repent?" echoed the dying sinner; "I don't see what I have got to repent of; I don't remember that I ever denied myself anything."

We may well suppose that such a personage would have readily voted for the Union, or for anything else.

Mr. ——, a wealthy merchant, had aristocratic aspirings. Having amassed great wealth in trade, as well by lucky hits as by persevering industry, he resolved to add a peerage to his acquisitions. A bargain was made with the Irish Minister; the ambitious merchant was to be created a baron for the stipulated payment of £20,000. The patent was forthwith made out, and the new peer took his seat in due form. The Government never entertained a doubt that his lordship would faithfully pay them the price of his new honours; and in this happy confidence they gave him his coronet without first securing the money for it. Six months passed, during which the Castle took for granted that the new baron would fulfil his engagement at his earliest convenience. At length the secretary wrote a "private and confidential" epistle, to give his lordship's memory a gentle refresher.

The noble lord made short work of the matter. He wrote back, denying all recollection of the engagement referred to, expressing great indignation that anybody should presume to accuse him of being a party to the sale or purchase of a peerage; and threatening, should the claim be renewed, to impeach the Minister in Parliament for so grossly unconstitutional a proceeding. The Government were outwitted, and the ex-merchant got his coronet, as perhaps he had got other things also, without paying for it.

Many such scamps were to be found in the Irish House of Lords; and English lucubrators upon Irish affairs triumphantly point to their unprincipled conduct, and ask—as if the question were conclusive against Repeal—"Would you revive *such* a Parliament?"*

No, certainly. We seek not to revive corruption. We desire to restore the Irish Parliament, cleansed, purified, and placed beyond the reach of all corrupt influences. The unprincipled class, moreover, to which Lord M——y and Lord —— belonged, cannot in any fairness be quoted against Irish claims or Irish rights. That class was manufactured by England in this country. It was prevented by English power and English artifice from becoming fully identified with Irish interests. When England, therefore, upbraids us with its moral rottenness, we retort that she was the instigator of its political crimes—that those crimes were disastrous to the great mass of the Irish

---

* Among the aristocratic eccentricities of the time was the Earl of Belvedere's *penchant* for people who had hideous noses. He is said to have given an annual entertainment called the Nosey Dinner, the guests being all remarkable for their large red noses, or for some other sort of nasal deformity. His lordship's great delight was to invite two opposite proprietors of outlandish noses to take wine with each other, and to watch the converging inclination of their hideous profiles.

people, who had no participation in them; and that the disgrace, consequently, rests not on us, but on England herself, and on the individual criminals who yielded to her seductions in this country.

The corruption of the Irish Parliament is also often mentioned by our English censors as if English Parliaments had always been immaculate, and as if Ireland alone presented specimens of senatorial profligacy. English history, however, informs us that this species of iniquity has occasionally flourished in the Parliament of England. Lingard, for instance, says that when Charles II. received, in January, 1677, a portion of his annual pension from the King of France, the whole sum was immediately expended on the purchase of votes in the English House of Commons; the result of which traffic gave the Court, upon questions of finance, a majority of about thirty voices. But English senators did not restrict themselves to a market so limited as the English Court.

"It seemed," says Lingard, "as if the votes of the Members of Parliament were exposed for sale to all the Powers of Europe. Some received bribes from the Lord Treasurer on account of the King; some from the Dutch, Spanish, and Imperial ambassadors in favour of the confederates; some even from Louis at the very time when they loudly declaimed against Louis as the great enemy of their religion and liberties." In 1678 a test was proposed for the discovery of such Members of Parliament as had received bribes or any other consideration for their votes, either from the English or any other Government. "The popular leaders," says Lingard, "spoke warmly in its favour; but before the last division took place, about an hundred members slipped out of the House, and the motion was lost by a majority of fourteen."*

Lord Macaulay calls the management by corruption of the English Parliaments of that period, and of much more recent times, "one of the most important parts of the business of a Minister;" and, speaking of the long period between the reigns of Charles II. and George III., he says that it was "as notorious that there was a market for votes at the Treasury as that there was a market for cattle at Smithfield." †

Mr. Lecky, in his "History of England in the Eighteenth Century," ‡ quotes the following passage from Sir E. May's "Constitutional History," i. 317:

"Great sums of secret service money were usually expended in direct bribery; and places and pensions were multiplied to such an extent that it is on record that out of 550 members there were in the first Parliament of George I. no less than 271, and in the first Parliament of George II. no less than 257, holding offices, pensions, or sinecures."

---

* Lingard's "History of England," *ad annos* 1676, 1678.

† Macaulay's "History of England," vol. iii. pp. 541, 546 8vo edition).

‡ Lecky's "England in the Eighteenth Century," vol. i. p. 436.

Mr. Lecky, speaking of Sir Robert Walpole, says: "He (Walpole) governed by means of an assembly which was saturated with corruption, and he fully acquiesced in its conditions and resisted every attempt to improve it. He appears to have cordially accepted the maxim that Government must be carried on by corruption or by force, and he deliberately made the former the basis of his rule. . . . He employed the vast patronage of the Crown uniformly and steadily with the single view of sustaining his political position, and there can be no doubt that a large proportion of the immense expenditure of secret service money during his administration was devoted to the direct purchase of Members of Parliament. . . . If corruption did not begin with Walpole, it is equally certain that it did not end with him. His expenditure of secret service money, large as it was, never equalled in an equal space of time the expenditure of Bute."*

English politicians sometimes say that the Irish Parliament was so corrupt that it deserved extinction. To reason thus is to confound the turpitude of particular Parliaments with the existence of Parliament. It is to deprive the Irish people of their birthright because certain parliamentary majorities have been base and venal. Would the gentlemen who reason in this way apply the same logic to England? Would they argue that the English Par-

---

* Lecky's "England in the Eighteenth Century," vol. i. pp. 365, 367, 368.

liament ought to be annihilated, and the English people deprived of self-government because English senators sold their votes to Dutch, French, Spanish, German, and native purchasers, and because the notoriety of the traffic equalled that of the public cattle-market?

If the Union struggle in the Irish Parliament developed on the one hand the political depravity which England had laboured so hard to produce, it also displayed on the other hand many brilliant examples of the most stainless and unpurchasable honesty. Every effort to debauch the Legislature had for a series of years been systematically made by the Government; and yet in 1799 the first attempt to carry the Union was defeated by men who might have made for themselves whatever terms they pleased with the Minister. And in 1800, after every possible exertion to pack the Parliament had been resorted to, there still remained 115 members, a tried and trusty band, who, although in a minority, were yet miraculously numerous when we remember the enormous powers of corruption which the Government derived from the number of close boroughs, and from their other resources. Of the men who were returned by the people a majority stood firm to their trust. The traitors were chiefly found among those men whom private influence had introduced into the Legislature.

The Viceroy could not help entertaining respect

for the anti-Unionists. On the 24th of May, 1799, he writes to General Ross :* "There is an opposition in Parliament to the measure of Union, formidable in character and talents."

The English Cabinet did not think that their Irish confederates were sufficiently active in pressing forward the Union. Lord Castlereagh, in a letter to John King, Esq., dated 7th of March, 1800, thus accounts for their imputed slowness: "It will be in the first place considered that we have a minority consisting of 120 members, well combined and united, that many of them are men of the first weight and talent in the House, that 37 of them are members for counties, that great endeavours have been used to inflame the kingdom, that petitions from 26 counties have been procured, that the city of Dublin is almost unanimous against it, and, with such an opposition so circumstanced and supported, it is evident much management must be used." †

When Lord Castlereagh boasted that the Union, by extinguishing a great number of pocket boroughs, would operate as a measure of Parliamentary reform, Charles Kendal Bushe immediately retorted that Lord Castlereagh's Union majority were to be found among the members for those very constituencies which his lordship proposed to abolish as a punishment for their impurity; and that it would be impossible

---

* "Cornwallis Correspondence," vol. iii. p. 101.   † *Ibid.*

for him to select one hundred members for the greater constituencies, amongst whom he would not find himself in a minority. "What, then," asked Bushe, "results from his own confession? This—that he is about to carry the Union against that part of the Parliament which he allows to be pure, and by the instrumentality of that part which he alleges to be corrupt. He does not merely state this as a matter of candour, but as a matter of boast. He glories in cutting off the rotten limb, and amputating the withered branch of Parliament, and yet, with that withered branch he beats down the Constitution."

Out of doors there was a nearly universal detestation of the Union, which would have been effectual in defeating it if it were not for the overpowering military force in the hands of the Government.

I have not sought to conceal the faults or vices of the Irish Parliament. It was an unreformed borough Parliament; and to the evils resulting from its construction must be added the mischiefs flowing from its sectarian bigotry during the long period between the restoration of King Charles II. and the relaxation of the penal laws. Yet, notwithstanding these very serious drawbacks, it is a fact of the highest importance that from the moment when, in 1782, this unreformed, bigoted Parliament acquired freedom from the usurped claims of England to legislate for Ireland, the prosperity of Ireland sprang forward at a bound, and its progress is attested by a host of unimpeachable witnesses, to whose evidence I shall advert in a subsequent chapter of this work. It is scarcely possible to conceive more effectual obstructions to the beneficial action of a free, resident Legislature than those which arise from the sectarian intolerance of its members, and from the prevalence of a close-borough system. Yet the Irish Parliament, despite those obstructions, conferred essential benefits on the country—benefits which greatly countervailed its evils. It kept the money of the country at home. It enacted several good measures. The individual interests of its members necessarily often ran in the same groove with the interests of the country; so that personal selfishness occasionally came in aid of patriotism. The very facts of residence and of discharging at home the high functions of Irish legislators produced in many of them sentiments of patriotic pride and of national honour. The general results appeared in the astonishing advance of trade, commerce, manufactures, and agriculture — an advance which forms a strong and melancholy contrast with the general decay that followed the Union, and the present condition of our flying population. By the Union, England obtained the dishonest control of the whole resources of Ireland; but she also obtained the lasting hatred of the people whose Legislature she had first corrupted and then destroyed. The Union laid a sure foundation for Irish discontent and disaffection. It disposed the people to look anywhere for friendship rather than to the power that had robbed them of their birthright by an act that capped the climax of innumerable deeds of aggression. Great national crimes have seldom been forgiven by the injured parties. Oblivion of wrong is best promoted by ample and honourable restitution. Restitution is, in our case, absolutely indispensable to our national prosperity and dignity. "Keep knocking at the Union," were among the last words of Grattan to Lord Cloncurry. "Come it soon, or come it late," said O'Connell, "my deliberate conviction is that if the Union is not peacefully repealed, a sanguinary separation will be the ultimate result." This is pretty much what Saurin said on the 27th of February, 1800. "I consider," said he, "the present measure (of Union) as most dangerous to that connexion" (with Great Britain). "My opinion has been uniformly that it is a project to change an union and connexion of safety and independence for an union of insecurity and dependence." Mr. (afterwards Earl Grey) said in the English House of Commons on the 7th of February, 1800: "Though you should be able to carry the measure, yet the people of Ireland would wait for an opportunity of recovering their rights, which, they will say, were taken from them by force."

I conclude this chapter with the following incident. On the night when the fatal measure passed the House of Commons, a large crowd who had assembled in College Green, waited until

Mr. Speaker Foster, the leader of the anti-Unionists, quitted the House. They took off their hats and followed him, sad, silent, and uncovered, to his residence in Molesworth Street. Ere he entered the house, he turned round, and sadly and solemnly bowed to the people, who then dispersed. No word was exchanged between the Speaker and the crowd. All felt the deadening pressure of a terrible national calamity. It was a sorrow too profound for utterance.

CHAPTER IV.

HOW IRISH DISCONTENT IS VIEWED BY SOME ENGLISH WRITERS.

"If it (the balancing check) keeps the three estates of Parliament together, all in their just proportion in each kingdom, why not depend on the same principle operating in the same way, and keeping the two Legislatures of both kingdoms in their just relations to each other, so as that their mixed powers, like those of the mixed Government, shall, by their separate exertions so checked, preserve the symmetry and union of the whole machine of the Empire, which a theoretic or unwise merging of the one into the other might so affect as to render incapable of working?"—RIGHT HON. JOHN FOSTER, 1799.

It is in the highest degree desirable that England and Ireland should entertain mutual sentiments of friendship, and that both should willingly occupy their appropriate positions as constituent parts of a great Empire. It is in the highest degree desirable that all the inhabitants of Ireland should have reason to render to the throne of these kingdoms the homage of hearty and unqualified loyalty.

Ireland is dissatisfied with her position. While the Union, in its present shape, exists, Irish discontent will be ineradicable. It is an inquiry worthy of a statesman whether the position of Ireland is such as she ought to occupy; whether it is compatible with her rights, with her interests, and with her honour. And if it be compatible with none of these, it is worth inquiry whether a more satisfactory position could not be substituted for one which results in national suffering, in unnatural emigration, and in extensive disaffection.

The present condition of Ireland is a scandal to the civilised world, a curse to its inhabitants, and a disgrace to the Imperial Government. If experience can teach anything, the whole experience of the Union unquestionably teaches that Imperial legislation is incompetent to render Ireland prosperous and happy.

When Irish discontent is spoken of, English writers sometimes suppose that it is merely a traditionary sentiment still lingering in the national mind—the surviving result of injustice that has long since passed away. For instance, the *Times*, in an article on Fenianism in September, 1865, thus deals with the existing discontent: " The greater our former injustice to Ireland, the easier it is to account for existing discontent without assuming any present injustice. If there be any such present injustice, let it be pointed out. Unless it be the maintenance of the Irish Church, we know not where to look for it; and assuredly no English interest will be allowed to protect this institution if Ireland be united in demanding its abolition."

When the *Times* named the State Church as

the only injustice subsisting in 1865, it forgot a greater and more grievous wrong—the Legislative Union. The State Church has since then been disestablished, and partially disendowed. It was doubtless a wrong of great magnitude, and created a severance of feeling between the two great sections of the Irish people which has survived its disestablishment. I wish with all my heart that the words "Protestant" and "Catholic," as symbols of political party, could be obliterated from our vocabulary. The State Church was bad; but the Union is far worse.

The *Saturday Review* also says that injustice to Ireland is merely a matter of past history. It admits, indeed, that grievances existed at a former period. "But to our minds," it proceeds to say, "all that is passed now. We have turned over a new leaf. We have for some years tried to govern Ireland as a part of England, as justly, as patiently, as mildly as we could. The case for an aggrieved, a separate, an alien Ireland has passed away."

This self-complacent journal is unable to comprehend why discontent exists in Ireland. "We have," it seems to say, "done our best for your ungrateful nation. We have destroyed your Parliament, and yet you are not satisfied. We have thereby trebled the absentee drain, extinguishing numberless home sources of industrial profit, yet you are not satisfied. We extort from your poverty an enormous tribute—yet you are not satisfied. We make you pay a smart share of our own pre-

Union debt-charge—yet you are not satisfied. We have drawn off to England the Irish surplus revenue, which the Act of Union promised should be appropriated to Irish purposes exclusively — yet you are not satisfied. We meet your demand for the redress of these grievances with chicanery and insolence; we call you sturdy beggars and we mystify financial statements—yet you are not satisfied. We have got hold of your manufacture market—yet you are not satisfied. We have governed you in such a mode that your race seems in a fair way of being expelled from their native country, much to the delight of the leading organ of British opinion; yet you are not satisfied. O incorrigible nation of grumblers, how is it possible you can be discontented or ungrateful when we lavish such blessings on you? For, look you! this is governing Ireland as if she were part of England."

The free paraphrase I have given of the words of the *Saturday Review*, shows, not unfairly, the contrast between English opinion and Irish fact. The journalist innocently says, "We have for some years tried to govern Ireland as a part of England." The experiment has not brought prosperity to Ireland. Nor is it possible that it could. For Ireland is not a part of England. God has stamped upon her the indestructible features of national individuality. Self-Legislation is her vital need.

To govern her, therefore, as a part of England, is, in effect, to govern her for the benefit of England

and not for her own benefit. We protest against that ruinous spoliation of her wealth, that insulting suppression of her individuality, which are termed "governing her as a part of England." We demand that she shall be governed as a distinct nation, with separate needs and separate rights, in accordance with the principles of the Irish Constitution of 1782, which, notwithstanding great obstructive influences, diffused unexampled prosperity through the nation during the period of its continuance.

In a part of the article of the *Saturday Review* to which I have referred, the writer, speaking of a projected Fenian invasion of Canada, says: "Fortunately the Canadians, by an overwhelming majority, are firmly attached to British rule." So they well may be. For the Canadians enjoy a free Parliament, and the uncontrolled regulation of their national interests. They are not robbed of their revenue for British uses. But Canadian attachment to Great Britain would sustain a rude shock if the Imperial Government attempted to rule Canada on the present Irish model; if it tried to govern Canada "as a part of England"—in other words, to destroy her Legislature, rifle her exchequer, and in every department of the State make English prejudice, English theory, or English sentiment supersede Canadian opinion. When in 1838 Lord Durham went to Canada to quell disaffection in the only statesmanlike way in which disaffection can be quelled—that is to say, by removing the grievances that caused it—he asked a question which we in Ireland may appropriately ask: What principle of the British Constitution holds good in a country where the people's money is taken from them without the people's consent? In Ireland our money is taken by the English Parliament without our consent; and the income-tax was imposed on us against the votes of a large majority of the Irish representatives.

Lord Durham's remedy for Canadian wrongs was precisely that which we claim for Irish wrongs. He advised that complete internal self-government should be given to the colonists; that the government of Canada should be put as much as possible into the hands of the colonists themselves. His advice was adopted; the Canadians got Home Rule; and the result shows a Transatlantic population transformed by that just and statesmanlike concession from a nation of insurgents into a nation of as loyal subjects to Her Majesty as can be found in any part of her dominions.

Among the most rational notions I have seen expressed by English journalists on Irish affairs is the following dictum of the *Pall Mall Gazette*, in an article on Fenianism in September, 1865: " The real prospect for Ireland is that of becoming in course of time a cis-Atlantic Lower Canada. It will no more amalgamate heartily with England than oil with water; but there is no reason why we should not be perfectly good friends, and very useful and convenient neighbours."

Not the least reason, if Ireland were treated as Canada is treated. Not the least reason, if Ireland had but the fair play of self-legislation, which is her indefeasible right. To call this dismemberment is to suppose that Foster, Grattan, Saurin, Ponsonby, and the other great opponents of the Union, were enemies of British connexion, instead of being, as they were, its firm friends.

The instinct of every Irishman—unless he is influenced by sectarian animosities and fears—will impel him not only to abhor the destruction of his country's Legislature, but to hate the destroyer also. There never was a greater blunder than to call the Union a bond of international affection. When I was a boy of ten years old, I was told by my seniors that we once had a Parliament in Ireland and that English influence extinguished it. I candidly acknowledge that my immediate impulse was to regard England with resentful abhorrence. Religious prejudices had nothing to do with the matter, for I was born of a Protestant family. I do not state this from the absurd notion that any importance attaches to myself or my sentiments I make the avowal because it records and explains my individual participation in a sentiment that at this moment actuates millions at home, in America, and in the Colonies, and which, by its general diffusion, assumes an aspect that is anything but contemptible.

Security of tenure for the tenant farmers, extinction of tithe-rent charge, which the Land Act of

1881 deprives the landlords of the means to pay—these, and other minor measures of relief would mitigate some of the external symptoms of the national malady. But nothing short of the restoration of the Irish Constitution—of the Government of the Irish people by the Queen, Lords, and Commons of Ireland—can reach the root of the disease.

"We may hope," said Grattan in 1780, "to dazzle with illuminations, and we may sicken with addresses, but the public imagination will never rest, nor will the public heart be well at ease—never! so long as the Parliament of England exercises or claims a legislation over this country."

And in his closing speech in 1800 against the Union, he predicts that although, for the present, the forces of military terror and corruption may overthrow the Irish Constitution, yet the country will at some future time throw off the incubus of foreign legislation and re-establish her rights.

"I do not give up the country: I see her in a swoon, but she is not dead; though in her tomb she lies helpless and motionless, still there is on her lips a spirit of life, and on her cheek a glow of beauty—

> "Thou art not conquered; beauty's ensign yet
> Is crimson in thy lips and in thy cheeks,
> And Death's pale flag is not advanced there.

"While a plank of the vessel sticks together, I will not leave her. Let the courtier present his flimsy sail, and carry the light bark of his faith with every new breath of wind; I will remain anchored here with fidelity to the fortunes of my country, faithful to her freedom, faithful to her fall."

CHAPTER V.

THE DIPLOMACY OF MARQUIS CORNWALLIS.

> As we are men and Irishmen,
>   Scorn for his curst alliance;
> As we are men and Irishmen,
>   Unto his throat defiance.
>
> BANIM.

THE Union having been accomplished, the prevalent desire amongst the Irish people was, of course, to obtain its repeal. For a few years no great effort was made for this purpose. The army of occupation, under the terror of which it had been forced upon Ireland, was to a great extent still continued in the country.

But the national desire for Repeal is coeval with the Union itself. It was not possible that a nation should sit quietly down in contented acquiescence in its own servitude. A sullen sentiment of enmity to England smouldered in the public mind. Men brooded angrily over the enormous crimes the English Government had committed against their country; and they felt (to use the language of Saurin, a lawyer of the highest ability) that "the exhibition of resistance to the measure became merely a question of prudence."

Ere I pass to later periods, let me pause for a few moments to notice a misrepresentation. It is frequently said that the Catholics supported the Union. The Catholics, as a body, are free from the imputed guilt. At a Catholic aggregate meeting held in Dublin in 1795, the Catholic leaders unanimously passed a resolution that they would collectively and individually resist even their own emancipation, "if proposed to be conceded on the ignominious terms of an Union with the sister kingdom." Imbued with this sentiment, O'Connell, in his maiden speech, delivered at a Catholic meeting held at the Royal Exchange, Dublin, to oppose the Union, on the 13th of January, 1800, declared that he would prefer the re-enactment of the whole penal code to the destruction of the Irish Parliament. On the 15th of January, the patriotic conduct of the Dublin Catholics was referred to in the House of Commons by Grattan, who said: "If she (Ireland) perish, they (the Catholics) will have done their utmost to save her. . . . They will have flung out their last setting glories and sunk with their country."

The Viceroy, Marquis Cornwallis, had made many attempts to gain Catholic support for the Union, and he had at one time flattered himself with hopes of success. But on the 12th of December, 1798, he wrote as follows to Major-General Ross:

"The opposition to the Union increases daily in and about Dublin; and I am afraid, from conversations which I have had with persons much connected with them, that I was too sanguine when I hoped for the good inclinations of the Catholics."

His failure to cajole the Catholic body is again mentioned in the following passage of a letter he addressed to the Duke of Portland, dated 2nd of January, 1799: "The Catholics, as a body, still adhere to their reserve on the measure of Union. The very temperate and liberal sentiments at first entertained or expressed by some of that body, were by no means adopted by the Catholics who met at Lord Fingal's, and professed to speak for the party at large." *

"On the 12th of April, 1799, Mr. Secretary Cooke wrote to William Wickham, Esq., as follows: "The Catholics think it (the Union) will put an end to their ambitious hopes, however it may give them ease and equality." †

I find in an interesting compilation entitled "The Very Rev. Dr. Renehan's Collections on Irish Church History," the following incidental notice of Catholic hostility to the Union:

"1799, July 1.—Dr. Bray (Catholic Archbishop of Cashel), in reply to urgent appeals to procure discreetly Catholic signatures in favour of the Union

---

* "Cornwallis Correspondence," vol. iii. p. 28. The meeting at Lord Fingal's was held 13th of December, 1798.

† *Ibid.*, p. 87.

in Tipperary and Waterford, says that Lord Castlereagh, at whose instance this application was made, should know that he, as a Catholic Bishop, had little influence. The Union might prove to be a useful measure; but bishops injure their own character and the cause of religion *by interfering against the wishes of the people.* It is plain that Dr. Bray intended this answer as a polite refusal. A few days after, he received a letter from the Archbishop of Tuam, expressing his fears lest some ecclesiastics should be seduced by the Government into approval of its measures, particularly the Union, from which he anticipated the worst evils."*

Despite martial law and Governmental interference to obstruct anti-Union petitions and to procure signatures in favour of the Union, we know that the signatures against it were 707,000, whilst those in its favour did not at any time exceed 5,000. Now, when we reflect that out of the 5,000,000 who then inhabited Ireland, 4,000,000 were Catholics, and also that the whole number of pro-Union petitioners, Protestants and all, was not greater than 5,000, is it not clear that the Catholic body stands exculpated from the ignominy of having supported the disfranchisement of Ireland? Lord Cornwallis, while trying to persuade the Bishop of Lichfield that, excepting Dublin, the general sense of Ireland was favourable to the

---

* Renehan's "Collections," vol. i. p. 375.

Union, inadvertently adds: "It is, however, easy for men of influence to obtain addresses and resolutions on either side."* If so, how did it happen, that notwithstanding the alleged popularity of the Union, the men of influence who favoured it could only stimulate 5,000 persons to sign petitions in its behalf; whilst the men of influence on the other side could muster an array of 707,000 petitioners? Lord Cornwallis discloses the truth. On the 31st of January, 1800, he writes to Major-General Ross: "The Roman Catholics, for whom I have not been able to obtain the slightest token of favour, are joining the standard of opposition."

To these proofs that the Catholics were not accomplices in the disfranchisement of Ireland I add the following extract from Daniel O'Connell's anti-Union speech, delivered on the 13th of January, 1800: "There was no man present," said O'Connell, "but was acquainted with the industry with which it was circulated that the Catholics were favourable to the Union. In vain did multitudes of that body, in different capacities, express their disapprobation of the measure; in vain did they concur with others of their fellow subjects in

---

* "Cornwallis Correspondence," vol. iii. p. 169. It is to be noted that in the accounts we possess of the public transactions of the period, the number of signatures to pro-Union petitions is sometimes set down at 5,000, and sometimes at 3,000; but as it is also stated that several of the petitions prayed, not for the enactment of the Union, but only that it might be discussed, I dare say the apparent discrepancy may be explained by assigning 2,000 of the signatures to the latter class of petitions.

expressing their abhorrence of it—as freemen or freeholders, as electors of counties or inhabitants of cities—still the calumny was repeated; it was printed in journal after journal; it was published in pamphlet after pamphlet; it was circulated with activity in private companies; it was boldly and loudly proclaimed in public assemblies. . . . In vain did the Catholics individually resist the torrent. Their future efforts, as individuals, would be equally vain and fruitless; they must then oppose it collectively."

I have quoted the above testimonies in order to rescue the character of the Irish Catholics from a disgraceful accusation. That accusation, I presume, originated in the fact that the Government succeeded in cajoling a few Catholic prelates to sanction their measure, and that Lords Kenmare and Fingal were ready to surrender their country. I think the episcopal traitors did not exceed ten. Sir Jonah Barrington says: "The Bishops Troy, Lanigan, and others, deluded by the Viceroy, sold their country, and basely betrayed their flocks by promoting the Union. But," Sir Jonah adds, "the great body of Catholics were true to their country." * This can be affirmed alike of the laity, the priesthood, and the majority of the Bishops.

The Protestants were not more favourable to the Union than their Catholic brethren. There were numberless resolutions of grand juries, Orange

---

* Barrington's " Rise and Fall of the Irish Nation," chap. xxvii.

guilds, and Orange lodges, denouncing the project in the strongest language. Saurin declared that although the Union "might be made binding as a law, it could never become obligatory upon conscience; and that resistance to it would be in the abstract a duty." Numbers of the Protestant ascendency party were inaccessible to the bribes of the Minister. Their political integrity deserves honourable record, and enduring national gratitude. Sir Frederick Falkiner had four executions in his house at Abbotstown on the very day on which he rejected a large offer of money from Lord Castlereagh. There were numerous other instances of noble and disinterested patriotism amongst the leaders of Orangeism.

The Government had tried to delude both parties—the Catholics, by holding out hopes of their emancipation from the Imperial Parliament; the Protestants, by instilling into their minds a belief that the Union would render emancipation either impossible, or, if it should be granted, innocuous to Protestant ascendency. It must be observed that in the beginning of 1795 there was no active or extensive hostility entertained by the Irish Protestants to Catholic emancipation. But the machinations of the English Government had been so successful in reviving and inflaming the animosities of sects and parties (animosities rendered inveterate by the horrors of the rebellion), that in 1800 the liberal and generous feelings which had influenced the Protestants five years previously were to a large extent superseded by a stolid hatred of the Catholics, and a fierce resolve to resist their admission to any political privileges. George III. adopted the notion that under an Union emancipation would become impossible. In his published correspondence with Pitt, he tells that Minister that he had consented to the Union in the full belief that it would "shut the door" for ever against the Catholic claims. It required much dexterity on the part of the Viceroy and his agents to infuse into the minds of the rival parties these opposite beliefs. Lord Cornwallis was, as we have seen, instructed by Pitt to assure the Catholics that the success of the Union was essential to the success of emancipation. At the same time his subordinate ally, Mr. Secretary Cooke, while amusing the Catholics with some indistinct hope of "additional privileges" (which he did not specify), assured the Protestants in the same paragraph that under an Union "the Catholics could not force their claims with hostility against the whole power of Great Britain and Ireland."*

Of Mr. Pitt's ambiguous utterances Mr. Speaker Foster said: "Mr. Pitt's language is of such a nature that one would imagine he had the two religions on either side of him, and one was not to hear what he said to the other." †

Lord Cornwallis's task was to create among the

---

* Mr. Secretary Cooke's "Arguments for and against an Union Considered," p. 30.

† Mr. Foster's Speech, 11th April, 1799.

Catholics a conviction that their claims would be much *strengthened* by incorporation with England. But what was the Viceroy's own conviction? Let him answer the question himself:

"The claims of the Catholics will certainly be much *weakened* by their incorporation into the mass of British subjects." *

This he wrote to the Duke of Portland at the very time when he was labouring to convince the Catholics that the Imperial Parliament would emancipate them. So it did, twenty-nine years later; and so it would *not* have done at that, or probably at any other time, had not O'Connell's agitation created a belief in the Duke of Wellington's mind that the only alternatives were concession or civil war.

It is interesting to notice the doubts of success which Lord Cornwallis occasionally felt. In a pamphlet by a barrister named Weld, the author, speaking of the bribed supporters of the Union, says, "their penitential tears fall fast upon the wages of apostasy."

This reluctance to perform the execrable task for which they took payment is seen by Lord Cornwallis, who writes to the Bishop of Lichfield, on the 24th of January, 1800: "There can, I think, now be no great doubt of our Parliamentary success, although I believe that a great number of our friends are not sincere well-wishers to the measure

---

* Letter to the Duke of Portland, 24th December, 1798. "Cornwallis Correspondence," vol. iii. p. 22.

of Union." The Viceroy was right. Those men had not virtue to resist the wages of iniquity; yet their lingering *amor patriæ* would have been rejoiced if their country had escaped the blow of the executioner.

Again, the Viceroy writes to General Ross on the 4th of February, 1800: "God only knows how the business will terminate; but it is so hard to struggle against private interests, and the pride and prejudices of a nation, that I shall never feel confident of success till the Union is actually carried." *

This admission that he was fighting a hard battle against the pride and prejudices of a nation, contrasts rather curiously with his statements in other parts of his correspondence that the national sentiment was in his favour. On the 18th of April, writing to General Ross on the Parliamentary supporters of the Union, His Excellency says: "I believe that half of our majority would be at least as much delighted as any of our opponents, if the measure were defeated." †

In fact they well knew that the measure struck a mortal blow at the best interests of their country, as well as at their own personal consequence. But the seduction of enormous bribes prevailed so far as to secure a majority for the Government in 1800. On the 27th of February in that year, Mr. Saurin described that majority as "consisting almost

---

* "Cornwallis Correspondence," vol. iii. pp. 169, 177.
† *Ibid.*, vol. iii. pp. 228, 252.

entirely of gentlemen holding offices or places at the pleasure of the Crown; of adventurers from the bar, of adventurers from the British army, of men who would have no scruple to subject the property of this kingdom, in which they have no share, to a foreign Parliament; to traffic the independence of Ireland for a personal independence for themselves."

In the English Parliament, Mr. (afterwards Earl) Grey thus described the Union majority in the Irish House of Commons: "There are 300 members in all. . . . One hundred and sixty-two voted in favour of the Union; of these 116 were placemen; some of them were English generals on the Staff, without a foot of ground in Ireland, and completely dependent on the Government."

The Union being carried against the will of nearly every inhabitant of Ireland, Protestant and Catholic, it appeared to the Government politic to conciliate the Protestants, as being the stronger party. Pitt indeed made a show of retiring from office, because the King's prejudices prevented him from carrying a Catholic Relief Bill. But he soon resumed office, having—as Lord Hawkesbury at a later period* publicly declared in the House of Lords—made a voluntary pledge that he never again would bring the Catholic question under the consideration of His Majesty. And in 1805 he positively refused to present a petition for Emanci-

---

* March 26, 1807.

pation to the House of Commons, or even to lay it on the table of the House; he went so far as to say that if the petition should be presented by any other Ministerial member, he would feel it his duty to resist it. At the same time he politely informed the deputation who brought the petition, "that the confidence of so very respectable a body as the Catholics of Ireland was highly gratifying to him."

The confidence of the great body of Irish Catholics, Mr. Pitt had never possessed; and the few gentlemen (ten Bishops included) who styled themselves "Catholic leaders," and who were weak enough, or base enough, to consent to the Union in the hope of its being immediately followed by Catholic Emancipation, and in the hope, also, of episcopal pensions from the Government — those gentlemen deserved their disappointment. They deserved it for their folly in trusting the vague, indefinite intimations of Pitt and others that the English Parliament would immediately remove their political disabilities. They deserved it for their unprincipled readiness to sacrifice the legislative independence of their country for any consideration whatever.

No doubt there were multitudes who rejoiced in believing with King George III. that the Union had "shut the door" for ever against the claims of the Catholics. Those claims seemed for a while to be forgotten. The Government allowed the Irish Protestants to monopolise the local control of the country as the most effectual means of reconciling them to the Union. They had the Castle, the courts, the public offices, and the enormous revenues of the State Church. They had everything that remained after the suppression of the Legislature. Yet this monopoly did not avail to extinguish altogether the national sentiment that had grown up under the influence of home legislation.

Grattan, the illustrious founder of the Constitution of 1782, retired on the enactment of the Union into private life, from which he did not emerge until 1805, when he was returned to the Imperial Parliament for the borough of Malton. On the first appearance of so distinguished an orator on the boards of St. Stephen's, there was necessarily great curiosity excited. There were in his style of speaking some marked peculiarities, and also in his voice some Hibernian inflections, which called forth an incipient titter of derision from certain of his English auditors. These symptoms, however, were checked by Pitt, who nodded his approval of the style and manner of the speaker.

What a type of Ireland's degradation! Her most honoured and venerable patriot exposed to the sneers of a foreign assembly, and indebted for exemption from insult to the patronising approbation of the bitter and triumphant enemy of his country! It was in the speech he then delivered that Grattan, in alluding to the fallen fortunes of Ireland, used the touching words, "I sat by her cradle; I follow her hearse."

In 1805 several of the guilds of Dublin met to prepare petitions for the repeal of the Union. The Stationers' Company met at their hall in Capel Street and appointed a committee of nine to draw up their petition. They were probably encouraged to commence the good work by Grattan's return to the English House of Commons. The Orange Corporation of Dublin followed the example of the guilds in 1810, and confided their petition for repeal to Grattan and Sir Robert Shaw, father, I believe, of the gentleman who for many years was the Recorder of Dublin. Both these gentlemen promised to support the Repeal, and Grattan emphatically said: "Whenever the question shall come before Parliament, I shall prove myself an Irishman; and that Irishman whose first and last passion is his native country."

It is curious to hear modern Orangemen and Tories denouncing Repeal as being no better than treason, when we remember that Repeal was proposed in 1810 by the most ultra-Orange municipality in the kingdom. The example of Repeal agitation was then given by that body, whose anti-Catholic prejudices were so violent and inflexible, that it admitted only five Catholics to be freemen of the city of Dublin during the period of forty-eight years, from 1793, when the Catholics became legally admissible, to 1841, when the Orange Corporation was dissolved by the Municipal Reform Act. Mr. Butt, while still a Tory, once arraigned the Repealers as traitors in a speech at the Rotunda. He apparently forgot that his ancient friends and clients, the Orange Corporation, should necessarily be involved in this censure. The "treason" of Repeal was long enshrined in the Orange sanctuary in William Street, and many a true Orange knee was bent in that temple before the altar of the national divinity. Shall we ever see the Orangemen return to their ancient anti-Union principles? Shall we ever see them adopt the political faith which seeks not the ascendency of a class or sect, but the greatness, the prosperity, the dignity, of the whole Irish nation?

I have mentioned that during the forty-eight years from 1793, when Catholics became legally eligible, to 1841, when the Corporate Reform Act disbanded the Orange Corporation, the Dublin corporators only admitted five Catholics as members of their body. Contrast their intolerance with the liberal conduct of the reformed Corporation of Dublin, in which there is an important majority of Catholics. Since 1841 to the year 1882, this reformed Corporation, in which Catholics predominate, has seventeen times elected a Protestant Lord Mayor; besides conferring on Protestants the situations of City Treasurer, City Engineer and Borough Surveyor, Assistant Engineer, Medical Officer of Health and City Analyst, Overseer of Waterworks, Superintendent of Fire Brigade, and Assistant-Superintendent. The names of these gentlemen will be found in the Appendix. The moral of the contrast is plain.

CHAPTER VI.

REPEAL AGITATION—SECTARIAN OBSTRUCTION.

> And will yo bear, my brother men,
>   To see your altars trampled down?
> Shall Christ's great heart bleed out again
>   Beneath the scoffer's spear and frown?
> *Spirit of the Nation.*

IN 1810 public meetings were held in sustainment of the Repeal, and in order to encourage the Corporation. George III. became ill, prior to his madness, and the loyal corporators suspended their agitation lest they should embarrass the royal invalid. In 1813 the Repeal demand was renewed in Dublin, and the Repealers of all creeds held a meeting to promote their object. O'Connell, who had joined the movement in 1810, now again came forward, and exerted himself in conformity with the earliest declaration he ever had made of his political principles. In 1822 Mr. Lucius Concannon, a member of the House of Commons, gave notice of a motion for the Repeal of the Union. Mr. (afterwards Sir Robert) Peel inquired "if the honourable gentleman could seriously ask the House to violate that solemn compact?" Just as if a measure which was literally forced upon Ireland at the point of the bayonet, could be rationally called a compact! From that period forward the Repeal was constantly mooted in private society. In 1824 Lord Cloncurry wrote a letter, which was read by O'Connell at the Catholic Association, recommending the Catholics to abandon for a time the struggle for Emancipation, and to coalesce with the Protestants in a struggle for Repeal. But this advice was premature; the Protestants of Ireland could not just then have been induced to combine with the Catholics for that or any other purpose. The demon of religious hatred was in the ascendant. Catholicity was familiarly designated "the beast" and "the accursed thing," by Protestant controvertists; and the more bigoted Protestant preachers inculcated envenomed hostility to the creed of the Catholics as a Christian duty paramount to all others. When sectarian hate is incessantly enforced it is speedily transferred from the creed of misbelievers to their persons. Those who recollect the exertions of the Biblical party in 1824, 1825, and 1826, have reason to rejoice that their pernicious activity has been to a considerable extent relaxed. The controversial excitement through the country was actually frightful. The Protestants were taught to look on the religion of the Catholics as a grand magazine of immorality, infidelity, and rebellion; while the Catholics, in their turn, regarded their enthusiastic assailants as the victims of a spiritual insanity derived from an infernal source, and as disastrous in its social results as it was bizarre in its exhibition. The kindly charities of friendship were annihilated; ancient intimacies were broken up; hatred was mitigated only by a sentiment of scornful compassion.*

Such were too frequently the mutual feelings of the two great sections of the Irish community—the one party having the immense preponderance in number, the other in wealth. Mr. Plunket, then Attorney-General, had declared that "the cauldron was already boiling over in Ireland; and that it

---

* Lord Farnham was a leading patron of these Biblical exploits. One cannot help regarding with a feeling of melancholy interest the curious scenes to which the system patronising proselytes from Popery gave rise. I knew more than one Protestant clergyman, remote from the headquarters of religious excitement, who had been asked by distressed wretches, "How much will I get from your reverence if I turn Protestant?" The universal conviction on the minds of the lower order of Catholics was that nobody "turned," as they called it, except for lucre, and that an enormous fund existed, under the control of the Protestant leaders, for buying up the religious belief of all Papists who were willing to conform. Weekly bulletins of the number of new converts from Popery were placarded on the walls, or suspended from the necks of persons who were hired to perambulate the public streets. Fourteen hundred and eighty-three converts were at one time announced as the fruit of Lord Farnham's exertions in Cavan; but when Archbishop Magee went down to confirm them their number had shrunk to forty-two. Lord Farnham was doubtless a sincere enthusiast; but his fanatical folly was excessive, and he was greatly imposed on. He kept open house for the crowds of proselytes, who were furnished with soup, potatoes, and in some was not requisite that a polemic contest should be thrown into it." *

The advice was wasted. Many motives impelled the Biblical party to persevere. First of all, to do them every justice, there were some fanatics among their number who conscientiously believed that they were divinely commissioned to dispel the gross darkness of Popery. They were, as they conceived, authorised to walk forth, wielding "the sword of the Spirit, which is the Word of God." Then there were the political speculators, who looked on the furious theological excitement as affording a useful diversion of men's minds from the grievances of tithes and legal disabilities to the abstract topics of purgatory, transubstantiation, and Saint Peter's

---

instances with clothes. Pauper Protestants are said to have sometimes enjoyed his hospitality under the pretext of being "converts" from Popery; and it is said that such Catholics as thought they could escape recognition among the multitude of strange faces, contrived to be "converted" three or four times over, in order to prolong the substantial advantage of being fed in a dear season at the noble lord's cost. When the supply of food, etc., was discontinued, they returned to their former Church. This Lord Farnham had been a determined opponent of the Union in 1800; and not long before his death, he declared at a Conservative meeting that his hostility to Repeal arose from a religious, and not at all from a political motive. Alas! Lord Farnham was not the only man in whom sectarian fanaticism spoiled a good patriot.

* But although Mr. Plunket said this, he is also stated—I do not know with what accuracy—to have helped to set the cauldron boiling by advising Dr. Magee, the Protestant Archbishop of Dublin, to institute a controversial movement against the Catholic religion, which it was hoped would produce numerous conversions to Protestantism.

supremacy. Again, it was hoped and expected by others that the ceaseless abuse launched at Popery would disincline Protestants to become emancipators, and possibly withdraw from the Catholics the political support of many who already had joined them.

It is probable that some of the Liberal members of Parliament, at that period, had but little sincerity in their emancipating zeal. The profession of Liberal politics effected two things for them—it obtained an agreeable popularity, and also what they considered the honour of seats in Parliament. Such persons voted for the Catholics year after year, entertaining, I verily believe, a full conviction that Emancipation would never be conceded. They thus enjoyed the cheap distinction of being senators on the easy terms of supporting a measure for which they cherished no affection, but of whose defeat they indulged in a comforting certainty. How ludicrously disappointed must such men have been when Peel and Wellington suddenly became champions of Emancipation in 1829!

Religious jealousy and sectarian distrust, like the poisonous exhalations of the upas tree, blighted and withered the natural, inborn sentiment of nationality in many a well-meaning man. When Lord Cloncurry, in the letter already alluded to, publicly advocated Repeal, a worthy Protestant gentleman said to me that it would be an excellent thing if we had a Parliament of our own in Ireland —"but then," he added, "the Papists are so numerous they would soon get the upper hand." I asked him what harm their emancipation would do him or any one? His reply was to the effect that they would rival the Protestants in everything; if a Papist was more eloquent or a better lawyer than a Protestant, he might get the start of the Protestant in Parliament, or he might he promoted to the Bench, while the Protestant of inferior talent lost the race. As matters stood, the Protestant could not be beaten in the race, for the Papist could not run; an advantage that should not be surrendered on any account.

I mention this trifling incident because it illustrates the sort of jealous feeling which operated, not only to enlist Protestants against the Catholic claims, but also to smother their national spirit as Irishmen. The mischievous efficacy of this jealous terror will be more apparent when I add that the gentleman in question had been connected with the United Irishmen in 1797. The impressions received from that connexion were effaced by the malign influence of sectarian partisanship. And yet there was no great bitterness, nor was there any personal hostility in his politics. He did not hate Catholics; he was not unkind to them in his landlord capacity; but he had taken up the notion that the doctrine of absolution authorised crime. He had accurately expressed the sentiment that actuated thousands—a sturdy resolve to sustain the monopoly the Protestants had got, not only to preserve a party advantage, but from a belief that the spiritual merits of Protestantism entitled its professors to that monopoly.

Meanwhile, O'Connell worked the Catholic question indefatigably. He was an inexhaustible declaimer, and astonishingly fertile in argument, in expedient, and in topics of excitement. There had been from the commencement of his career this novel feature in his agitation—there was nothing secret in it: no locked doors, no secret committees, no hidden springs, no machinery to which he would not at any moment have admitted the whole corps of Government inspectors. Former political leaders had conceived that secrecy was an indispensable element of success. But O'Connell early saw the perils of every scheme of which concealment formed a part. The very fact of supposing a junto secret would necessarily induce ill-regulated spirits to give utterance to illegal or treasonable sentiments. There was the presumed protection of silence. Then there instantly arose the danger of treachery; any rascal who was sufficiently base to betray his associates, any Reynolds or Newell, might instantly compromise the safety of the entire association by revealing the indiscretion, or the illegality, or the treason, of a single member. O'Connell's sagacity swept away all such danger. By resolving to hide nothing, his associates were sure to say and do nothing that required to be hidden.

O'Connell's immediate predecessor as a Catholic leader was John Keogh, a Dublin merchant.

Keogh was far advanced in years at the time when O'Connell first became very celebrated; and it is believed that the old leader felt jealous of the popular talents as well as of the influence acquired by the younger one. It is certain that he sought to persuade O'Connell that the Catholics, instead of continuing their agitation, should relapse into silence and inertion, and try the effect of regarding the Government with a surly, awe-inspiring frown, indicative of hostility too deeply rooted to petition or negotiate. Keogh, in fact, proposed and carried a resolution to that effect at a public meeting at which his rival attended. O'Connell proposed and carried a counter resolution to that effect at the same meeting, which pledged the Catholics to unremitting activity.

Nothing could have gratified the Government more than the adoption by the Catholics of Keogh's advice. It would have released them from the annual Parliamentary bore of the Catholic question. It would have retarded the success of that question incalculably. The policy of endeavouring to scare a hostile Government by a grim and silent scowl, was too melodramatic to avail on the political stage.

O'Connell, of course, persevered. In 1813 he was called "an agitator with ulterior views." He immediately accepted the designation, and declared that the ulterior object he had in view was the Repeal of the Union. When urged at a much later period to postpone the agitation of the

Catholic claims to that of Repeal, he refused to comply, alleging as his reason that Emancipation, by removing one great subject of national difference, would facilitate the junction of all Irishmen to regain their national independence. O'Connell undoubtedly entertained at that time too favourable a notion of the patriotism of the Orange party. He did not anticipate the stubborn, inflexible, enduring Orange bigotry which has survived the emancipation of the Catholics, and thus outlived the chief pretext for its exercise. No doubt there were other pretexts too; there were the corporations and the iniquitous Church Establishment; the former have been taken from the Orangemen; but the so-called "disendowment" of the State Church has been so partially effected that it is in truth a re-endowment, not indeed of its original magnitude, but sufficiently large to make the Church a profitable institution to its officers, who are principally subsidised at the expense of the nation. So long as an anti-national institution is supported at the national expense, so long will the party that gains by its existence refuse to co-operate with the general mass of their countrymen.

John Keogh's belief in the inutility of political agitation is instructive. Lord Fingal was latterly impressed with that belief, and alleged it as his reason for declining to preside at a Catholic meeting in Dublin. How often have I—how often have all whose memory extends back to the latter years of the Catholic struggle—heard from all sides the exclamation, "Oh! they will never get Emancipation! The Government never will grant it! How are the Catholics to frighten the Government into concession? O'Connell is wasting his time; he has been haranguing for nearly thirty years, and has brought his dupes no nearer to it yet."

Thus do we hear the struggles of Ireland for domestic legislation denounced as a delusion, and in much the same language. That our claim should be derided by our enemies is natural. Among its friends—that is to say among the great bulk of the people of Ireland—there is too often an impatience of persevering agitation, a disposition to relinquish a pursuit that is not speedily successful. To all fickle patriots I would observe, firstly, that the object to be gained—namely, the restoration of the Irish Parliament in connection with the Crown of Great Britain—is our indefeasible right, and is vitally necessary to our national prosperity. It is a political pearl beyond price. Secondly, I would remind them that the pursuit of Catholic Emancipation occupied fifty-one years. The first relaxation of the penal laws occurred in 1778; the admission of Catholics to the Bench and to Parliament was not gained until 1829. Fifty-one years! Here is a lesson for impatient patriots. During that protracted period how many were the dreary intervals of hopeless depression! How often did ultimate success appear desperate! How many a heart was weary of the long, long struggle, which often seemed a vain and feeble protest against omnipotent hostility! Yet for fifty-one years the friends of the Catholic cause struggled on with varying fortunes, until at last success crowned their persevering efforts. And we must not forget that some of the worst enactments of the penal code had become law more than fourscore years before the earliest legal mitigation of that code's severity.

Hence we may learn a lesson of unfaltering perseverance in pursuit of Repeal. I do not underrate the difficulties of the task. England is now strong, and we are weak. Yet it is quite possible that political complications may arise which would render it worth England's while to purchase the fidelity of Ireland at the expense of that grand act of restitution. Repeal of the Union has ever had, has now, and ever will have, the great strength of incontrovertible justice and right. Let the people of Ireland be ever on the watch for a time when Imperial expediency may enforce from our rulers the concession of our righteous claim to self-legislation. Fenianism in America, despite its blunders and the glaring rascality of some of its leaders, is a portent too mighty to be despised. It is an exhibition to the world of the insatiable resentment of a people expelled by misgovernment, fiscal and political, from the land which "the Lord their God had given them" to inhabit. When, after 1798, the Marquis Cornwallis was congratulated because "the rebels were all crossing the Atlantic," His Excellency answered: "I would

rather have three rebels to deal with in Ireland
than one in America." Fenianism, as we have
seen its exhibition in America, showed a great
waste of power. The Fenians possess the raw
material of great strength; but their strength is
neutralised by mistakes in their programme, and
by the turpitude of scheming leaders, who have
filled their own pockets by trafficking on popular
credulity.

The hatred entertained to England by the expatriated Irish, whom the Union has expelled
from their native land by stripping it of the
means of supporting them, has occasionally
puzzled English commentators on Irish affairs.
But the fact can be easily explained. England first
corrupted the Irish Parliament, and then destroyed
it. The destruction of home government was
necessarily followed by national decay. Deprived
by the competition of English capital of the resource
of manufacturing industry, the great bulk of the
people were thrown on the land as their sole means of
subsistence. Mr. Mitchell Henry, member for the
County Galway, stated in the English House of
Commons on the 9th of February, 1880, that there
were no more than 273 manufactories in Ireland, and
that these included the flax-mills at Belfast. He
added that the manufactories only gave employment
to 80,000 persons in a population that then exceeded
five millions. The people, almost exclusively dependent on the land for the means of existence, were
in numberless instances persecuted by rapacious

landlords, whose insatiable greed was often accompanied with fierce sectarian hatred of the tenants whom they fleeced. The landlords were generally Protestants. The tenants were generally Catholics. The whole ecclesiastical State revenues of Ireland had been wrenched by English power from the Catholics and given to the members of the English religion, whose ministers, naturally drawn towards the power that had given them the revenues, and as naturally hating the Catholic people who were wronged by that gigantic fraud, occasionally stimulated the religious zeal of their flocks by such utterances as the following:

"Again, sir," said the Reverend Francis Gervais at a meeting at Dungannon, held on Tuesday, 9th of December, 1828, "I consider the religion of Rome as under the curse of the Almighty, distinctly denounced against it, and that the time is at hand when the Divine judgment will fall on it, and everything connected with it—political institutions as well as others."

The report says these sentiments evoked "great applause."

In July, 1843, Doctor Robert Daly, Protestant Bishop of Cashel, delivered a charge to his clergy, principally against the Tractarians, in which his lordship thus expressed himself:

"It was said by a shrewd and pious man that Popery was the masterpiece of Satan, and that he never would bring into the world a second scheme of evil equal to it in cunning and mischief; and the scheme now introduced (Puseyism) is not another—it is only a modification of the Popish views."

Isaac Butt, in his admirable "Plea for the Celtic Race," cites the following passage from a speech delivered at a great Protestant meeting in 1834 by the Reverend Marcus Beresford, afterwards Archbishop of Armagh:

"I trust that every good and faithful minister of his God would sooner have potatoes and salt, surrounded with Protestants, than to live like princes, surrounded with Papists."

It will be admitted that such utterances as these were not calculated to promote friendly feelings between the Protestant landlords and the Catholic peasantry. Enthusiastic clergymen vied with each other in assailing the popular creed.

The absence of manufactures necessarily caused a great subdivision of land. The interests of the landlords suffered from the overcrowding of their estates with human beings for whom there was no manufacturing outlet, and whose numbers exceeded the capacity of the land, as it was then cultivated, to support them. The system of clearing estates of their human inhabitants was vigorously acted on. The late Mr. Sharman Crawford showed, from parliamentary returns, that in the five years from 1838 to 1843 inclusive, ejectment proceedings had been taken against 356,985 persons; and he said he was prepared to show that the extermination of the people was going on in a rapidly increasing ratio. He called it "a dreadful and heartless persecution." The crowbar brigade has been actively employed from that day to this; and between its operations, and the general impoverishment of Ireland resulting from the want of home government, our population, which in 1841 was 8,196,597, has sunk in 1885 to 4,900,000. Lord Macaulay instances as a proof of the destructive effects of war that the Prussian population was diminished ten per cent. by the wars of Frederick the Great. The Irish population has lost more than thirty per cent. under the Union since 1841; and if it be said that it increased between 1800 and 1841, we reply that it multiplied in misery during that period. There were not then the modern facilities for emigration, and the Union starved our people in their own country. Now that magnificent steamers waft them cheaply and swiftly across the Atlantic, they emigrate, bearing in their hearts an ineradicable hatred of the power that has driven them into exile.

Can we conceive a condition of things more calculated to demoralise a nation, or to engender international animosity? Mr. Godkin, editor of a New York journal, contributes to the *Nineteenth Century* for August, 1882, the following testimony of Irish feeling towards the English Government:

"I confess," he says, "I have until recently under-estimated the strength and permanence of Irish hatred of England, which the English hatred of Irishmen has at last produced. . . . In America it is apparently cultivated by the Irish as a sort of religion, and is transmitted to the second generation, which knows Ireland only by hearsay. . . . The Irishman in this country and his son and grandson are tormented neither by landlord nor police, and never see an Englishman or the English flag, and yet they hate the English Government with a kind of frenzy."

This American writer ascribes Irish antipathy to England to the habitual hatred and contempt of Ireland which pervade English literature and conversation. That cause doubtless operates; but a much more potent cause exists in the material injury and insult inflicted on Ireland by the Union. That measure permanently dislocated the social frame of Ireland, checked the growth of manufactures, intensified the mutual enmity of classes, overspread the land with pauperism by draining it of public revenue and private income, and became the prolific parent of crime by producing a hideous condition of social and political distortion and disease.

I respectfully suggest to the Irish in America and in the Colonies, that in order to achieve legislative freedom for Ireland, they must renounce every principle that repels the great body of the Irish Repealers at home. They are sometimes accused of intending to substitute a republic for the Irish throne of Queen Victoria. It is our ardent desire that Her Majesty should govern Ireland through an Irish Ministry and an Irish Legislature, just as

Francis Joseph now governs Hungary through a Hungarian Ministry and a Hungarian Legislature. The Fenians—I speak of the multitude of Irish-American emigrants, not of some ten or twelve dishonest leaders—must bear in mind that the Irish Repealers inherit the constitutional principles of 1782, by which the legislative independence of Ireland was combined with untainted loyalty to the sovereign of these realms. Any deviation from these principles must be fatal to an alliance between them and us; fatal to the strength which such an alliance, if wisely formed, would constitute.

Calculated as the Legislative Union is to alienate Irishmen from the English connexion, it is not unnatural that our exiles who have sought refuge in the American Republic from the wrongs inflicted by that measure, should sympathise in the Republican principles of the land of their adoption. But it does not therefore follow that they will not loyally and faithfully adhere to the Royal Constitution of Ireland when the Home Government Bill shall have removed the evil of foreign legislation, and re-established on a stable basis our exclusive right to legislate for our country. Their unanimous support of Mr. Gladstone's Bill sufficiently indicates their sentiments.

English writers have complained that they have now two Irelands to deal with, one on each side of the Atlantic. This is true; and in order that these two Irelands should effectively combine for the recovery of their rights, the Ireland now in exile must carefully shape her course in accordance with the principles and exigencies of the Ireland at home.*

It is needless to point out the political contingencies in which British statesmen may find it their true policy to give Ireland that contentment which can alone result from our possessing the sole control of our own national concerns. War-clouds are blackening in various quarters of the horizon. It is vitally important to the integrity of the Empire, that in the event of foreign war, Ireland should be the fast and firm friend of England. There is but one way of making her so, and that is by the restoration of her stolen property, her power of self-legislation—in a word, by repealing the Union.

All this is of course unpalatable to the English lust of domination. But we in Ireland have our own experience of that domination. In an article on Fenianism in 1867, the *Times* asserted with sad truth that England " does but hold Ireland in the very hollow of her hand." Much more recently the *Economist*,† in an article on Secret Societies, repeated the same statement in these words : " It is the English people who hold Ireland."

True: we are strangled in the English gripe, and the results of this Imperial pressure are

---

* There are also other Irelands growing up in Canada, Australia, and other British colonies.

† The *Economist*, quoted in the *Irish Times*, 1st of July, 1882.

disclosed by the special correspondent of the *Times*, who writes from Cork to that journal on the 23rd of March, 1867. "In the country districts," says the *Times* correspondent, "the depopulation of Ireland is not brought to one's notice so forcibly as in the towns. The peasant's cabin, when its last occupant has gone across the blue water, is pulled down, and no trace is left that it ever existed. But town dwellings 'to let' and empty shops remain, sad witnesses of a population that has been and is not. To the Irishman this is a trite subject; the English traveller, accustomed at home to the rapid growth of numerous small towns in most of the counties he visits, is startled in this country by the almost uniform decay of towns, both small and great."

Yes; Ireland is held, as the *Times* says, in the very hollow of the hand of England; and the deadly consequence of that unnatural position appears in the evanishment of her people and in the decay recorded by the *Times* correspondent. It is well to bear in mind that when we were *not* held in the hollow of her hand—when, after 1782, we enjoyed for some years the priceless blessing of self-government — every element of national prosperity developed itself with a force which, contrasted with our present degraded and despoiled condition, demonstrates the absolute necessity of domestic legislation.

"It is the English people," says the *Economist*, "who hold Ireland."

This is the explanation of the ulcerated state of Ireland. The English people have no more right to hold Ireland than the French or German people have to hold England. No condition can be more unnatural, more provocative of crime, more prolific of turbulence, more conducive to misery, than that of a nation gripped fast in the talons of another.

The extermination of great masses of the Irish people appears, from time to time, to have been a favourite object of English statesmanship. In the reign of Elizabeth, Lord Deputy Gray so conducted the Government that, as Leland informs us, the Queen was assured "that little was left in Ireland for Her Majesty to reign over but ashes and carcases."*

The Governmental raid on human life is thus described by Mr. Froude: †

"In 'the stately days of great Elizabeth,' the murder of women and children appears to have been the every-day occupation of the English police in Ireland; and accounts of atrocities, to the full as bad as that at Glencoe, were sent in on half a sheet of letter-paper, and were endorsed like any other documents with a brevity which shows that such things were too common to deserve criticism or attract attention."

In Mr. Prendergast's "Cromwellian Settlement," the author says: "Ireland now lay void as

---

* Leland, book iv. chap. 2.

† See his article in *Fraser's Magazine* for March, 1865, "How Ireland was Governed in the Sixteenth Century."

a wilderness. Five-sixths of her people had perished."*

In the gracious reign of Queen Victoria more than three millions of the Irish race have been got rid of between 1846 and 1885. This is being held in the very hollow of the hand of England. The diminution still goes on; and so long as we enjoy that affectionate pressure, the same result may be expected. The *modus operandi* has indeed been changed from ancient times. In the days of Elizabeth and Cromwell there were sanguinary raids against the people, and troops were employed in destroying the green corn and carrying off the cattle in order to starve out the Irish race. The people perished because their means of support were destroyed or abstracted. And the people of our own time perish or emigrate precisely because their means of support are taken away from them —not, indeed, by the coarse, rude methods of a former age, but by the equally effectual methods devised by modern statesmanship. The Union, with its consequent drain of Irish wealth in absentee taxes and absentee rental, and its destruction of the nascent manufacturing industries of Ireland by irresistible British competition, achieves the thinning out of our race which was formerly wrought by the sword. It deprives Ireland of the means of supporting the Irish; and it thus effectively replaces the murderous policy of Elizabeth

* Page 146.

and Cromwell. The work once performed by military violence is now accomplished by an economic process, and under legal, peaceful, and constitutional forms.

An Irishman who believes in the retributive justice of Providence may well be excused for doubting if such a system of iniquity is destined to be perpetual. *Quousque, Domine, quousque?*

CHAPTER VII.

THE EMANCIPATION STRUGGLE.

"I think the character of the Irish Protestants not radically bad; on the contrary, they have a considerable share of good-nature. If they could be once got to think the Catholics were human creatures, and that they lost no job by thinking them such, I am convinced they would soon, very soon indeed, be led to show some regard for their country."—EDMUND BURKE.

DURING the struggle for Emancipation it must often have sorely galled the Catholic leaders to encounter the patronising condescension of Protestant nobodies, who took airs of protection and arrogated high consideration in virtue of being emancipators. Prompt payment in servility was expected for the assuasive courtesies which seemed to claim a measureless superiority over the Catholic *protégés* on whom they were bestowed. "We have now shaken off our chains," said Sheil after Emancipation; "and one of the blessings of freedom is release from petty and contemptible political patronage. If a Protestant vouchsafed to be present at any of our meetings, it was, 'Hurrah for the Protestant gentleman! Three cheers for the Protestant gentleman! A chair for the Protestant gentleman!' And this subserviency, readily tendered by some, was perhaps the most provoking small nuisance of our grievances."

A species of humiliating advocacy consisted in alleging that although the religion of the Papists was damnable, idolatrous, diabolical, degrading and so forth, yet its wretched votaries might be safely admitted to political equality, inasmuch as the preponderating Protestant strength of the Empire would always avail to counteract any mischief that might be devised by the Papists. Nay, Emancipation might possibly be instrumental in converting the Papists to a purer faith; inasmuch as their legal disqualifications rendered perseverance in Popery a point of honour with its professors, whereas admission to equality of privilege would remove the suspicion which might otherwise attach to their motives in conforming to Protestantism.

Among the parliamentary advocates of Emancipation who took the occasion of supporting the Catholic claims to vituperate the Catholic religion was Mr. Perceval. He delivered a speech in which the ultra-virulent abuse of Catholicity was only to be equalled by the language of some orator at Exeter Hall, on a grand anti-Papal field-day; at the same time recommending the repeal of all disqualifying laws as conducive to the religious enlightenment of the Catholics. It scarcely needs be said that advocates of Mr. Perceval's class were among the politicians who would have clogged Emancipation with the royal veto on the appointment of Catholic Bishops. On this one point— that is, in supporting the veto—the illustrious Grattan went wrong. Mr. Daniel Owen Maddyn, in a work on Irish politics, upbraids O'Connell with having "laboured to make the venerable Grattan as unpopular as possible."

The accusation, when translated into the language of simple truth, merely means that Mr. O'Connell, with characteristic sagacity, opposed every scheme of accompanying Emancipation with measures calculated to secularise the Catholic Church in the slightest degree, or to bind up the priests in the trammels of the State. Grattan would have taken Emancipation, though encumbered with the veto; and although a Roman Catholic may condemn such a policy, yet he scarcely can blame Grattan for adopting it. Grattan was a Protestant, and, of course, could not fairly be expected to possess the watchful solicitude for the independence of Catholic spiritualities which should animate an intelligent Catholic, anxious as well for the religious interests of his Church as for the political freedom of his countrymen. In truth, the only point on which O'Connell differed from Grattan was the question of the veto.

But if Grattan needed any apology for the part he adopted, he could have found it in the fact that among the Catholics of note were some men who conceived that Emancipation should be purchased at the expense of handing over to the Government the appointment of the Catholic Bishops under the name of a veto. One of these Liberal Catholics was the late Chief Baron Wolfe, then a rising barrister on the Munster Circuit. He came into collision with O'Connell on this subject at a public meeting held in a church in Limerick, and made a powerful and effective speech from the front of the gallery in favour of the veto. O'Connell, in reply, told the story of the sheep who were thriving under the protection of their dogs, when an address, recommending them to get rid of their dogs, was presented by the wolves. He said that the leading *Wolfe* came forward to the front of the gallery, and persuaded the sheep to give up their dogs; that they obeyed him, and were instantly devoured; and he then expressed a hope that the Catholics of Ireland would be warned by so impressive an example against the insidious advice of any *Wolfe* who might try to seduce them to give up their proved and faithful guides and protectors. The hit was received with roars of applause, and the vetoists were routed.

Among the Protestant emancipators who combined patronage with insult, was the statesman immortalised in Disraeli's "Coningsby" under the pseudonym of Nicholas Rigby, a dexterous and lucky adventurer, of whose career a few brief incidents may not be uninteresting.

Rigby's father held a Government office near Dublin, and gave his son a college education. The young gentleman, whose critical taste was early on the outlook for subjects to dissect, published a metrical satire on the *corps dramatique* of the Theatre Royal, as it existed under the management of Mr. Frederick Jones. This production saw the light in 1804, and was entitled "Familiar Epistles to Frederick Jones, Esq." The authorship was not avowed until after the work had passed through two editions. The versification was easy and correct; the personal sketches flippant and piquant; the text, in short, was good of its kind, but the notes which encumbered every page were of helpless dulness, which quality was rendered the more striking by the perpetual and clumsy attempts of the author to be pointed and brilliant.

The dreary and ponderous pleasantry of Rigby's notes, irresistibly reminded the reader of the stupid German commemorated by Boswell, who, being charmed by the exuberant spirits of some humorist, endeavoured, when alone, to emulate his friend's vivacity by jumping over the tables and chairs, explaining the purpose of this saltatory exercise to an acquaintance who surprised him in the midst of his antics by saying, "*J'apprends d'être vif.*" Rigby's prosaic efforts to be *vif* were clumsy failures. But there was really a good deal of pungent sarcasm in his verses.* The amusing personalities of the "Familiar Epistles," rendered the book very popular in Dublin, and a good deal of interest was excited to discover the author. So long as the Epistles were anonymous, several of the small *literati* acquired a transient importance from imputations of the authorship—imputations which some of them encouraged. But at length the real poet came forth to claim his laurels;

E.g., the sketch of Richard Jones :

> But who is this, all boots and breeches,
> Cravat and cape, and spurs and switches,
> Grin and grimace, and shrugs and capers,
> And affectation, spleen, and vapours?
> Oh, Mr. Richard Jones, your humble !
> Prithee give o'er to mouth and mumble.
> Stand still, speak plain, and let us hear
> What was intended for the ear;
> For, faith! without the timely aid
> Of bills, no parts you've ever played.

Another sketch :

> Next Williams comes, the rude and rough,
> With face most whimsically gruff;
> Aping the careless sons of ocean,
> He scorns each fine and easy motion.
> Tight to his sides his elbows pins,
> And dabbles with his hands like fins.
> Would he display the greatest woe,
> He slaps his breast and points his toe.
> Is merriment to be expressed ?
> He points his toe and slaps his breast.
> His turns are swings, his step a jump,
> His feelings fits, his touch a thump;
> And violent in all his parts,
> He speaks by gusts and moves by starts.

and Mr. "Nicholas Rigby" immediately began to lionise on the strength of his literary glories. Literary ladies asked him to their assemblies; dinner-giving dilettanti invited to their tables the young satirist who had revealed so just an appreciation of the scientific *gourmandise* of Frederick Jones. The "Familiar Epistles" soon rendered their author more familiar with champagne and turtle-soup than perhaps he had previously been.

One of the personages who bestowed their attentions on young Rigby was the late eccentric Baron Smith, father of Thomas Berry Cusack Smith, Attorney-General for Ireland at the time of the State trials of O'Connell and others, and subsequently Master of the Rolls. I have heard that the Baron warmly admired the sportive rhymes of Rigby; but however this may be, he bestowed some flattering attentions on their author, and affectionately invited him to his country-seat.

The Baron was proverbial for his oddity. Possessed of an acute and metaphysical mind, his great intellectual powers were often distorted by unaccountable caprice. One of his traits was the suddenness of his attachments and dislikes, the lightning rapidity with which he could adopt and discard an acquaintance. He would ask you to spend a month at his house with an air of affectionate cordiality. If you accepted the invitation, and seemed disposed to take your host at his word, you would speedily receive an unequivocal hint that the sooner you ended your visit the better.

He tried the experiment on Rigby. He asked him to stay for a month. Rigby accepted the Baron's hospitality, and was received with the blandest courtesy. For the first two days everything was *couleur de rose*. The Baron was enchanting; his guest was delighted with his condescension. Rigby was introduced to the company who filled the house as a young gentleman of extraordinary genius, and his host's most particular friend.

On the third day things were changed. The Baron scarcely deigned to glance in the direction of Rigby; or, if he did look towards the place where Rigby sat, it was with that wandering gaze that seems unconscious of the presence of its object. Rigby stood his ground unmoved. He, on his part, seemed unconscious of any alteration in the manner of the Baron. He rattled away, quite at his ease; lavished his stores of entertaining small talk on the company, who were charmed with the Baron's agreeable guest. At dinner the Baron did not speak to him; treated him with marked and supercilious coldness; and indicated by the mute eloquence of manner that Rigby had exhausted his welcome.

Next day Rigby took his usual place at the breakfast-table, conversed with delightful animation, and wore the appearance of a man so well satisfied with his quarters that he had not the least notion of changing them. The Baron, finding that silence had no effect in dislodging his pertinacious guest, at last determined to speak out. Meeting him alone in the domain soon after breakfast, he thus addressed him: "I had hoped, Mr. Rigby, that you would have spared me the pain of telling you what I think that my manner sufficiently indicated—that your visit is no longer agreeable. Is it possible you cannot have discovered this?"

"Of course I have discovered it," returned Rigby. "You do not suppose me such a fool as not to have perceived that you became capriciously rude—from what cause I am wholly unable to guess. But this I know, that you invited me to stay for a month, and for a month I *will* stay. Your station in the world is fixed, but mine is not. Before I quitted Dublin I boasted among all my acquaintance of the flattering invitation you gave me. I told them I was going to spend a month with you. If I returned at the end of a few days I should be their laughing-stock; my social position would be seriously damaged, and my prospects would be more or less injured. No, no. You certainly cannot be serious, Baron, in the intention of converting your kindness into a source of mischief to me."

These words, spoken in a tone of civil but resolute impudence, tickled the Baron's fancy; he saw that his guest was no every-day character, and, being an admirer of originality, he broke into a good-humoured fit of laughter, and permitted Rigby to remain until the month was expired.

The anecdote is very characteristic of the energetic perseverance which has marked through life the politician celebrated in Disraeli's novel as "The Right Honourable Nicholas Rigby."

Rigby's next adventure of importance was his return to Parliament. There was an election for the borough of Downpatrick.* The contest was expected to be very close. One of the candidates was detained by an accident, and his friends, in order to prevent his rival from getting ahead of him, set up Rigby—who happened to be in the town—as a stalking-horse. Rigby was proposed and seconded—harangued the electors against time—a poll was demanded, and *one* vote was given, which, with the votes of the proposer and seconder, gave him *three* of the voices of the electors of the borough. Just at this stage of the proceedings the bonâ fide candidate arrived. Rigby retired from the hustings, but made no formal resignation of his claims. Fierce raged the contest. There was on both sides a tremendous expenditure of bribery. The election ended in the triumph of the man who bribed the highest; and in due course of time his antagonist petitioned against his return. The sitting member was unseated for gross and corrupt bribery; but the petitioner was not seated, for bribery to a great extent was clearly proved to have been committed by him also.

There had been, however, a third candidate, who had committed no bribery—a candidate who had got three votes. The committee accordingly reported that "Nicholas Rigby, Esquire," had been

---

* Query—should this be Athlone?

duly returned for the borough. This decision astonished the public, who had looked on Rigby's standing for the borough as a mere electioneering ruse, and who, in fact, had forgotten the circumstance in the interest excited by the more important candidates.

Here was a frolic of fortune. It is not every day that senatorial honours are flung at men's heads, and Rigby determined to make the most of his sudden and unlooked-for elevation. The gentleman as whose *locum tenens* he had been originally proposed to the electors wrote him a very friendly letter, requesting he would resign his seat, as the writer wished to offer himself again for the borough. But Rigby resolved to keep what he had got. What, resign his seat? How, in point of justice to his constituents, or consistently with his sacred duty to the country, could he surrender the important trust the electors had kindly confided to his hands? Forbid it honour! conscience! patriotism! Rigby's friend was compelled to submit to Rigby's virtuous determination.

Our hero, in the year 1808, published a pamphlet, entitled, "A Sketch of the State of Ireland, Past and Present," in which he bestowed a species of contemptuous advocacy on the Catholic claims. His arguments went to support Emancipation on the ground of its being too insignificant a boon to be worth refusing. He styled it "an almost empty privilege." He held the opinion that Emancipation would facilitate conversions to Protestantism.

"Trade," he wrote, "when free, finds its level. So will religion. The majority will no more persist—when it is not a point of honour to do so—in the worse faith than it would in the worse trade. Councils decide that the Confession of Augsburg is heresy, and Parliaments vote that Popery is superstition, and both impotently. No man will ever be converted when his religion is also his party. But expedient as Catholic Emancipation is, I think it *only* expedient, and concede it not without the following conditions."

He then enumerated four conditions, of which the most important were the payment of the priesthood by the State, the approval of the prelates by the Crown, and the disfranchisement of the forty-shilling freeholders. Curious timidity, that sought these protective conditions in return for conceding "an almost empty privilege"!

It is creditable to our hero that in his "Sketch of the State of Ireland" he has anticipated the aphorism that acquired for the late Under-Secretary Drummond such extensive popularity. "A landlord," said Rigby, "is not a mere land merchant; he has duties to perform as well as rents to receive, and from his neglect of the former spring his difficulty in the latter, and the general misery and distraction of the country. The combinations of the peasantry against this short-sighted monopoly are natural and fatal."

Candidly and boldly expressed. This evidence, coming from such a quarter, is worth something.

Rigby had previously given an accurate description of the rack-rent system. He, however, took care, *more suo*, to insult the objects of his advocacy: "The peasantry of Ireland are generally of the Roman Catholic religion, but utterly and disgracefully ignorant; few of them can read—fewer write." (Thanks to the Protestant Code that had made their education penal—but Rigby does not tell us so.) He goes on: "The Irish language, a barbarous jargon, is generally, and in some districts exclusively, spoken; and with it are retained customs and superstitions as barbarous. Popish legends and pagan traditions are confounded and revered." He elsewhere calls the people "utterly dark and blind."

I have mentioned Baron Smith. That wayward functionary was a member of the Irish Parliament, and supported the Union with a zeal which in due time was rewarded with elevation to the Bench. In 1799 he issued an ingenious pamphlet, entitled "An Address to the People of Ireland," recommendatory of the Union. He went largely into the question of the competence of Parliament to annihilate itself, which competence most of the anti-Unionists denied. He told the Catholics that he did not know whether an Union would better their chance of admission to the Senate, but suggested that at any rate it would not diminish it. On the question of commercial advantages he availed himself extensively of the *petitio principii*, assuming, as if it were an incontrovertible axiom, that the incorporation of the Legislatures would, *ipso facto*, incorporate the nations, extinguish their reciprocal jealousies, and identify their interests. How far he was sincere in the profession of these views it would now be useless to inquire. But as a sample of the readiness with which he accepted, or pretended to accept, empty professions for substantial securities, it is not uninteresting to record that he quotes the following passage from a speech of "that enlightened Minister," as he calls him, Mr. Pitt, to prove that Irish commercial and manufacturing interests would sustain no injury after an Union from English rivalry or jealousy:

"I will say," said Mr. Pitt, "that for a hundred years this country (England) has followed a very narrow policy with regard to Ireland. It manifested a very absurd jealousy concerning the growth, produce, and manufacture of several articles. I say that these jealousies will be buried by the plan (of Union) which is now to be brought before you." Having quoted the above words, Mr. Smith exclaims: "I can entertain no fears that the statesman who thinks thus liberally and speaks thus frankly, will, after an Union, make the influence of all Irish members submit to the mechanics of a single English town."

The English policy towards Ireland, described by Mr. Pitt as "very narrow," has more recently been described by Lord Dufferin in one of his letters to the *Times* in the following vigorous language: "From Queen Elizabeth's reign to the Union," says Lord Dufferin (he should have said from Queen Elizabeth's reign until 1779), "the various commercial confraternities of Great Britain never for a moment relaxed their relentless grip on the trades of Ireland. One by one, each of our nascent industries was either strangled in its birth, or handed over, gagged and bound, to the jealous custody of the rival interest in England, until at last every fountain of wealth was hermetically sealed."

But Mr. Pitt's frank and liberal acknowledgment that this policy was "narrow," and his generous promise that an Union would render such narrowness impossible, inspired the confiding breast of Mr. William Smith with implicit and unlimited trust in Great Britain. It is not thus, however, that men bestow their confidence in private life. Suppose, for example, that Brown says to Robinson; "My excellent friend, I acknowledge that I have always robbed and swindled you, I have counterworked your honest industry, deprived you of a market, and done my utmost to starve your wife and beggar your children. All this, I confess, was very narrow policy. But, my beloved Robinson, let us henceforth join forces. Give me, O friend of my heart! the key of your strong box and the control of your estate; and you shall see with what noble and affectionate generosity I shall treat you for the future." If Brown, having plundered Robinson, thus addressed him, and if Robinson gave Brown the control of his estate and the key of his strong box, we should certainly set down Robinson as a lunatic.

Pitt had admitted the past hostility, which, in truth, was undeniable. The leopard cannot easily change his spots. There was absolutely nothing in the Union to extinguish that hostility. On the contrary, there was everything to increase and perpetuate it. The Union invested our hereditary enemy with legislative power over Ireland. Irish commercial, manufacturing, and trading interests were then prosperous, because the Volunteers had won Free Trade for Ireland in 1779. Prior to that period, the British Parliament, deriving strength from the religious divisions of this country, had usurped the power of enacting prohibitory statutes and enforcing embargoes. British statesmen might calculate that after an Union the destruction of Irish industrial interests, which the prohibitory statutes and embargoes of a former period had achieved, could thenceforth be effected by the enormous hemorrhage of Irish income, whereby Ireland would be deprived at once of her domestic markets, and of the capital which is indispensably necessary to create or perpetuate manufacturing establishments." *

---

* The English jealousy of Irish prosperity sometimes peeps out in the shape of an apology for any suggestion that might seem calculated to promote Irish interests. The following appeared in the *Dublin Evening Mail* in September, 1861:—
"The dread of a cotton famine has so demented the Lancastrians that one, writing in their behalf to the *Daily News*, advises a recourse to Irish linen as a temporary substitute. But the audacity of the proposal is so glaring that an apology is found necessary for counselling anything so desperate. '*Without wishing*' (says

Baron Smith did not like the agitators. He got into the habit of introducing political dissertations into his charges to grand juries. A speaker at some public dinner at Tullamore in 1833, had said that "Catholicity now held aloft her high and palmy head, unshaken by the stormy blasts of persecution." The Baron thought this bombast worth quoting and censuring in one of his charges. He used to come into court at two o'clock in the afternoon; and, when opening the commission, he carried a vast manuscript, the terror of grand jurors. This was his charge; and even although his auditors in the grand-jury box might concur in the political views which he announced, yet it is said that they were wont to cast many a weary glance at the ponderous composition, whilst the Baron perused page after page of a document which, to their impatience, appeared to be interminable.

It should be stated, to the Baron's honour, that as a judge he was humane, considerate, and painstaking. He went to the trouble of studying the Irish language in order to render himself

---

this friendly gentleman) '*in any way to promote Irish interests*, I venture to suggest, at this dull, season, whether Irish linen might not in many cases be used instead of cotton?' If Irish linen could be grown near Glasgow or Preston, there might be no objection; but to encourage its manufacture on the west of St. George's Channel is only to be justified by the urgent pressure of necessity. Such inadvertent admissions betray the jealousy with which the efforts of this country to achieve a commercial independence for herself are regarded by a great portion of the trading community in England."—*Dublin Evening Mail*, quoted in the *Cork Examiner*, 12th September, 1861.

independent of interpreters when witnesses were unable to speak English. Of his views on Catholic Emancipation I cannot speak with certainty. He tells us in his "Address to the People of Ireland" that he supported the Catholic claims in 1795; but it is clear that he considered that the preservation of the State Church Establishment and of Protestant ascendency should be carefully provided for in any measure of Catholic concession. I presume he held views on the Catholic question not dissimilar from those expressed by Rigby.

Advocacy which was blended with a lofty assumption of superiority, or with actual insult, could scarcely be acceptable to the Catholics. This sort of insolent patronage was symptomatic of the general Protestant feeling of contempt for Papists which I have already noticed.* In truth, this was to some extent the fault of the Catholics themselves. I have known a Catholic family of respectable station seize, with alacrity which seemed servile, the proffered acquaintance of Protestant neighbours who, at least in the article of wealth, were in no respect their superiors. Similar instances are consistent with my knowledge. A Protestant lady of fashion, angry with a female friend (also a Protestant) for introducing her to some ineligible acquaintance, exclaimed that she would avenge the affront by inviting the parish

---

* I once asked a baron (the son of an Union peer) whether any of his relatives were Catholics. "Oh, none," he replied, "except the bastards."

priest to meet the offending fair one at her house. This mode of punishing an affront, by inflicting the parish priest on the offender, was thoroughly expressive of the Protestant estimate of Catholic society.

Without disparaging the Catholic gentry, it must be owned that as a class they were inferior to the Protestants in all the refinements of polished life. Exceptions, no doubt, there were; but such was the general fact. The penal laws were the cause of this inferiority. It is uttering an obvious truism to say that the exclusive possession of power, official dignity, and political station, must necessarily have imparted to the habits and manners of the favoured class all the social ease which results from the consciousness of command. Their peculiar advantages placed within their reach every facility of refinement. Their monopoly of so many other valuable things gave them almost a monopoly of civilisation. It was a proverb, even so late as the first quarter of the present century, that you might know a Catholic in the street by his crouching appearance. The iron of the penal laws had entered into the souls of the people, and branded their manners with strong marks of their inferiority. The subservient spirit has long since passed away; but I am not quite sure that in other respects Catholic society has yet fully acquired the polish which, from the causes already stated, is to be found amongst the upper classes of Protestants.

On the other hand, there is no vulgarity so

odious, so offensive, so pestilent, as that of the Orange squireen. It is the ingrained vulgarity of mind, of soul, of sentiment. It is the loathsome emanation of "malice, hatred, and all uncharitableness" in all its coarseness and deformity, unchecked and unconcealed by the conventional amenities of civilised life.

Decipit exemplar imitabile vitiis.

The squireen class could imitate the bigotry of their betters, but they could not imitate the graces of manner which sometimes invested the aristocratic bigot with something of a chivalrous and dignified air.

The Irish *noblesse* and leading gentry of the last century lived magnificently. The edifices they erected, both in town and country, the scale of their household establishments, their equipages, were magnificent. In their manners there was *l'air grand;* their very rascality was of magnificent dimensions. There was no paltry peddling about them. You could hardly have found one of them capable of selling himself, like the Scotch Lord Banff, for the paltry trifle of eleven guineas. The *abandon*, the *laisser-aller* principle was carried amongst them to the greatest extent compatible with social politeness. Whatever was bad, bigoted, or unnational in the aristocracy was duly adopted and improved on by their industrious imitators, the small squires. Whatever tended to mitigate the evils of bigotry was beyond the imitation of the squireen class, because it was beyond their comprehension. How deeply are the Catholics of Ireland indebted to O'Connell for removing from them the galling indignities entailed by their political inferiority to such a thoroughly contemptible class!

An amusing volume might be written on the exploits of the Orange squires of Ireland.

Vulgarity of soul was of course often found among the possessors of thousands a year, as well as of hundreds. The squireen magistracy were a curious generation. While the smaller sort of justices occasionally rendered their judicial decisions auxiliary to the replenishing of their poultry-yards, those whose wealth gave them greater weight were in frequent communication with the Castle, recommending "strong measures" to keep down the people, such as the increase of the constabulary or military force, the proclaiming of disturbed districts, the enforcement of the Insurrection Act, or the suspension of the Habeas Corpus. Complaints against obnoxious individuals were frequently made in these communications. The Government were earwigged by the "Loyalists," as the oppressors of the people thought proper to term themselves; and doubtless many a poor devil who never dreamed of plots or conspiracies, has been indicated to the executive as concerned in revolutionary projects.

One ludicrous instance of this species of volunteer espionage is deserving of record. The officious informant of the Government flew at higher game than ordinary. He was a magistrate, a grand juror, a man of family and fortune. The object of his attack was also a magistrate and grand juror, and of lineage and station at least equal to his own, They were both " good Loyalists." The former gentleman amused his leisure hours with a corps of cavalry yeomanry of which he was captain, and which he seemed to consider indispensable to the stability of British connexion.

These dignitaries quarrelled with each other. It was a private dispute—I do not know its nature; perhaps it concerned the comparative merits of their foxhounds. The Accusing Angel (whom I shall call Mr. A.) conceived that the most exquisite revenge he could take would be to procure the dismissal of his foe (Mr. B.) from the commission of the peace.

Mr. A. was in constant communication with the Government. He wrote frequent letters to the Viceroy or his secretary, expatiating on the demoniac disposition of the people, on the perpetual perils besetting the well-affected, and in especial on his own great merits. The literary qualities of his correspondence must have amused the official critics at Dublin Castle, for his orthography was unfettered by the usual rules, and he sometimes introduced a colloquial oath by way of giving additional emphasis to his statements. His despatches, with some such announcements as these, that " By ——! the country was in a truly aweful situation"—that "they ought to look sharpe to Mr. Murtogh O'Guggerty," etc., had been usually received with such respectful consideration by official persons that at last he began to consider himself all-powerful with the Irish Administration. His correspondence was private and confidential; so that he revelled in the double confidence of power and secrecy.

He accordingly wrote to apprise the Lord Lieutenant that Mr. B. was a political hypocrite, who, while wearing the outward marks and tokens of loyalty, was destitute of its inward and spiritual graces. One specific accusation, of which I was informed by Mr. B.'s son, was that persons of disloyal politics were hospitably entertained at his father's table. Mr. B. was represented as a dangerous character, who ought promptly to be struck off the list of magistrates. Mr. A. did not entertain a doubt that the return of the post would bring with it a supersedeas for his enemy from the Lord Chancellor; and he chuckled with anticipated ecstasy over B.'s mortification, and his ignorance of the quarter whence the arrow was aimed.

Although they had quarrelled, yet they had not quite discontinued their acquaintance. Mr. A., therefore, was not very much astonished when he saw Mr. B. one morning approaching his house on horseback. "Perhaps," thought he, "B. is coming to make up matters, if he can. I wonder has he heard of his dismissal yet?"

The visitor, seeing the man of the house on his hall-door steps, hastened forward, reached the mansion in a few moments, sprang from the saddle, and, horsewhip in one hand, presented with the other a written paper, saying:

"There, sir, is the copy of a document signed with your name, which I have received from Dublin Castle by this morning's post. It foully and falsely accuses me of being a disloyal subject, and demands my dismissal from the magistracy. I have come to ask whether you are the author of this rascally document?"

Mr. A. was so thunder-stricken at the suddenness, the total unexpectedness, of such an accusation, that he was quite at a loss what to answer. He stammered out an admission that he had written the letter.

"Then," said B., "walk into the house this instant, and write a contradiction of it, which I shall dictate."

Mr. A. could not choose but comply. B. immediately dictated a very full and unqualified contradiction, which A. duly wrote, and of which, the instant it was written, B. took possession. He then quitted the house with scant ceremony, and despatched to the Chancellor the exculpation he had extorted from his accuser. Of course he was not dismissed from the magistracy. Nor was his accuser dismissed; the Government probably attributing his escapade to an exuberance of loyal zeal.

Of the accusing justice the following anecdote

was told me by a beneficed clergyman of the Established Church. His worship had an inveterate habit of profane swearing. At a meeting of magistrates, presided over by the Protestant rector of the parish, who was also a magistrate, he, as usual, gave emphasis to his opinion by a blasphemous oath. The rector, scandalised at the impiety, said: "I shall fine you tenpence, sir, for swearing in court."

"Here it is, by ——!" said the other, handing up the tenpenny-piece (it was before the days of the shillings) and accompanying the coin with a repetition of the blasphemy.

"Another fine for that," said the rector. The justice tendered a second tenpenny with a similar profane accompaniment. And so on, the magistrate swearing, and the rector fining him, until he had emitted some eight or ten oaths, and got rid of a corresponding number of tenpennies. His worship probably considered the affair an excellent joke.

This gentleman was the juror who, at the Cork assizes, presented to the court, in the character of foreman, the verdict of "guilty," which he had spelled "gilty."

"That's badly spelled," said the counsel for the defence,* who was near the box, and seized the paper *in transitu*.

"How shall I mend it?" inquired the foreman, abashed and confused at this public censure.

---

* Harry Deane Grady.

"Put n, o, t, before it," returned the counsel, handing back the paper for the emendation, which the former immediately made, in bewildered unconsciousness of the important nature of the change.

"There—that will do," said the counsel, taking the amended document, and handing up "Not Gilty" to the Court. A fortunate interposition. The juror in question had a mania for hanging. He had, in his impetuous haste, handed in the issue paper without consulting his brethren of the jury-box. But if the prisoner in that instance escaped death, in how many instances were the miserable victims sacrificed? A verdict of guilty was easily obtained from jurors who belonged to a class that deemed accusation sufficient to establish criminality, and with whom the received policy was that of hanging the accused, "to make an example, and to preserve the quiet of the country."

CHAPTER VIII.

THE ZEAL OF A PACIFICATOR.

A man he was, to all the country dear.
                                    GOLDSMITH.

THERE occurred in 1816 an incident strikingly illustrative of the Protestant ascendency policy of making examples to preserve the quiet of the country.

The gentleman who officiated as peace-preserver on the occasion to which I now allude, was the Rev. John Hamilton, Protestant Curate of Roscrea, in the King's County, and a magistrate. The reverend gentleman had been transplanted to Roscrea from the County Fermanagh. In politics he was an enthusiastic Orangeman; his personal disposition appears to have been romantic and adventurous.

Mr. Hamilton, on receiving his appointment to the magistracy, promised, as he afterwards boasted, to distinguish himself by his zeal in discharging the duties of his office. He speedily set about redeeming his promise. The Monaghan militia commanded by Colonel Kerr, were at that time quartered in Roscrea. They were all of red-hot Orange principles; and it was the familiar practice of the reverend gentleman to obtain from the commanding officer parties of the men, who scoured the country, firing shots, playing party tunes, and thus exhibiting their ardent loyalty in a sort of irregular ovation of perpetual recurrence. But these triumphant *feux-de-joie*, and the accompanying martial music, could not long furnish serious occupation to a spirit so adventurous as that of the Rev. John Hamilton.

There resided at Roscrea two highly respectable Catholic distillers, the Messrs. Daniel and Stephen Egan. There was also in that town a rival distiller named Birch, a wealthy Protestant, in whose family the reverend gentleman had officiated as tutor for some time after his appointment as curate.

It occurred to the Rev. Mr. Hamilton, J.P., to evince his magisterial zeal by implicating the Messrs. Egan in a criminal conspiracy to murder the Protestant gentry of the neighbourhood. He possibly also desired to serve the commercial interests of his patron, Mr. Birch, by getting the rival manufacturers of whisky hanged. He was bustling, active, and artful; and finding in many of his neighbours the ready credulity of prejudice, he soon succeeded in creating serious alarm in their minds. He procured the aid of a confederate named Dyer, who was groom or stableman in the employment of Mr. Birch (the reverend gentleman's patron); and Dyer, being duly drilled by Mr. Hamilton, swore informations, bearing that several persons engaged in the murderous conspiracy aforesaid, occasionally rendezvoused in a valley called the Cockpit, situated in the domain of the Hon. Francis Aldborough Prittie, M.P., for the purpose of concerting their organisation, and also of practising the manœuvres of military exercise.

Matters were not yet ripe enough to explode the plot against the Egan family. An assistant for Dyer was procured from Dublin, a dexterous practitioner in informations, named Halfpenny, alias Halpin. He was then in the police, an *attaché* of Major Sirr's office. He had, in 1798, displayed great activity as an informer. On this man's arrival at Roscrea, he was taken into the councils of the Rev. Mr. Hamilton.

That reverend gentleman, his wife, and Halpin, dressed up a straw figure in a suit of Mr. Hamilton's clothes. They placed this figure in a sitting attitude, at a table in a parlour on the ground floor of Mr. Hamilton's house; its back was turned towards the window; on the table before it was expanded a large Bible; a pair of candles stood upon the table. From without, the appearance of the pantomime was precisely that of the reverend pastor of the Roscrea Protestants, deeply immersed in the study of the Word of God. The scenic illusion in the parlour being thus prepared, the reverend gentleman furnished a pistol to Halpin, who, with

Dyer, had received his instructions to fire through the window at the stuffed figure. A man named Quinlan was inveigled to join the shooting party. Dyer and Halpin, in obedience to Mr. Hamilton's injunctions, fired through the sash at that reverend gentleman's straw representative, the window shutters having been left open for that purpose. The figure was hit in the back with a bullet—the Bible was dislodged—two bullets struck the opposite wall.

Dire was the commotion that instantly prevailed through the town. The shout rang from mouth to mouth that the excellent pastor had been fired at while studying the Bible. He had escaped—hurrah!—by the special interposition of Providence. His preservation was, doubtless, miraculous; but who could say that the same overruling care would be vouchsafed to the other Protestant inhabitants, whose lives were equally menaced by the Popish conspiracy which had thus been mercifully baulked of its first intended victim? The Protestants clearly must defend themselves.

The drums beat to arms. Parties of the Monaghan militia paraded the streets. In half-an-hour the Messrs. Egan, who were quietly sitting with some friends, were arrested by a piquet, and conveyed to the guard-house, where they were detained for a whole night on a charge of conspiring to murder the Rev. Mr. Hamilton. These events all took place on the night of the 28th of December, 1815.

Next morning the two Egans were bailed out with great difficulty by the strenuous exertions of their friends. For some days a calm succeeded, interrupted only by the occasional nocturnal visits of Mr. Hamilton and the police to Mr. Egan's house, under pretext of searching for arms.

It was surmised—I pretend not to say with what truth—that the Government felt rather disinclined to follow up the prosecution in consequence of the excellent character always borne by the parties accused. But Lord Norbury and the Earl of Rosse so vehemently urged the prosecution, that the scruples, if any, of the Government were overruled. A fresh witness to sustain the accusation was procured in the person of one Hickey, brother-in-law of the first witness, Dyer.

Meanwhile, the rampant delight of the Orange inhabitants of Roscrea was evinced in the most noisy and extravagant manner. Colonel Kerr was an active partisan of the Rev. Mr. Hamilton. He permitted the tattoo to be beaten through the town every evening, the drums being followed by a large military escort, at whose head the reverend gentleman ostentatiously strutted, arrayed in an orange cloak, and wearing round his waist a belt studded with pistols. This melodramatic exhibition was enlivened by such tunes as "Boyne Water," and "Protestant Boys," played on the military fifes.

On the morning following the attack on the stuffed figure, the Hon. Mr. Prittie, son of Lord

Dunally, visited the Rev. Mr. Hamilton to inquire the particulars, and asked him whether his (Mr. H.'s) son had not had a great escape?

"Yes, sir," replied Mr. Hamilton.

"*Where were you sitting,*" demanded Mr. Prittie, "*when the shot was fired at you?*"

"There, sir," answered Mr. Hamilton, pointing to a table in the room. Mr. Hamilton thus sought to confirm Mr. Prittie in the belief which that gentleman had, in common with the public, then adopted—namely, that the shot had been actually fired at himself. This attempt at deception should be carefully borne in mind, because it neutralises the defence which the reverend gentleman set up for his conduct at a subsequent stage of the affair.

On the 11th of January, 1816, the Messrs. Egan were arrested under a warrant of the Rev. Mr. Hamilton's. They were placed in the custody of a party of soldiers and marched to the inn, where they found some eight or ten persons in custody on the charge of being also involved in the murderous conspiracy. The last-named parties were confined for the night in the guard-room.

At ten o'clock on the following forenoon all the prisoners set out for Clonmel, which is forty miles distant from Roscrea, escorted by a large body of military and police. The Egans travelled in a chaise which proceeded at a footpace; the other prisoners walked, handcuffed, after the carriage. The first day's journey was to Templemore. It was rendered extremely fatiguing by the slowness of the pace and the inclemency of the weather. The rain poured down in torrents, and the prisoners, on arriving at Templemore, were conducted to a miserable den without a fireplace, appropriately named the Black Hole, in which they would have spent the night but for the humane interposition of Sir John Carden, who obtained for them the accommodation of the inn.

Next day they proceeded to Cashel, where they were consigned to a small, dreary, damp apartment, without any sort of furniture. They applied for permission to occupy the inn, but met a refusal on the plea that the disturbed state of the country would render compliance dangerous. It was, however, resolved to forward them at once to Clonmel.

A curious incident occurred within a few miles of that town. Two of the escort appeared to quarrel with each other, and in the course of the dispute they fell from their horses. The steeds, released from their riders, ran away, and the whole escort, with the exception of a single policeman, made off in pursuit of them. The solitary guard approached the Egans and strenuously urged them to escape. "I will follow my comrades," said he, "in pursuit of the runaway horses, and you can then act as you please." But the prisoners, apprehensive of some trick, rejected the advice thus urgently offered, and quietly awaited the return of the party of police.

Arrived at Clonmel, they were met in jail by the Rev. Mr. Hamilton and Mr. Corker Wright,* a magistrate, who had sedulously interested himself in the prosecution. Mr. Wright on the following morning visited the prisoners, affecting great friendliness, and strongly advised them to confess all they knew of the "conspiracy," promising to exert his influence to procure their pardon. Of course an indignant disclaimer of all knowledge of any conspiracy was the only reply elicited by this treacherous suggestion. The Egans were then invited to see the various apartments of the jail. In one room they were shown the hangman busily preparing ropes for the next execution. But this sight failed to scare them into the false and foolish act of self-crimination.

In a few days the special commission was opened by Lord Norbury and Baron George. The

---

* This Mr. Corker Wright's house, near Shinrone, was the scene of a bloody tragedy in 1815. A party had been got up to attack the house, it is supposed with his knowledge, and arranged by his steward, Hoey. At all events, the plan was fully known before it was acted upon; for a party of soldiers were in the house awaiting the assailants, in company with whom it is alleged that they marched for a part of the way. Arriving before the assailants, the soldiers were stationed on the stairhead. The aggressors entered without any opposition. One of them, lighting a candle, exposed the whole party to the soldiers, who immediately fired and killed them all. Not a man was left to disclose the agency by which the attack was concerted. The bodies were paraded on cars through the neighbouring villages on the following day, as trophies of the victory obtained by Mr. Corker Wright.

Crown Prosecutor was Charles Kendal Bushe, then Solicitor-General, and afterwards Lord Chief Justice. The public augured very gloomily for the prisoners when it was known that Lord Norbury was to try the case. Norbury had a terrible reputation for severity. "We'll have great hanging next assizes—Lord Norbury's to come," was a phrase that familiarly heralded his lordship's approach to assize towns on the circuit.

Two witnesses came from Roscrea to bear testimony to the excellent character of the Egans. One of these was the Rev. Mr. L'Estrange, Protestant Rector of Roscrea. The other was a Protestant layman, Mr. William Smith, who informed the prisoners that shortly previous to the firing at the straw parson through the window, he had been present at a dinner-party given by Mr. Birch, of Roscrea, at the Rev. Mr. Hamilton's instance. It was there stated that the Egans were accused, on Dyer's sworn informations, of drilling men in the domain of the Hon. Mr. Prittie, for treasonable purposes; and Mr. Smith was then told that he should be apprised of the mode in which it was intended to proceed against them, provided that he took an oath to keep secret the particulars. Mr. Smith rejected this condition, stating his conviction that the Egans were incapable of the imputed criminal acts; and that, to his own personal knowledge, Dyer had sworn falsely, inasmuch as the Egans were in another place at the very time when they were sworn by that person to have been drilling men in Mr. Prittie's grounds.

Dyer was of course the principal witness. He gave his evidence with great self-possession and dexterity. He deposed to several meetings for military exercise in Mr. Prittie's domain. He was obliged to confess, on cross-examination, that he was in the receipt of five shillings a week for suppressing his evidence against one Francis Cotton,* on a trial in which the said Cotton had been charged with the murder of a man named Quigley. The admission of his own infamy in compounding the felony of murder, necessarily deprived his evidence against the Egans of weight with the jury. Contradictions in his testimony were also elicited on cross-examination.

The Rev. John Hamilton was the next witness. The trick of the stuffed figure had transpired, and as he knew that a cross-examination on the subject awaited him, he resolved to put a bold face on the matter. Accordingly, in his direct evidence, he spoke of the effigy as a stratagem, employed for the purpose of ascertaining if Dyer's previous informations were true; but on his cross-examination he was constrained to admit that he had left the Government, as well as several of his brother magistrates, under the impression that the firing at the effigy was an actual firing at his person. The reader will remember that, when

---

* This Cotton, and also Dyer, were subsequently in the employment of Mr. Birch, the distiller, at Roscrea.

Mr. Prittie, on the morning following the attack on the straw figure, said to the Rev. Mr. Hamilton, in that gentleman's house, "Where were you sitting *when the shot was fired at you?*" Mr. Hamilton answered, "There, sir," pointing to a table in the room, and thus attempting to confirm, in Mr. Prittie's mind, the belief that he had been actually fired at.

When the reverend gentleman's testimony closed, the court-house rang with execrations, and the judges had some difficulty in restoring order.

Halpin, and Dyer's brother-in-law, Hickey, were next examined. Halpin gave his evidence with the composure and readiness of an expert informer. He inculpated Quinlan in the guilt of firing at Mr. Hamilton's effigy, under the belief that the effigy was the reverend gentleman himself. Hickey's evidence tended to exonerate Quinlan from having fired; but he swore that Mr. Stephen Egan had administered to him an oath to assist any one who should attempt to take Mr. Hamilton's life.

The infamous nature of the prosecution being manifest, the jury without the least hesitation unanimously acquitted the prisoners. Lord Norbury, deprived of an opportunity of hanging anybody, escaped from the court under the pretext of sudden indisposition, leaving Baron George alone on the bench.

Dyer, with the concurrence of the learned Baron, was placed in the dock by the order of the Solicitor-General, and indicted for wilful and corrupt perjury. But the grand jury, thinking, perhaps, that he might be useful on some future occasion, committed the disgraceful act of ignoring the Bill.*

The liberated prisoners were warmly congratulated by their numerous friends. They had a narrow escape. Had the Rev. Mr. Hamilton's dexterity of execution been equal to the ingenuity of his invention, it would have fared hardly with them. He wanted only the opportunity to become a second Titus Oates. It was a romantic experiment, doubtless—that of the Orange divine who

> Stuffed a figure of himself—
> Delicious thought!—and had it shot at,
> To bring some Papists to the shelf,
> Who could not otherwise be got at.†

The Egans on their return were obliged to enter Roscrea by a back lane, in order to avoid the sanguinary ferocity of about one hundred of the Monaghan militia who had turned out, half intoxicated, ready for a desperate riot. There were also a large number of Orangemen, armed and prepared for mischief, who excited alarm by firing squibs through the town. Colonel Kerr was with some

---

* In 1844 Dyer was still living at Roscrea; he was then old, and seemed penitent for his former awful crimes. The witness Hickey was sent out of the country on the failure of Hamilton's plot by the parties who employed him, and is supposed to have gone to America.

† "Fudge Family in Paris."

difficulty induced, by the strong remonstrance of a military gentleman, to draw the soldiers into the barracks. Mr. Hamilton published a pamphlet in his own vindication. He expatiated on his magisterial zeal—on the innocent nature of the exploit of getting men to fire at the effigy, which exploit, he loudly protested, was merely an ingenious device resorted to with the view of ascertaining whether designs against his life were really harboured by the persons whom Dyer had accused. He disclaimed having represented to the Government that the firing at the effigy was a firing at his own person; he alleged that he had made Major Sirr privy to the trick, and that he had requested the Major to convey that information to the Castle authorities. If he did so at all, it was somewhat of the latest.

The most amusing part of Mr. Hamilton's pamphlet is his solemn complaint that the Messrs. Egan showed no gratitude to Colonel Kerr. He was also dissatisfied with Peel, who was then Irish Secretary. "It is evident," says the ill-used clergyman, "that Mr. Peel's sole object was to vindicate the Lord Chancellor for not superseding me, and that he had no wish to defend me on my own account."

One would think that Mr. Peel, in all conscience, had quite enough to do to palliate the retention of such a person in the magistracy, without entering on a defence of his machinations against the Egan family.

My account of the transactions described in this chapter is derived from a manuscript narrative lent me by one of the Egan family, Alderman Egan of Dublin, and a pamphlet published by the Rev. Mr. Hamilton.

When we look back upon those dreary times; when we contemplate the social and political depression of the Catholics, and the supremacy of their enemies in all the departments of the State; when we think of the enormous influence possessed by a virulent faction; the vast array of selfish interest, deeply-rooted prejudice, and impenetrable ignorance, which had to be encountered and overcome; it is difficult to form an adequate estimate of the political merits of that leader whose voice inspired the timid and spiritless, whose sagacity restrained the intemperate and rash, and whose influence combined together the millions in that memorable organisation which wrung from reluctant bigotry the concession of the Catholic rights. O'Connell stated that a majority of the very House of Commons which in 1829 enacted Emancipation, had been returned in 1826 on pledges to resist that measure. As to the King, Lord Eldon has portrayed His Majesty's virtuous agonies at being compelled to give the royal assent to the Relief Bill. "What can I do?" exclaimed the disconsolate monarch. "What can I now fall back upon? I am miserable—wretched. My situation is dreadful—nobody about me to advise with. If I do give my assent I'll go to the baths abroad, and from thence to

Hanover; I'll return no more to England; I'll make no Roman Catholic peers—I will not do what this Bill will enable me to do—I'll return no more. Let them get a Catholic King in Clarence—— The people will see that I did not wish this."

The Great Agitator triumphed, *pro hac vice*, over King, Lords, and Commons.

CHAPTER IX.

ANTI-TITHE AGITATION OF 1831-2.

He vowed before the captive's God to break the captive's chain,
To bind the broken heart, and set the captive free again.

ANON.

O'CONNELL'S transition from the lawyer to the statesman was a change for which his long course of political agitation had prepared him. He intimately knew the people whom he was now to combine for the revival of the national Legislature, and whose scattered strength he was to consolidate. The Catholic Association was pronounced to be an *imperium in imperio* of vast magnitude and influence. And so it truly was. But the Repeal Association which O'Connell founded on the 15th of April, 1840, gradually swelled to larger dimensions than its predecessor. In 1843 it surpassed the Catholic Association in the number of its members, in the extent of its funds, in the steady enthusiasm of its friends, and in the exquisite perfection of detail with which its organisation reached every nook and corner of the country.

The sentiment of nationality had ever been a ruling idea in O'Connell's mind. It broke forth at first in his memorable declaration prior to the passing of the Union, that he would rather behold the re-enactment of the penal code than consent to the destruction of the Irish Parliament. With that declaration most of his subsequent acts have been consistent. That he who fleshed his maiden sword in opposition to the Union should devote his matured abilities to the repeal of that measure was naturally to be expected. He struck the right chord; the sympathies of his countrymen responded. In September and October, 1830, he addressed four letters to the Irish public on the subject of Repeal. Those letters produced a deep and general sensation; and if public adhesion to the cause was not then as universally declared as at a later period, the reason why men paused was the great magnitude of the measure, which led even those who most ardently desired it to fear that it was impracticable.

O'Connell's appeal to his countrymen was readily responded to. But it is a total mistake to suppose that such response originated solely in the leader's influence. It originated in the deeply-rooted conviction in men's minds that they were the worse for the suppression of their native Legislature and would be the better for its restoration. What O'Connell openly uttered every man had felt before. The leader did no more than rehearse the popular sentiment.

By-and-by public meetings began to spring up in different quarters. The opposition to the tithe-impost at that time convulsed every parish in the land; and the two great questions of the Repeal of the Union and the Disendowment of the State Church were soon agitated together on nearly every rural platform.

The landlords in great numbers espoused the anti-tithe cause. Protestantism they affectionately loved, but the cheaper they could have it the better. Best of all if they could enjoy it gratis. I knew in 1823 a landlord of Conservative politics in collusion with his own Catholic tenant to defeat the exorbitant demands of the rector. The reverend gentleman claimed his tithe; but the landlord, by collusive distresses for rent, contrived for some time to outwit him. The landlord, disgusted at the grasping propensities of the rector, dropped his acquaintance, and the alienation continued for some years. It is said that the same landlord lay in ambush with a gun to shoot the parson's proctor, who presumed to enter his Protestant premises in order to make a valuation of the growing crops, and that the angry gentleman was only restrained from some deed of violence by the strong remonstrances of a friend on the consequences which the act must have entailed on the perpetrator. I knew all the parties. The anecdote was given me as a fact; but I think it must have originated in an angry threat which was interpreted too literally. Even thus modified, the story indicates a feeling of rage against the tithe system. In fact, a great proportion of the Protestant proprietary hated that system as intensely as the Catholics did; as intensely as it had been hated by their own Protestant predecessors, the members of the Irish House of Commons, who in 1735 passed the memorable Agistment Resolution that exempted all pasture-lands from the claims of the State clergy, and threw the burden of tithe exclusively on tillage.*

"Down with the tithes," then, was the cry of many a Protestant landlord in 1831 and 1832. With some it was a purely selfish cry—a cry of men who simply preferred not paying money to paying it, and who dignified their conduct with the sounding phrases of "indignant resistance to an unjust and abominable impost," "sympathy in the sufferings of a Catholic people compelled to pay a Protestant priesthood," and similar expressions of generous and lofty principle. Unjust and abominable was the impost, doubtless; and a flagrant

---

* This Resolution is generally described as having thrown the burden of tithes from the Protestant aristocracy on the Catholic tenantry. It indeed relieved the owner of pasture-land; but this relief imposed no additional burden on the owner of tillage. The man who tilled his land paid neither more nor less tithe after than before the passing of the Agistment Resolution. Moreover, tillage, in the early part of the eighteenth century, was so little practised in Ireland that the Legislature, not twenty years previously to the extinction of tithe of agistment, had passed a law to compel every occupier of a hundred acres to keep at least five acres tilled. Grazing was general, and the Catholic tenant who grazed his land partook of the exemption secured to pasture by the Resolution of 1735.

spoliation of the Catholics, from whom the Church property had originally been torn, and on whom, consequently, the support of two Churches was thrown by the egregious malversation of the ecclesiastical State revenues; but the animus of some of the anti-tithe landlords in 1832 was rather selfish than national. Many, however, were actuated by a purer motive.

There was another section of the Protestant landlords, more important in respect of their wealth and position, and including many of the nobility, who rallied round the parsons at their utmost need, paid their own tithes, compelled (where they could) their tenants to pay theirs, and entered into large subscriptions to enable the parsons to recover all arrears by legal process.

The anti-national Church Establishment, thus supported at home, and backed from without by the power of England, outlived a storm of well-earned popular vengeance that shook every stone and timber in the edifice. It was an institution totally indefensible on any ground of justice, honesty, or common sense. The remark is now trite that Ireland is the only country on the face of the earth, in which the whole ecclesiastical State revenues have been grasped by the pastors of a small fractional part of the population. Such a monstrous outrage on the great principles of equity, and on the great majority of any nation, may be elsewhere vainly sought, either in or out of Christendom. In truth, it was an outrage which no thoroughly free country would submit to for a single day. It has now been disestablished and partially disendowed; but what is termed its disendowment has been so adroitly managed, that the tithes, under the name of tithe rent-charge, still remain an oppressive burden on the landed property of Ireland.

The anti-Irish State Church has been so important a factor in Irish affairs, that a short retrospective view of its origin, of the objects of its authors, and of the results of its establishment, becomes necessary in a general sketch of the condition of Ireland.

Bacon recommended the "princelie policie" of fomenting the internal divisions of the Irish people as a means to facilitate their subjugation. It was "*Divide et impera.*" A more effective mode of carrying out this policy could scarcely be devised than the violent confiscation of the old Catholic ecclesiastical State revenues of the kingdom, and the transference of those revenues to an alien hierarchy, chiefly imported from England, and whose mission, accredited by the English Government, was to uproot, if they could, the ancient creed of the people whose Church property had been seized by the apostles of the new religion.

Whether that religion was right or wrong, I do not here discuss. I have only to do with its political results. The Irish were universally Catholics in the sixteenth century, as their ancestors had been from the days of Saint Patrick. Spenser, writing in

1596, says: "They be all papists by profession." The Rev. Maziere Brady has shown by the evidence of the highest Elizabethan functionaries,* that the instruments of the new apostolate were "fines, imprisonments, tortures, and death, unscrupulously employed by the ecclesiastical as well as the civil agents in that alleged reformation." Nor was their violence accompanied by the ascetic virtues which might have given an air of sincerity to the boisterous apostleship of the agents of the Reformation. Spenser deplores their immorality; he says:

"The clergy there (excepting the grave Fathers which are in high place about the State, and some few others which are lately planted in their new college) are generally bad, licentious, and most disordered."—*View of the State of Ireland.*

Sir William Drury (April 16th, 1577) mentions "the students of Ireland that are in Louvain, and come from thence." At that time our ecclesiastical students were under the necessity of seeking their education in foreign lands; and when they returned to keep the lamp of religion from extinction in their own country, they did so at the risk of their lives. Spenser marvels at their zeal, and in a well-known passage contrasts it with the sloth of the Reformed ministers.

"It is," he says, "great wonder to see the odds which is between the zeal of Popish priests, and

---

* Preface to "State Papers concerning the Irish Church in the Time of Queen Elizabeth," edited by the Rev. Maziere Brady.

the ministers of the Gospel; for they spare not to come out of Spain, from Rome, and from Remes, by long toil and dangerous travelling hither, *where they know peril of death awaiteth them*, and no reward or riches is to be found, only to draw the people into the Church of Rome; whereas some of our idle ministers, having a way for credit and estimation thereby opened unto them, without pains, *and without peril*, will neither for the same, nor any love of God, nor zeal of Religion, nor for all the good they may do by winning souls to God, be drawn forth from their warm nests to look out into God's harvest, which is even ready for the sickle, and all the fields yellow long ago."—SPENSER'S *View of the State of Ireland*, pp. 210, 211, 12mo edition, 1750.

The comparative ideas of religious toleration respectively held by the Irish Catholics and the Protestant Government in Spenser's time, are incidentally revealed in the above passage. The Catholic priests were in "peril of death" from Protestant intolerance, while the Protestant ministers could, had they so pleased, have assailed the old faith of the kingdom "without peril" from Catholic violence. It is, and always has been, a glorious trait in the character of our Catholic countrymen that their unshaken fidelity to their own religion is associated with the utmost tolerance of the religion of others.

Spenser says the Protestant preachers could "do small good" in converting the Irish, until the

Irish "be restrained from sending their young men abroad to other universities beyond the sea, as Remes, Doway, Lovain, and the like."

A religion which emanated from England, and which was enforced in Ireland by "fines, imprisonments, tortures, and death," was naturally productive of two important consequences. It excited the abhorrence of the people to whom it was introduced by this species of sanguinary apostleship; and its position as a new and hostile element in Irish politics inevitably generated in its followers a strong anti-national sentiment, which is unfortunately inherited by too many of their successors at the present time.

In truth, no other results could have been reasonably expected. The new clergy, subsidised with the spoils wrenched from the old Church, could not, by the most tortuous exercise of sophistical ingenuity, have contrived to consider themselves anything else than intruders. When they looked around they saw a flock by whom their ministry was repudiated. Looking over to England they there beheld the power that sustained them in possession of the spoils of the Irish Catholic Church, in defiance of the natural resentment of the Irish Catholic population. Occupying such a position, it was inevitable that their affections should be given to England who supported their usurpation, and withdrawn from the Irish people to whom that usurpation was abhorrent. In November, 1626, the assembled Protestant hierarchy, having successfully ousted the Catholic Church from its ancient temporalities, issued the following declaration against tolerating the creed of the people they had robbed:

"The religion of the Papists is superstitious and idolatrous; their faith and doctrine erroneous and heretical; their Church, in respect of both, apostatical. To give them, therefore, a toleration, or to consent that they may freely exercise their religion, and profess their faith and doctrine, is a grievous sin; and that in two respects: for, first, it is to make ourselves accessory not only to their superstitions, idolatries, and heresies, and, in a word, to all the abominations of Popery; but also (which is a condition of the former) to the perdition of the seduced people which perish in the deluge of the Catholic apostasy."

In its nature the English Church thus established in Ireland was a potent engine of national discord. The practice which from the date of its origin had prevailed of largely importing English clergymen to occupy its benefices, excited the wrath of the Protestant settlers, who had got confiscated estates, and who deemed themselves entitled to monopolise Church patronage for the benefit of their families. Ecclesiastical incomes were in many cases rendered more attractive because they did not involve the necessity of residence. The incumbents were frequently non-resident. In many instances they had the excellent plea for non-residence afforded by the fact that their parishes contained no Protestants. They had no flocks requiring their ministry, and they knew that their prospects of preferment would be bettered by residence in Dublin.

Pluralities were numerous. In 1764 the County Clare contained seventy-six parishes, of which sixty-two were sinecures. The whole seventy-six parishes paid tithe to fourteen rectors, many of whom habitually lived in the metropolis. No doubt they never were missed by their Catholic parishioners. Without the slightest disparagement of the many excellent persons belonging to the Anglican religion, it cannot be denied that its existence as a State Church in Ireland was a grim burlesque on ecclesiastical establishments.

But the grim burlesque was so useful to the policy of *divide et impera* that in 1800 its preservation was specially provided for as an article of the Union; and the Union was defended on the express ground that it would render the grim burlesque impregnable. That nine or ten per cent. of the inhabitants of Ireland should style their Church the Irish Church was ludicrous. Mr. Under-Secretary Cooke accordingly argued that an Union would remove the anomaly by incorporating the people of this kingdom with their English neighbours, and thus converting the Irish Catholic majority into an Imperial Catholic minority. "With the Union," said he, "Ireland would be in *a natural situation;* for all the Protestants of the Empire being united, she would have the proportion of fourteen to three in favour of her [Church] Establishment, whereas at present there is a proportion of three to one against it."

This is a good sample of Unionist reasoning. The autonomy of Ireland was to be demolished, and her vital rights were to be trampled in the dust, in order to perpetuate the oppressive ascendency of the alien Church Establishment. And this monstrous subversion of all national and moral right was called putting Ireland in "a natural situation." The Catholics, however, could not see that the wicked suppression of the Irish Parliament rendered it a whit less dishonest to tax them for Protestant purposes.

The practice of bringing over Englishmen to enjoy the ecclesiastical revenues of Ireland had been to a great extent discontinued during the present century; and the State Church became a fruitful preserve for the junior members of the Irish landed aristocracy. Before the Composition Acts came into force the income divided among the ministers, great and small, of the Establishment, was probably a million per annum. After the enactment of the 1st and 2nd Victoria, chapter 109, which converted the tithe into a rent-charge, payable by the landlords to the rectors, and recoverable by them from the tenants, the gross income of the State Church has been calculated by the Rev. Maziere Brady at £700,000 per annum.

Before I come to the period of Disestablishment, I wish to note some instances in which nobility of heart, and the instinct of honourable nationality, enabled Irish Protestants to escape from the demoralising influence of an establishment which was eminently calculated to make its followers bad Irishmen. Foremost among these stands Henry Grattan, a Protestant, whose belief was sincere and fervent, and who declared that his first and last passion was his native country. The fact was, that Home Legislation, except where English intrigue corrupted it, had the strongest tendency to generate national feeling among the Irish Protestants; and national feeling gravitated towards the inclusion of the Catholics in all constitutional privileges. Among the Protestant friends of Catholic Emancipation must be reckoned Plunket, Sir Lawrence Parsons, the Protestant Bishop of Derry,* Curran, Wolfe Tone, Valentine Lord Cloncurry, Lord Edward Fitzgerald, the Emmetts, Arthur O'Connor, Hamilton Rowan; the Belfast Volunteers, who, so far back as 1783, had instructed their deputies to the Dublin Convention to support the unqualified emancipation of the Catholics;† the numerous Protestants in the body of United Irishmen; the students of the Protestant University of Dublin, who, in their noble address to Grattan in April, 1795, expressed their

---

* Earl of Bristol in the English peerage.

† "Life of Wolfe Tone," p. 50 (M'Cormick's edition). Tone states (p. 77) that twelve Belfast citizens subscribed £250 each to establish a journal called the *Northern Star*, in which Catholic Emancipation was advocated.

hope "that the harmony and strength of Ireland will be founded on the solid basis of Catholic Emancipation;" and, I may add, on the authority of Earl Fitzwilliam, a majority of the Protestants of Ireland, many of whom asked for, and few in 1795 opposed, the repeal of all the then remaining Catholic disqualifications. Such was the state of good feeling, fraught with the promise of national prosperity and happiness, which was destroyed by the machinations of Pitt and his agents.

CHAPTER X.

THE DISESTABLISHMENT CAMPAIGN.

"I well remember a phrase used by one not a foe to Church Establishments—I mean Mr. Burke: 'Don't talk of its being a Church! It is a wholesale robbery!'"—LORD BROUGHAM (1838), *on the Anti-Irish Church.*

I HAVE recorded the general outbreak against tithes in the years 1831 and 1832. The English Parliament gave the anti-Irish State Church a new lease of its life by transferring the liability of payment from the occupying tenant to his immediate landlord. The Act (2nd and 3rd Victoria, chapter 109) to which I have already adverted, empowered the landlord to recover the tithe rent-charge from the tenant in the shape of additional rent. This was sometimes done. There were numerous instances in which it could not be done; instances where the landlord found it difficult enough to obtain his original rent. The law assumed that he could recover the whole of an equivalent to the rector's tithe, and enabled him to retain twenty-five per cent. of such rent-charge to compensate his trouble in becoming that reverend gentleman's tithe proctor. But it was frequently impossible to obtain more than the seventy-five per cent. from the tenant; so that in every such case the landlord got nothing for his trouble and liability.

In May, 1856, Mr. Miall, member of Parliament for Rochdale, submitted to the House of Commons a resolution declaratory of the justice and expediency of impartially disendowing all churches in Ireland, and of applying their revenues to purposes of secular utility. He was in a minority of 93 in a House of 312. There were twenty-six pairs. The English Dissenters felt themselves aggrieved by being compelled to contribute to the support of the Established Church from which they or their ancestors had seceded. They therefore proclaimed the principle of voluntaryism; which principle had been preached from a thousand Irish platforms during the anti-tithe movement of 1831 and 1832. Our English allies also knew that in order to emancipate themselves from the incubus of State Churchism, they should first, by an active union with the Irish Catholics, effect the disestablishment, and, as they hoped, the disendowment of the anti-Irish State Church. Their efforts were responded to in Ireland by a meeting held at Clonakilty in the County Cork, on the 15th of August, 1856, at which resolutions were unanimously passed, expressing thorough approbation of the principles announced by Mr. Miall, gratitude for his advocacy, and promising to co-operate with his party in effecting the overthrow of the pernicious institution which he assailed.

The progressive steps of our agitation may be briefly summarised. The English voluntaries were active, intelligent, and indefatigable. Their alliance was indispensable to success. Yet, in seeking to promote that alliance, I encountered some difficulties. A Catholic Member of Parliament whose assistance I solicited, seemed averse to the proposed co-operation, not only because he deemed the theological principles of the English voluntaries violently anti-Catholic, but because whenever any measure affecting Catholic interests came before the House of Commons, their parliamentary representatives invariably "went into the wrong lobby." The objection thus started was by no means confined to the gentleman who made it. There was, however, a more practical and rational view of the question taken by an eminent Catholic dignitary, the Most Reverend Doctor Leahy, Archbishop of Cashel; he saw the great importance of accepting the assistance of the English voluntaries. I was honoured with much of his correspondence at the time when the English alliance was debated; and to his Grace's influence I consider the adoption of that alliance by the Irish Catholic hierarchy is chiefly attributable.

Shortly after the Clonakilty meeting I was visited by Mr. C. J. Foster, Chairman of the Parliamentary Committee of the Liberation Society. He was accredited by a letter from Mr. Miall, who introduced him as his *alter ego*. On both gentlemen I impressed the necessity of keeping attacks on Maynooth as much as possible in the background; not that the disendowment of Maynooth was to be relinquished, but that as heretofore every attack on that college had been made on purely sectarian grounds, it would be hard to separate an aggression on it, in ordinary Catholic apprehension, from an assault on the Catholic religion; even although the present assault was not at all sectarian, but merely directed against it as an endowed institution.

The agitation went on, slowly at first, but gradually acquiring momentum. Something more than eight years after the Clonakilty meeting an association was formed in December, 1864, for the threefold purpose of obtaining educational justice for the Catholics, a satisfactory settlement of the land question, and Disendowment of the anti-Irish Church. Our inaugural meeting was held in the Dublin Rotunda. Many Catholic prelates were present. To Archbishop (afterwards Cardinal) Cullen and myself was committed the Disendowment question. The Archbishop's resolution condemned the existing malversation of Church property in Ireland. My resolution affirmed the principle of voluntaryism, and disclaimed all desire on the part of the Catholics to acquire sectarian ascendency. Thenceforth the agitation proceeded with vigour. The English Liberationists were invaluable auxiliaries; held numerous meetings, disseminated pamphlets written with distinguished ability, while their able, accomplished, energetic secretary, Mr. Carvell Williams, essentially contributed by his personal exertions to prepare the public mind in England for the impending change. The question had now advanced so far that Sir John Gray, M.P. for Kilkenny, and proprietor of the *Freeman's Journal*, was induced to give it the support of his influential newspaper. He also issued a commission to inquire into the local details of the ecclesiastical anomaly in the different parts of the kingdom. Meanwhile petitions to Parliament for the abolition of State-Churchism were circulated for signature by the National Association, of which Alderman M'Swiney, Lord Mayor of Dublin in 1864, was one of the principal founders. These were extensively signed; and the signatures would have been greatly more numerous only for a strong popular distrust in the utility of asking the foreign Parliament for any measure of national justice.

In 1867, Sir John Gray introduced the question into the House of Commons in an able speech. His motion was supported by 183 votes against 195. His defeat by only twelve votes showed the great progress the anti-State Church cause had made, and encouraged the English voluntaries to redouble their efforts in behalf of Disestablishment. Early in 1868, Mr. Gladstone moved his celebrated Resolutions in the same direction. He was supported by 331 Ayes against 276 Noes. There were twelve pairs. Mr. Gladstone then introduced a Bill for suspending appointments to any Church benefices in Ireland which might become vacant prior to the final legislation of the following year. The Bill was easily carried in the House of Commons, but it was thrown out by the House of Lords on the 29th of June, 1868, by 192 votes to 97. A dissolution of Parliament soon followed. At the ensuing general election the Disestablishment of the State Church was made the principal test at every hustings. A large anti-State Church majority was returned to the House of Commons. The Bill was easily carried by Mr. Gladstone, and was then sent up to the Lords, by whom its provisions were so much mutilated that if it had passed as they returned it to the Commons, it would have increased, instead of diminishing, the ecclesiastical grievance.

A compromise between the conflicting parties followed the adverse action of the Lords. The Bill, as finally passed, dissolves the Union effected in 1800 between the anti-Irish State Church and the Church of England; dissolves the connection between the former and the State; protects the life-interests of its clergy; enables them to capitalise their incomes at a given rate of purchase, the Treasury advancing the money; appropriates the surplus of Irish ecclesiastical property to such secular uses as Parliament shall direct; and it provides for the total extinction of the tithes in fifty-two years from the date at which the landlords shall have gone through the form of what is termed "purchasing" them.

An impression extensively prevailed among the Irish landlords that the tithes, or tithe rent-charge, would expire in fifty-two years from the 1st of January, 1871, the day on which the Act came into operation. This was a mistake. Mr. Gladstone, with characteristic ingenuity, had introduced into the Act a clause which rendered the form of "purchase" a condition precedent of expiry; so that the payer of tithe-rent charge "purchasing" it now, or at any future period, is not credited in the purchase-money with one farthing of the hundreds, perhaps thousands, of pounds he shall have paid for tithe-rent charge since 1871. The fifty-two years are to be computed from the date of the purchase, not from the date of the Act. Thus an important obstacle has been placed in the way of extinction; as numerous landlords, unaware that the form of "purchase" was required by the Act, continued to pay the tithe-rent charge in the belief that the annual payment of the impost for fifty-two years would extinguish it at the end of that period.*

---

* The 32nd section of the Act requires "purchase." The Commissioners sell at twenty-two-and-a-half years' purchase, with the alternative of fifty-two annual payments as stated in the text.

CHAPTER XI.

STATE CHURCH ARGUMENTS EXAMINED.

"In parishes where there were no Protestants, or but the fewest, and which yielded their hundreds of pounds a year in tithes for dignitaries and incumbents, non-resident, and without duties, there were hundreds and thousands of Roman Catholics. That there was a tithe war is not to be wondered at; the only wonder is that any Protestant church was left standing, or any Protestant clergyman's life spared."—*The Irish Church*, by Herbert S. Skeats, an English Dissenter, p. 26.

It is not uninteresting to record the pleas assigned by the friends of the ex-State Church for the preservation of that unprecedented injustice. Before entering on this retrospect, however, I wish to show the reader the view in which the injustice presented itself to a Dublin Quaker, Mr. James H. Webb, who seems to have been a rope-maker in St. Audeon's parish. The rector of the parish, the Rev. James Howie, had seized certain goods in Mr. Webb's warehouse in satisfaction of parochial dues; on which the aggrieved Quaker addressed the following matter-of-fact appeal, "To the inhabitants of St. Audeon's parish belonging to the sect called the Church of England:

"10, Corn Market, *Dec.* 7, 1848.

"DEAR FRIENDS ;

"Well and truly may your pastor, James Howie, declare that 'he has done that which he ought not to have done;' for he has taken advantage of an Act of Parliament to take my property without giving me value. His collector called on me and made a demand of 18s. 6d. for certain prayers, sermons, &c., performed by James Howie; but as I had never employed him for such a purpose I declined paying the demand. On the 28th of November the collector, Joseph Conway, again called, in company with two bailiffs and two policemen, and on my again refusing his demand he carried away two pounds fifteen shillings' worth of my goods. I think it right that you should be aware that the person to whom you look for spiritual instruction makes out his livelihood by thus disobeying the simplest commands of Christ, and I ask you how you can be benefited by the teachings of such a man? It is as disgraceful to have other people's property taken for your religion as it would be to have it taken for your bread and butter. If you require such a person, you ought to make up a sum which would enable him to live honestly. It is well you should know that the same James Howie, by his collector, &c., took from me last June six pounds' worth of cords, for prayers, sermons, &c., valued by him at twenty-eight shillings.

"Yours truly,
"JAMES H. WEBB."

The terse, shrewd way in which the aggrieved Quaker puts his case may be taken to epitomise the national wrong, so far as its dishonesty was concerned. The pecuniary injustice, however, was the least of the evils engendered by the alien Church. It was a fertile source of irritation by which the social frame was grievously disjointed. It was impossible that the classes who were affected by the ecclesiastical outrage—those whom it benefited, and those whom it injured—could regard each other with the cordial friendliness essential to the national interests.

Let us here recapitulate the principal pretexts put forth in behalf of the anti-Irish Establishment.

I. It was urged by the transcendental pietists of the Protestant party, that the State is bound to provide for the dissemination of true Christian knowledge among the community.

But those gentlemen had been in the habit of vociferating that "the Bible alone" is the sole arbiter of controversy. Yet here they made the State, and not the Bible, the arbiter of what is, and what is not, true Christian doctrine. It may be asked what authority the State, as such, possesses to define theological doctrines, and in virtue of such definition to tax the public of all creeds for their diffusion? The State in England has been Roman Catholic, has been Puritan, has been High Church Anglican, has been Latitudinarian. If the State have the right to hand over the national ecclesiastical endowments to the clergy who happen to accept its theological views, then it will follow that as often as the Government sees fit to change its religious belief, it may lawfully enforce a corresponding change in the destination of Church property.

II. The argument was sometimes put in this way: "The State is entitled to offer religious truth to the acceptance of the nation."

The nation, it was answered, has at least a good a right to deny, as the State has to affirm, that the commodity thus offered is religious truth. The State had been making that offer to the Irish people (at their bitter expense) for more than three centuries; and the people, strong in their own religious faith, persisted in believing that the article offered by the State was a counterfeit. Even if it were assumed that the Irish people erred in so believing, yet who, unless he were stone-blind from prejudice, could deny that a species of State-apostleship which the experience of three centuries had shown to be efficacious only in irritating, not converting, stood *ipso facto* self-condemned?

I desire in this work to keep clear of all doctrinal controversy. But without entering upon any, it may be observed that independently of all doctrinal grounds for rejecting the State Church, there is the significant fact that it is scantily believed in by large numbers of its own ministers. The Irish State clergy perpetually claimed identification with the State Church in England. The Union, they said, had incorporated the two Establishments. The Churches were "no longer twain, but one flesh." The Irish Protestant clergy imagined that they strengthened their position by hooking themselves on to the Anglican Establishment. But for several generations great numbers of the English State clergy had been clamouring against the hard necessity of subscribing their own doctrinal code. In 1772, and again in 1815, petitions from numerous Churchmen for exemption from what they called "the grievance" of subscription to the Thirty-nine Articles, were presented to Parliament. If the reverend petitioners really believed the Articles, they could not have termed their subscription a grievance. The Irish State clergy were apparently hard run for support when they sought strength in identification with a Church which was officered by a host of clerical unbelievers.

On the 15th of January, 1863, a meeting of 300 "evangelical" clergymen of the English Church was held at Bishop Wilson's Memorial Hall, Islington. At that meeting the Rev. Hugh Stowell thus delivered himself: "The astounding fact was now developed that numbers had avowed themselves believers in the Revelation of God, had actually taken upon themselves to teach that Revelation, and were yet all the while hollow of heart and unsettled in conviction." The reverend chairman of the meeting thus indicated the species of doctrine taught by these "numbers" of clerical dissidents: "The peculiarity of our present position is this, that the sceptical sentiments of the present day proceed, not from the school of Paine or Voltaire, but from those who are within the pale of our National Church—from men who, by their station and profession, are pledged to uphold themselves, and to teach to others, the doctrines of our holy religion." *

On the 9th of June, 1863, Mr. Buxton, M.P., brought a Bill into Parliament to abolish the necessity of subscription to the Thirty-nine Articles. He acted at the instance of ministers of the Anglican religion and candidates for ordination, who, as he described their pitiable case, felt their consciences tormented by the dire necessity of declaring their belief in doctrines in which they did not believe.†

Yet the Anglo-Irish Protestant clergy claimed to retain their grasp on the whole ecclesiastical State revenues of Catholic Ireland, on the pretext of diffusing among us a doctrinal code which their clerical brethren in England were trying to fling off as an intolerable burden on their consciences. To some extent the recalcitrant clergy were successful. By the Act, 28th and 29th Victoria, chap. cxxii., entitled, "An Act to amend the Law as to

---

* London *Liberator*, 1st February, 1863.
† *Ibid.*, 1st July, 1863.

the Subscriptions and Declarations to be made and Oaths to be taken by the Clergy of the Established Church of England and Ireland," a less stringent form of Declaration of Assent is substituted for the previous forms of Declaration and Subscription. The short title of the Act is, "The Clerical Subscription Act," and it is dated 5th of July, 1865. I cannot see that the dissident clergy have gained much by the change. Although the language in which profession of belief is henceforth to be made is undoubtedly to some extent relaxed, yet it still is, in express terms, a " Declaration of Assent"; which cannot, I think, be satisfactorily used by men whose real sentiment is Dissent. But whether the State clergy believed, or disbelieved, or doubted, or denied, the truth of their own religion, the Irish nation for more than three centuries had been taxed for the support of that religion; the Act of Union professed to perpetuate its grasp on the national purse; and the 32nd section of Mr. Gladstone's Act of Disestablishment has dexterously thrown an obstacle in the way of the final extinction of the burden.

III. It was said in defence of the Establishment, "The earliest Christians of Ireland were Protestants, whose belief was the same as that of the modern Anglo-Irish parsons. The parsons, therefore, are entitled, in virtue of their spiritual descent from the Irish Protestant Christians aforesaid, to enjoy the Church temporalities of Ireland."

To this plea we answered: firstly, that the

statement was untrue; and secondly, that if it had been true, it could not establish any right to the national Church revenues on the part of the Protestant clergy of the present day.

The statement is untrue. For proofs of its untruth I refer the reader to a book by the Rev. Dr. Rock, entitled "A Letter to Lord John Manners," sold by Delman, of London. Dr. Rock's book overflows with irresistible demonstrations. A volume on the same subject by the Rev. Mr. Gaffney, sold by Duffy, Dublin, may also be consulted with advantage. A work by the Rev. Dr. Moran* is also worth the careful study of those who are interested in the history of the early Irish Church. Independently of the direct proofs contained in the works now referred to, there are historical statements made by the Rev. J. H. Todd, of Trinity College, in his "Life of St. Patrick," which seem wholly incompatible with the theory of early Irish Protestantism; and which are the more remarkable, inasmuch as Dr. Todd rejects the Roman origin of St. Patrick's mission.

Dr. Todd says: "The deadly hatred of England and of anything English, which has for so many centuries unfortunately rankled in the native Irish heart, was not at first created by any difference in religion."*

---

* "Essay on the Origin, Doctrines, and Discipline of the Early Irish Church," by the Rev. Dr. Moran, Vice-Rector of the Irish College, Rome. Dublin: Duffy, 1864.

† "Life of St. Patrick," Introduction, p. 242.

This is an important statement. The creed of the English invaders was admittedly Roman Catholic. Now, if the creed of the native Irish had not been also Roman Catholic, it is plain that religious dissensions between the two parties, exasperated by their national antipathies, must have widely prevailed through the kingdom. But while history is full of the struggles for political power between English and Irish, it is silent as to any theological warfare between them. The only rational solution of this silence consists in the fact that their creed was the same.

Accordingly, Dr. Todd candidly says: " There were two Churches in Ireland, separated from each other, *without any essential difference of discipline or doctrine*, at a period long previous to the Reformation." *

Observe the important admission, " without any essential difference of discipline or doctrine." Now, one of these two Churches, or, more accurately speaking, these two hierarchies, is admitted on all hands to have been Roman Catholic. The other hierarchy, therefore, which did not differ essentially from Roman Catholic discipline or doctrine, cannot possibly have symbolised with the modern Protestant anti-Irish Church, which differs most essentially from both.

The doctrinal and disciplinary identity of the ancient Irish and Anglo-Irish hierarchies is further

---

* "Life of St. Patrick," Introduction, p. 241.

shown by Dr. Todd, who says: "At a subsequent period, when the Anglo-Irish Church had accepted the Reformation,* the 'mere Irish' clergy were found to have become practically extinct. *Their Episcopacy had merged into, or become identified with, the Episcopacy which was recognised by the law.*"—Ibid., p. 242.

This quiet identification into one body of the two hierarchies shows that their religious belief was identical. This is evident when we consider the impossibility of such identification, or common merger into one hierarchy, of two Churches having different creeds. For instance, the identification of the present Anglican Church in Ireland with the Irish Roman Catholic Church is impossible. Fancy the Most Rev. Dr. Trench, the Protestant Archbishop of Dublin, celebrating mass in the Church of the Conception; or Cardinal Cullen preaching

---

* Which alleged acceptance is disproved by the Rev. Maziere Brady, D.D., and rejected as a monstrous historical error by so earnest a Protestant as Mr. Froude. Immediately following the passage last cited in the text, Dr. Todd, speaking of the post-Reformation period, says: "Missionary bishops and priests, therefore, ordained abroad, were sent into Ireland to support the interests of Rome ; and from them is derived a *third* Church, in close communion with the see of Rome, which has now assumed the form and dimensions of a national established religion" (p. 242). What Dr. Todd here calls "a third Church" was precisely the same great mass of Irish and Anglo-Irish Catholics whom he admits to have been in communion with Rome up to the date of the Reformation. He seems, by the words, "a third Church," to ignore the lay element of the Church, which constitutes the great body of its members, and which formed neither a third nor a second Church, but remained unchanged in its

up the Thirty-nine Articles in St. Patrick's Cathedral! But Dr. Todd informs us that such an identification of the ancient Irish Church and the Anglo-Irish Roman Catholic Church had actually occurred before the Reformation; an identification which could not have occurred unless their religious belief had been previously identical.

But it may be suggested that the English invaders had, perhaps, infused their Roman Catholic notions into the minds of the Irish.

To such a supposition Dr. Todd supplies the answer when he tells us of "the deadly hatred of England and of everything English which for so many centuries unfortunately rankled in the Irish heart." That deadly hatred would have necessarily extended to any English religious opinions not previously held by the Irish themselves. The Irish were not likely to accept the apostleship of

hereditary fidelity to Rome. It is true that the ferocity of the Reformed Government deprived the Catholic people of home education for their clergy, who were therefore compelled to pursue their ecclesiastical studies in foreign seminaries, whence they returned to preach the old faith in Ireland, where, according to Edmund Spenser, "peril of death" awaited them. But the people of Ireland were, and are, unable to understand how the tricks which the secular power played with religion in the sixteenth century could destroy their own inherited identity with the Church of their ancestors, even supposing that the alleged conversion of nearly all their bishops to Protestantism were historically true, instead of being, as it is, totally destitute of historical foundation.

Dr. Todd's work displays much research and possesses great interest, even for readers who do not acquiesce in all his views.

invaders whom they held in mortal abhorrence. The inference is inevitable; the Irish did not receive, and could not possibly have received, their undoubted Roman Catholic belief from England. Whence, then, did they derive that belief? There is but one answer—they derived it from the original founders of Irish Christianity. In fact, the difference between the early Irish and Anglo-Irish hierarchies was purely political or national, and not at all doctrinal.*

But in truth, the question whether the Church of Saint Patrick was Catholic or Protestant, was totally irrelevant to the claims of the anti-Irish State Church. Even if Saint Palladius and Saint Patrick had taught the Thirty-nine Articles, and

---

* Among the proofs of the connection of the early Irish Church with Rome is a rule, or canon, contained in the ancient Book of the Canons of Armagh, which enjoins that disputed matters, which could not be settled by the local ecclesiastical authorities, should be referred to the Roman See for final adjudication. Here is the canon as translated by the late Professor Eugene O'Curry: "Moreover, if any case should arise of extreme difficulty, and beyond the knowledge of all the nations of the Scots [*i.e.*, the Irish, who were then called *Scoti*], it is to be duly referred to the chair of the Archbishop of the Gaedhill—that is to say, of Patrick—and the jurisdiction of the bishop (of Armagh). But if such a case as aforesaid, of a matter of issue, cannot be easily disposed of [by him] with his counsellors in that [investigation], *we have decreed that it be sent to the apostolic seat—that is to say, to the Chair of the Apostle Peter having the authority of the city of Rome.*

"These are the persons who decreed concerning this matter, viz., Auxilius, Patrick, Secundinus, and Benignus." See "O'Curry's Lectures on the Manuscript Materials of Ancient Irish History," pp. 373, 611. Dublin: Duffy, 1861.

converted the Irish of the fifth century to Anglican Protestantism, the modern Protestant hierarchy would not have been a whit the nearer establishing a righteous title to our national ecclesiastical revenues. For, in the first place, the legislator of our day has to deal, not with the fifth century, but with the nineteenth. Again, if the aboriginal Irish parsons of those early times were Protestants, they must have been an exquisitely good-for-nothing set of gentlemen, since it is clear that they suffered the whole nation to slip through their fingers into the hands of the Popish priests. On the modern "evangelical" hypothesis, those early pastors must have been given the Church-revenues as the salary for teaching Protestantism to the Irish people. But they did not keep their part of the bargain, for they suffered all their flocks to lapse into Catholicity. They did not give value for the money, and they consequently became disentitled to claim it.

How preposterous, then, to assert for the anti-Irish clergy of the present day, a right as derived from a long extinct generation of parsons, who, if they ever existed at all, manifestly forfeited all title to Ireland's Church property some thousand or twelve hundred years ago! Were such a plea valid, it would follow by parity of reasoning that if all the original holders of Irish Church property had been Mohammedans, then a hierarchy of Turkish muftis would, at the present day, have a rightful claim to our ecclesiastical State revenues.

IV. It was strenuously urged that as nearly all the Irish Roman Catholic Bishops at the period of the Reformation accepted Protestantism, they became entitled, in virtue of their corporate identity, to carry the Church property into the new creed of their adoption.

But, firstly, the story of their conversion is a figment. The Rev. Maziere Brady and the Rev. Dr. Moran have conclusively disproved it. Next, if the whole Catholic hierarchy of the Elizabethan period had adopted Protestantism, I do not see how their conversion could have justified them in carrying into the Protestant Church the Catholic ecclesiastical property of which they had been given the use on condition of their fidelity to the Catholic Church. On the contrary, it seems clear that by deserting Catholicity they would have forfeited their sole original right to enjoy the Catholic endowments. Suppose the whole English hierarchy were suddenly to become Anabaptists to-morrow, would they have a moral right, in virtue of their corporate identity, to carry the whole national Church property of England into the Anabaptist communion?

V. It was urged that the disendowment of the anti-Irish State Church would invalidate or shake the title to all other kinds of property. Sir Hugh (afterwards Earl) Cairns expresses the objection in the following words: "It was utterly impossible they could attempt to destroy any kind of property in the country without loosening the security of property of every kind. . . . They could not confiscate benefices without loosening the bonds that secured property of every kind in the kingdom."

I quote the following answer to the above objection from the report of a speech which I delivered at the National Association of Ireland on the day of its inauguration:

"Just as if the ecclesiastical endowments, which Grattan called 'the salary of prayer,' stood on the same basis with private property! The law creates the endowments. But the law only protects other kinds of property. The revenues instituted by the State as the salary or remuneration for the performance of certain specific public functions, are legitimately liable to interference on the part of the State that created them. But this gives no precedent for interference with property which the State did not create; property acquired from industry, inheritance, or gift. So much for the principle. Then, as to the fact. All this bugbear about loosening the security of secular property if the ecclesiastical revenues were meddled with—all these menaces were dinned in our ears when Parliament, about thirty years ago, struck twenty-five per cent. off the Irish tithe-rent charge. But what private property was loosened or lessened by extinguishing one-fourth of the parochial revenues of the Irish State clergy? Can Sir Hugh Cairns, can any man, show that private property was shaken or diminished to the extent of one farthing by what the learned gentleman would doubtless call the confiscation of a fourth part of the Irish benefices?"*

VI. It was asked, "Would you make the tithe rent-charge a present to the landlords by a simple act of disendowment?"

When this question was asked, the landlords occupied a position very different from that in which the Land Act of 1881 has placed them. It was at that time fair to answer that the revenues of the State Church should be secularised, and applied to public uses of general benefit. Mr. Miall proposed that the tithe rent-charge should be sold to the landlords at ten years' purchase. It was also suggested that the poor-rate should be partially paid from the tithe rent-charge. The State Church property was a great national trust fund; and honesty imperatively demanded that it should be appropriated so as to benefit the whole Irish nation. Now, we said that although it was the trust estate of all, it was dishonestly monopolised by a small fractional part of the people. The Catholics had been robbed of it in the sixteenth century, and the robbery was perpetuated on hypocritical pretexts and defended by shallow and insulting sophistry. Restitution, we said, could be

---

* Page 14 of my speech, which was printed as a pamphlet by the English Liberation Society, from whom it can be had at 2, Serjeants' Inn, Fleet Street, London. Nobody can pretend that the recent agitation against excessive rents had any connection with the disestablishment of the State Church. It arose from various other causes, of which one was the existence of the rack-renting system.

made in either of two ways—by reinvesting the Catholic Church with the ecclesiastical revenues, or by appropriating those revenues to secular objects for the benefit of the whole people. The former mode was heartily deprecated (and for excellent reasons) by nearly all the Irish Catholics. The latter mode, as matters then stood, commended itself as being an effectual and satisfactory mode of restitution.

I say, as matters then stood; for matters stand quite otherwise now with the Irish landlords. This we shall see when the next plea in behalf of the State Church comes to be examined.

VII. It was said, by way of showing that the Catholics had no right to complain, that the incidence of tithe, or tithe rent-charge, fell upon the landlords, who were chiefly Protestants, and not upon the tenants, who were chiefly Catholics.

This was in most cases a delusion. The English Parliament took care to leave the burthen of tithe rent-charge on the tenants, by enabling the landlords to exact the amount from them in the shape of additional rent. Only the impost, when paid by the tenants, was to be called "rent," and not "tithe;" and was recoverable as rent by the landlords. Compositions for tithe had frequently been made by the tenants with the Protestant rectors. It was not unusual, while the system of "middlemen" prevailed, that two, three, sometimes even four lessees and sub-lessees were interposed between the head landlord and the actual occupier of the land. To enable the landlords, when saddled with tithe rent-charge, to extract it from their subordinate lessees and sub-lessees, the Act 1st and 2nd Victoria, chap. cix., provided a process of recovery which is thus described in the marginal summary of the 10th section of the Act:

"If any person who would have been liable to tithe-composition hold mediately or immediately under the person liable to such rent-charge, *the amount of such rent-charge may be recovered as rent from the next tenant and so downwards to the person primarily liable.*"

Thus the occupying tenants were reached by the parsons, not indeed directly as of yore, but by the device of transforming the landlords into tithe-proctors. The tenants paid the impost to the rectors through the receivership of the landlords, instead of paying it as formerly through the receivership of the old tithe-proctors. To be sure the name was changed; but "a rose by any other name would smell as sweet;" and the tithe, whether styled rent, or rent-charge, or modus, or whatever else you please, had as foul a stench in the nostrils of justice as in the days of Captain Rock and the tithe-riots.

Many landlords added the tithe rent-charge to the previously reserved rent. In all such cases the burden fell upon their tenants, in full accordance with the spirit of the Act to which I have referred. But there also were many cases in which the landlords found it extremely difficult, occasionally even impossible, to obtain the tithe rent-charge from their tenants; and of course in such cases the burden unquestionably fell upon themselves. It was, and is, paid in such cases from their rents, unassisted by the additional rent which Parliament empowered them to extract from their tenantry.

An erroneous impression prevailed in some quarters that the Rent-charge Act conferred a boon upon the landlords, because, in rendering them responsible to the rectors for the tithe, it professed to allow them to retain twenty-five per cent. for collecting and handing to the clergy the remaining seventy-five per cent. Judging from my own experience, from my knowledge of the country, and from my communications with other landlords, I feel certain that very few landlords, if any, pocketed a farthing of the twenty-five per cent. The tithe rent-charge was paid out of a gross rental which was greatly diminished by the repeal of the corn laws, while the septennial valuation of the impost was measured by comparison with the standard of high prices that preceded that repeal.

So stood matters up to 1881. But the Land Act of that year has essentially changed the position of the landlords, and largely increased the grievance of the impost. The Land Courts, constituted by the Act, have, on the average of Ireland, reduced the rents of landlords by from twenty to twenty-five per cent. This reduction of the rental cuts away the source from which the

Rent-charge Act empowered the landlords to obtain the tithe rent-charge for which they were responsible to the rectors, and since Disestablishment, to the Commissioners of Church Temporalities.

Let us suppose the case of a landlord whose original rental was £1,000 per annum, and the tithe rent-charge on whose estate was £100 per annum. The Rent-charge Act enabled him to recover £1,100 per annum from his tenants; at the same time requiring him to hand the tithe rent-charge to the rector from the additional £100 per annum. But now comes the Land Act of 1881. The landlord is brought into court. A judicial rent is fixed. The Court takes twenty or twenty-five per cent., often more, from the rent; thus sweeping off much more than the portion of the landlord's income which had been previously appropriated to the payment of tithe rent-charge. The tithe rent-charge is extorted, while the means of paying it is taken away by the law. A plainer case of injustice than this one can hardly conceive. If the English Parliament were actuated by a spirit of fair play, that body would advance from the Treasury a sufficient sum to buy off the anti-Irish clergy. They advanced twenty millions of money to buy off the slave-owners, an excellent precedent to follow in the present case. In point of justice England ought to pay the cost of purchasing out her clergy in Ireland, inasmuch as it was England that forced Protestantism on the Irish people. England committed the wrong by which Ireland for three centuries had been fleeced and otherwise afflicted; and England, having now discovered that the imposition of the Anglican Church on Ireland was a wrong, should emphasise her penitence by paying the pecuniary penalty. This, however, has not been done. The negro slaves were not required to repay the £20,000,000 advanced from the Imperial treasury for their emancipation. The Irish landowners *are* required to recoup that treasury for the cash advanced for Disestablishment.

VIII. Some Protestant clergymen pleaded that the State Church revenues of Ireland were little enough for the support of their order; and on this ground they deprecated reduction or alienation. For ministering to a small fractional part of the Irish people they were not ashamed to claim the whole ecclesiastical State property of the country. It was, they said, little enough. It was, as I have remarked, about £700,000 a year.* If this were little enough for the Church purposes of a fraction, let us ask to what annual sum should the payment of the Irish clergy of all denominations, rated on the same scale, amount? If the State Church

---

* The Rev. Maziere Brady, in a letter to *The Times*, March, 1867, having enumerated various items of Church revenues and Church property omitted from an annual income of £420,000, which Lord Dufferin appeared to think was the whole, says: "If those sums were added to the £420,000 a year of which Lord Dufferin spoke, the total would, perhaps, exceed £700,000; but in the absence of any reliable return, it is impossible to calculate with certainty the present revenues of the Establishment."

clergy, with flocks not more then eleven or twelve per cent. of the whole, required £700,000, then the collective Irish clergy of all denominations would have needed something about six millions sterling per annum. It was lucky for Ireland that her Catholic priests and her Presbyterian ministers had less inflated notions than the State Church clergy entertained respecting the pecuniary value of their ministrations.

I have now noticed a few of the current sophisms which were employed to defend the infliction of a Protestant State Church on Catholic Ireland. As an institution of the State, it was a marvellous system of incorporated fraud and insolence. It robbed the people and it insulted their religion. When its advocates, clerical and lay, had exhausted their eloquence in sounding its praises, we had only to look it in the face—to look at its shameless monopoly of a nation's Church property for the benefit of a small and wealthy minority—in order to condemn it as an abominable outrage on every principle of justice and of honest policy. Englishmen were often asked to make our case their own; to tell us what they would think of a Roman Catholic Church Establishment quartered by law on every parish of Protestant England; of fiery Roman Catholic polemics extorting payment from English Protestant flocks for ferocious vituperation of Protestantism?*

---

* It would be most unjust to inculpate all the Protestant clergy of Ireland as firebrand polemics. Great numbers of them

Why, it may be asked, was the anti-Irish State Church so long upheld by English statesmen ? Why did they persist for three centuries in inflicting on us a wrong to which the English nation would not submit for an hour ?

The true answer, I doubt not, is to be found in the traditionary Irish statecraft of English parties —in the belief that Ireland could not be governed without a plentiful application of exasperating injustice. To keep Ireland down, it was deemed necessary to perpetuate the distractions and miseries of her people. The policy was not new. "Some of her (Elizabeth's) counsellors," says Leland, "appear to have conceived an odious jealousy which reconciled them to the distractions and miseries of Ireland. 'Should we exert ourselves,' said they, 'in reducing this country to order and civility, it must soon acquire power, consequence, and riches. The inhabitants will thus be alienated from England; they will cast themselves into the arms of some foreign power, or perhaps erect themselves into an independent and separate State. Let us therefore connive at their disorders; for a weak and disordered people never can attempt to detach themselves from the crown of England.'"
—LELAND's *History of Ireland,* book iv., chap. 3.

In the species of statecraft here described by

---

were incapable of the insulting malpractices referred to in the text, and were personally very estimable; but there were also many whose controversial zeal rendered them intolerable nuisances. All alike were in a false position.

the historian, we discern the policy that inspired the establishment of an anti-national State Church in Ireland. "Let us connive at their disorders." It would tax human wit to connive at our disorders more effectually than by forcing on the country a corporate incubus of which social hatred and heart-burning were the necessary consequences; which generated an angry sense of wrong on the one side, and a sentiment of arrogant superiority on the other. With such a social gangrene among us, it cannot be matter of surprise that a thousand acrid humours diffused their poison through the nation's veins, and kept the body politic in a chronic condition of disease.

This was the true purpose and mission of the anti-Irish State Church.

Before I close this chapter I shall say a few words on the proposals which previously to Disestablishment had been from time to time suggested, to purchase the clergy by pensions, or glebes, or some other sort of State endowment.

Statesmen regard the endowment of any Church by the State in the light of a bribe to the clergy. Thus, Lord Castlereagh speculated on purchasing the support of the Presbyterian clergy for the Union by an augmentation of the *Regium Donum*. On the 23rd of November, 1798, he wrote as follows to William Wickham, Esq. :

"Of late they (the Presbyterians) are rather tired of the treason in which they had very deeply embarked; perhaps they may be inclined to compromise with the Union; *some additional provision for the clergy, connecting the Church more closely with the Crown, would probably disarm the opposition, if not secure the support, of that body.*" *

In the recently published "Correspondence of Earl Grey," † we find the following passage in a letter addressed by Sir Herbert Taylor to that nobleman: "Your lordship is aware that I was private secretary to King George III., when the correspondence took place with the Administration of which you were a member, on the Catholic question, and I was of course privy to all that passed (His Majesty being blind), and had opportunities of learning his sentiments not consigned to paper. I am almost confident that he more than once said that he should not object to a proposition for giving a stipend to the Roman Catholic clergy, and that he observed that no better expedient could be found for reducing the influence of the Pope in Ireland, and transferring their dependence to the Government from which they would derive their means of support. I have heard the late Duke of York express the same opinion; and the King assures me that the late Mr. Perceval had frequently stated it to him as an arrangement he should be glad to effect."

It is needless to observe that the Catholic clergy

---

* "Cornwallis Correspondence," vol. ii. p. 247.
† "The Correspondence of Earl Grey with King William IV. and with Sir Herbert Taylor." Edited by Henry, Earl Grey. London: John Murray, 1867.

give no allegiance to the Pope inconsistent with their temporal allegiance to their sovereign. What demands our attention is this—that the project of giving them a pension was considered in the light of a bribe by its authors—a bribe which was to buy them off from certain principles which it was presumed that they held. And in the light of a bribe would any possible scheme of endowing the Catholic clergy of Ireland by an English and Protestant State be inevitably regarded—not only by the Government, but, what is more important, by the people of Ireland. If the clergy of the people became the paid officers of the English Government, they would utterly and finally forfeit the confidence of their flocks. We shudder to contemplate the scenes of anarchy and irreligion which would follow from such a loosing of the bands that now unite the people and their pastors. Let us hope that in the wisdom, the honesty, and the Christian fidelity of the priesthood, a sufficient security exists against such a terrible result.

In Cardinal Cullen's Pastoral at the beginning of Lent, 1866, he said, with reference to the pensioning project, *" Timeo Danaos et dona ferentes."* Now, in whatever shape the *dona* may be offered, whether in glebes, in pensions, or in any other mode whatsoever, it is certain that the offer would be meant as a bribe to purchase off the priesthood from the national interests of their country. Both English Whigs and English Tories—combined in hostility to Mr. Gladstone's Home Government measure—are resolved on preserving the Legislative Union as long as they can. That is to say, they will do their best to perpetuate the legislative disfranchisement of Ireland; to prolong a system that deprives her of the sole control of her own national interests, and that gives to Great Britain about nine parts in eleven of the formal control of those interests, and in real fact, the whole of it; to prolong a system that results in the wholesale spoliation of the wealth which God has bestowed upon our island, and in the consequent depopulation that afflicts almost to madness every man who has a heart to feel for the wrongs of his expatriated brethren, and a conscience to abhor the diabolical wickedness of plundering a country of its riches and driving out the inhabitants.

All this the Union does, and the people of Ireland know it. How could they retain their confidence in a priesthood capable of accepting any species of endowment from a Government resolved to perpetuate that Union?

The scheme of dividing the national ecclesiastical endowments between the Protestant and Catholic Churches was started by a gentleman whose personal character, position, and abilities entitled him to our respect. I publicly stated my objections to this scheme. The attempt would have been extremely impolitic, for it would have turned against us our only reliable allies, the English voluntaries. Desirous, as a matter of principle, to obtain the disendowment of the State Church in England, from which they or their progenitors had gone forth, and irritated by being made to contribute to its support, they knew that the ultimate success of their attack on it would be much facilitated by the overthrow of the State Church in Ireland. Hence, in working for us they worked for themselves. To attempt an endowment for Irish Catholicity would have deservedly forfeited their support. Moreover, such an attempt would have entailed upon our cause the weakness of division. For the mass of Irish Catholics would not have deserted the voluntary banner under which they had previously rallied, in order to fraternise with the claimants for Catholic endowment. Our agitation would have been encumbered with miserable by-battles between the friends of total Disendowment and the gentlemen (few, though indefatigable) who demanded the division of the spoil between the Churches. Thus, we should have furnished to the Whigs a plausible pretext for leaving the giant evil undisturbed. They would have been only too glad of an opportunity of telling us that until we were agreed among ourselves as to the proper remedy, they would deem it inexpedient to interfere with existing arrangements.

We proclaimed that the Catholic Church in Ireland had thriven and flourished for more than three centuries on the voluntary system; that it had struck its roots deep into the hearts of the Irish people, not only unsustained by, but in defiance of, the powers of this world. We said that among the human motives which act in harmony with the principle of Divine faith, supporting that principle and in turn receiving strength from it, a leading motive was the deep, enduring, passionate love of country that burns in the hearts of our people. We warned the claimants for Catholic endowments from the alien State against the terrible experiment of separating our devotion to the Catholic Church from our Irish nationality. "Let no fantastic theorist," we said, "seek to reduce us to the awful alternative of abandoning our accustomed ecclesiastical obedience; or of rendering that obedience to a hierarchy who would have forfeited our confidence by accepting endowments from a Power that, whether nationally or religiously, cannot possibly have any common sympathies with Catholic Ireland."

There was not, however, much real chance that the advocates of a State endowment for the Irish Catholic Church would succeed in their movement, which was chiefly supported by one bishop, a lay gentleman of much poetic talent, and a handful of West-British Whigs. Against their scheme was the vast and powerful array of British voluntaries; the British anti-Papal multitude, who would have resented the endowment of "Popery" as treason to Protestantism; and, finally, the great body of Irish Catholics, clerical as well as lay, who felt that the union between the clergy and their flocks would be rudely shaken by placing the former under pecuniary obligations to the alien Government.

During the prevalence of the Fenian conspiracy, an intelligent priest in the south of Ireland, conversing with me on the efforts the Catholic clergy had made to check Fenianism, said: "The people were just hanging on to us—we could hardly hold them in; but if they had been able to point to an endowment in our hands we could not have held them in at all."

Of the general principle of State endowment of religion I shall here say nothing. But of its particular application by the Protestant Government of another country to our national Church, I will say this: Every Church which is endowed by the State must to some extent rely upon temporal support; but "the vital power of religion is generally found to exist in an inverse ratio to its reliance on temporal support."*

This is at any rate true of Catholicity in Ireland. And may God defend us, and defend our remotest posterity, from the fatal pecuniary alliance between our national Church and an alien, uncongenial Government!

---

* Rev. H. B. Liddon.

CHAPTER XII.

PROGRESS OF THE ANTI-TITHE MOVEMENT.

> Then who's the wretch that basely spurns
> The ties of country, kindred, friends;
> That barters every nobler aim
> For sordid views—for private ends?
> One slave alone on earth you'll find
> Through Nature's universal span,
> So lost to virtue, dead to shame:
> The Anti-Irish Irishman.
> *Spirit of the Nation.*

I HAVE said that "Repeal" and "No Tithes" were associated on the platforms. The journals in the State Church interest, and the speakers and writers, lay and clerical, by whom that interest was defended, generally represented Repeal as a purely Popish scheme, designed to overthrow Protestantism, and fraught with peril to the properties and persons of Protestants. The true merits and facts of the question were carefully suppressed; the most baseless falsehoods were boldly affirmed and reiterated; the fanatical engine was incessantly worked; and a profound impression was made on the credulity, the ignorance, and the religious prejudices of a large class of Protestants.

So far as concerns the miserable wrangling of adverse religionists, let it pass for what it is worth. A ferocious polemical divine imagines that he has discharged a telling shot when he has let off some fanatical impertinence about "idolatry," or "wafer-gods," or "the priest-ridden people." Well, he has been impertinent; what matter? None, surely—unless we get too much of his impertinence. I bear no enmity to any man for calling me a limb of Antichrist, and telling me I must go to the devil as a follower of the Pope. Certainly such language is not civil, and I am convinced it is not true. But there is little wisdom in quarrelling with men for mere incivility, or for a mistaken view of my chances of salvation. It is impossible to conceive anything more intrinsically unimportant than the anti-Catholic speculations and incivilities of our polemical assailants. "Antichrist" shouted at a Catholic by some delirious enthusiast should no more excite his wrath than "d——n your blood" from a drunken trooper. But the case is altered when abuse of our faith becomes the watchword of a powerful party. When it becomes the rallying cry of men who avail themselves of the spirit, it excites to assail our pockets or abridge our liberties, we are called on to resent it; to resist the party who use their fanaticism as an engine wherewith to work out our oppression.

It was preposterous to talk of the anti-Irish Church Establishment as a religious institution. Of the personal piety or of the doctrinal convictions of its numerous estimable members, I say nothing disrespectful. I speak of it solely as a State Institution. During the period of its Establishment it was in Catholic eyes a political instrument designed and calculated to create and intensify class animosities. I fear that a good deal of the bitterness which it engendered has survived its disestablishment.*

Its advocates defended it on the plea of its being what they termed "a Missionary Church." It was supposed to have a mission from the State to convert the Catholics. From a Protestant standpoint it cannot seem, in this sense, valuable; for it has not converted the Catholics of Ireland to

---

* In a paper entitled "Ritualism in its Missionary Aspect," by an Anglican clergyman—the Rev. Dr. Littledale—that reverend gentleman says of the State Church in Ireland: "Though called by some of its panegyrists a Missionary Church, how completely it has broken down in dealing with the Roman Catholic population need not be insisted on. It is enough to say that even if the reports of the proselytising societies were as true as they are unscrupulously mendacious, the results would be a very poor return for three centuries of monopoly."—From *The Church and the World: Essays on Questions of the Day*. By various writers. First Series. Edited by the Rev. Orby Shipley, M.A. Second Edition. London: Longmans.

Archdeacon Stopford, in order to demonstrate the vast success of the State Church in converting the Irish from Catholicity, published in 1853 in his work called "Income and Requirements of the Irish Church," a table professing to give the number of State Protestants in forty-eight selected parishes in 1834 and the Protestant religion. They were but as three to one during part of the last century; now they are seven to one as compared with the Protestants of the Episcopal Church—poor evidence of its missionary efficacy.

Has it diffused through the land the Christian fruits of peace, goodwill, and mutual tolerance? There for three centuries it stood—hating and hated, plundering and execrated; in past times prolific of tears, outrage, and wailings; in our own day prolific of bitter politico-sectarian animosity between classes who ought to have one common interest as Irishmen. The people regarded it as a monument of English power and Irish degradation.

These were the qualities that constituted its real value in the estimation of our Whig and Tory rulers. The Whigs, when out of office, had often made political capital by denouncing it as an in-

---

1851 respectively, by which he made it appear that the Protestant inhabitants were greatly increased by conversions, and amounted in 1851 to no less than 12,372 persons. Mr. Herbert Skeats, in his excellent pamphlet styled "The Irish Church; a Historical and Statistical Review," follows the Archdeacon through each of his forty-eight parishes, and finds, by comparing the Archdeacon's figures with the figures of the (then) last census, that if there were really 12,372 Protestants in those parishes in 1851, there must have been "the most alarming declension, in ten years, of the number of converts, or of members of the Established Church, that has probably taken place in any part of Ireland or in any other country." And well might Mr. Skeats say so, for the census of 1861 only gave a total of 6,939 State Protestants in the parishes in question. The other alternative suggested by Mr. Skeats is probably the true one—namely, that the Archdeacon's statement was inaccurate.

tolerable grievance. The Whigs, when in office, were accustomed to look with complacent philosophy at the intolerable grievance, and would to this day have continued equally sympathetic and equally inactive, if the English Liberation Society had not forced the question on the notice of the nation and of its rulers by such a vigorous and persistent agitation that the Government were at last compelled to abate the great scandal by complete disestablishment, and by a partial and inadequate disendowment.

Looking back on the anti-Irish Church, on its English origin and its historical sympathies, it would be impossible to conceive a more useful auxiliary to English Whigs and Tories in the misgovernment and robbery of Ireland. It held out rich rewards to an important class to sustain in every possible mode the (so-called) interests of imperial England as opposed to those of their native country. The injury of being thus rendered subservient to the powerful rivalry of another land became the more galling, when, as in the case of Ireland, the depressed nation was compelled to be the paymaster of those officers who enforced and perpetuated its own servitude. A man who supposed he could smooth his path to station and salary by crying, " Up with England ! Down with Ireland ! " found the inducement to anti-national politics much augmented, when to the motive of self-interest was added the stimulant of sectarian partisanship.

That such a wealthy exclusive institution as the State Church should have kept a considerable portion of the Protestant body from merging into the great national mass, is not greatly to be wondered at. Religious bigotry, combined with pecuniary profit, has availed to perpetuate the original hostility to Ireland of the Elizabethan, Cromwellian, and Williamite adventurers in the breasts of their descendants of the present day. This long-cherished hatred of a domestic faction to their countrymen has no parallel in any other country. You will find all Frenchmen, of whatever party in the State, zealous for the glory of France; all Germans ardent for the honour of Germany; Spaniards for Spain, and so on. It is in Ireland only that you will hear from the lips of her unnatural children the frequent expressions, "this odious land!" "this detestable people!" "England will drag her triumphant cannon over your prostrate carcases if you dare to resist;" * with innumerable similar ebullitions of venomous hatred of the unoffending people among whom their lot is cast, and whose only crime is that they agitate for the common liberties of their revilers and themselves. I recollect reading some years since in a Limerick paper a letter written by an English gentleman named Potter, who had spent some time in Ireland, and who expressed his surprise that all the Irish Protestants he met seemed to him to have

---

* I found this anti-national brag in the report of a speech delivered by Mr. Emerson Tennent.

been trained to hate their native country. A trivial circumstance will illustrate the satanic activity with which, under the pretext of religion, hatred of the Irish Catholic peasantry is instilled into the Protestant mind. I chanced to converse with a young lady who had been carefully brought up under parsonic influences. She abused our poor countryfolk as a set of ferocious and immoral savages. Of course she had derived that impression from her intercourse with teachers and companions. I tried to undeceive her, and stated one or two reasons to show she was mistaken.

"Ah!" said she, "I wish you had been the other night at the lecture we heard from the Rev. Mr. ——! He said the country people were a dreadful set, and told us how, when going among them, his life had been more than once in danger from the ferocity of fellows who were hounded at him by the priests. I can tell you he was well cheered."

I have no doubt he was well cheered. On my fair friend's table was a "religious" work, in which it was affirmed that the Irish Catholics considered it a greater sin "to eat meat on Friday, than to murder a Protestant for a consideration." These details may seem trivial. But such prejudices are not trivial in their consequences when kneaded into the minds of possibly well-meaning people, the current of whose affections has been thereby turned from the land that supplies them with their means of living, and from the people whom they ought to love.

What, I ask, is the inexhaustible fountain of this pestilential hatred of Ireland by Irishmen? What feeds the stream of ceaseless calumny, insult, and political enmity? Prior to the Disestablishment of the English Church in Ireland, the obvious answer to this query was—the anti-Irish State Church, acting through the interests it affected. Since Disestablishment we must ascribe the antinational feeling partly to the bigotry bequeathed by that pernicious institution to its disestablished successor, but also in some measure to the violent onslaught on the whole body of Irish landlords got up by Mr. Parnell, which fatally widened the traditionary chasm between them and the people —a chasm which we, of the Repeal Association and the Home Rule League, had laboured hard to close.

Despite the lapse of ages, despite even the connexions formed by marriage with many of the native families, the hostile spirit of the invader is as fresh, as vivid, in the modern descendants of the ruthless soldiery of Essex or St. Leger, of the sanguinary fanatics of the Commonwealth, or of the military settlers of the Williamite era, as it was some centuries ago in the breasts of their forefathers. They have never become blended with the people. I have heard language redolent of the most contemptuous and envenomed hostility to the national population of Ireland proceeding from tongues whose rich Hibernian brogue contrasted ludicrously with the anti-Hibernian sentiments they uttered. Even the ignorant Orange tradesman still fancies himself a sort of Englishman in virtue of his English creed, and the long habit, not yet extinguished by emancipation, of regarding its profession as a badge of social superiority.

To any dispassionate observer at a distance, not aware of the source of the unnatural hostility of Ireland's domestic enemies to their country, how strange, how unaccountable must that hostility appear! How strange that no national yearnings should be excited in their minds by the hallowed associations of home, the ties of kindred, the casting of their lot in the old land of their birth; that the blending of their forefathers' dust for many a generation with Irish earth, should yet leave the living descendant as alien in feeling—nay, as hostile, as if no such associations existed to bind his heart to his fatherland! Strange that the mystic voices of the breeze that stirs the sycamores over his ancestors' graves should not whisper to his spirit to love Ireland—to strive for her liberties! Strange that he should have no pride of country; that not only is he destitute of the ordinary sentiment of patriotism indigenous to every other land on earth, but that from *his* tongue should emanate the bitterest insults to Ireland and her sons—from *his* brain should proceed the wickedest devices to enthral his own countrymen! I once heard a jovial Irish squire of Cromwellian descent, whose estate lay in as peaceable a district as any in the world, exclaim that if it were not for the personal supervision his property required from him, he would quit "this abominable country and go to live in England." An orator named Harte proclaimed at a meeting of the Dublin Conservative Society some years ago, that "it was perfectly notorious to every man who heard him, that to be a Protestant in Ireland was sufficient to render life insecure." These instances are not isolated. The party who display this astounding hatred of their country are indefatigable in their calumnies. The inspiring source of that hatred is clearly discernible in the pseudo-religious character of their attacks. Take two instances which accidentally met my eye some years ago; they are both typical. The first of these is an extract from the *Cork Constitution* newspaper of July 27th, 1844. It is headed:

"DOINGS IN DINGLE.

"On Sunday last, the Rev. Mr. Brasbie read his public recantation from the errors of Popery in Dingle Church. The fact of a priest abjuring Popery caused great excitement; and the magistrates, having got full notice that the mob were determined to execute lynch law on the priest on his road to the church, took full precautions to preserve the peace. Before service commenced, the townspeople were astonished to see the Hon. Captain Plunket, of H.M. steamer *Stromboli*, march into the town from Ventry with a force of about one hundred men, including the marine artillery and marines, with drums and colours. This fine body of men, armed to the teeth, having joined the seamen and marines of H.M. brigantine *Lynx*, under command of Captain Nott, presented such an imposing appearance that, we need not say, everything passed off very quietly. The coastguard from the surrounding stations were marched to church, fully armed, and conveyed the reverend gentleman to the house of the Rev. Mr. Gayer, where he at present remains. Mr. Gillman, our active sub-inspector, had all his police ready to turn out at a moment's notice. Dingle for the last twenty years never presented such a force."

Lord Aberdeen, about that period, apologised in Parliament for the non-transmission of a marine force to Morocco, as Her Majesty's war vessels were on duty on the coast of Ireland. His lordship ought to have explained the tremendous nature of the duty which deprived the Mediterranean of the presence of the British flag. He should have announced that the *Stromboli* and the *Lynx* were required to assist the " missionary Church " (as the *Evening Mail* delighted to term the Establishment) in the acquisition of the Rev. Mr. Brasbie to her fold.

The whole paragraph is redolent of Irish State Churchism. The transition from Popish error to Protestant truth is performed by the beat of drums and the flourish of military colours. The triumph of having caught a priest who will renounce holy water and purgatory is combined with the congenial triumph of saying to the mob, " My lads, we have 100 marines all armed to the teeth, who will make smithereens of any man that dares to wag a finger." The orthodox parade of " such a force as Dingle had not seen for twenty years," is requisite to give due *éclat* to the Rev. Mr. Brasbie's exchange of Pope Gregory XVI. for Pope Victoria as the head of his Church; and, moreover, to protect the sacred person of the convert from the truculence of the "mob," who in all probability did not care three straws for the exploits of the reverend gentleman.

The other instance is the allegation by the Rev. Mr. Nangle, of Achill, that eleven Achillonians had attempted to induce one Francis M'Hugh to enter into a conspiracy to burn Mr. Nangle's house. That reverend gentleman also printed in the *Achill Herald* (of which he was the editor) a statement that the Catholics of the island had conspired to break into his dwelling, and strangle the inhabitants. His charge of meditated murder and arson elicited from Mr. S. C. Hall, the well-known writer, an indignant letter to the *Times*, from which the following paragraph is an extract:

"The intention of the conspirators (writes the Rev. E. Nangle in his own newspaper, the *Achill Herald*—fruitful source of incalculable mischief!) was to have come down in considerable force at night, to have entered by one of the senior missionary's (*i.e.* Mr. Nangle's) houses, to have strangled him and the other heads of the mission in their beds, and, after robbing them, to burn their dwellings.

"Rely on it, sir, there is not a shadow of foundation for this 'horrible plot.' For the sake of mercy and justice, lend your powerful aid to prevent so foul a slander from obtaining credit in this country.

"Without meaning to insinuate that this cock-and-bull story of conspiracy to murder wholesale has been got up for the occasion, I may at least say that it occurs at a lucky moment for the colony, inasmuch as within the next month the Rev. E. Nangle will make his customary round of visits to several English towns, and deliver his annual oration at Exeter Hall; the result of which, once a year, is a freightage of English gold to his small colony at Achill. I append my name, which you will either print or withhold at your pleasure.

"S. C. HALL."

"Jan. 8th, 1844."

Mr. Hall is not only a Protestant, but a Conservative. I mention his religious and political opinions, not that his personal truth and honour are in the slightest degree thereby affected, but because there are readers who will more readily accept the testimony of a gentleman who holds his views than if it were the evidence of a Catholic nationalist. In fact it is extremely difficult to suppose that Mr. Nangle believed in the truth of his serious accusations. They were, of course, interspersed with affecting expressions of pious regret at the dense spiritual blindness of the people. Mr. Nangle prosecuted the alleged culprits. The charge of attempting to involve M'Hugh in a conspiracy to burn the house was sworn to at the Mayo assizes of July, 1844, by that person himself, who appeared to be a convert, probably of Mr. Nangle's manufacture. His sworn testimony was rejected by Judge Jackson as totally incredible.*

The work of pious slander is incessant. In July, 1863, a circular address was issued from "The Metropolitan House, Bachelor's Walk, Dublin," to the Protestant employers of Ireland. It is headed with the words, "Assassination—Self-Preservation," and seems to have been chiefly meant to work upon the nervous fears of ladies, inasmuch as it commences, "Dear Madam." I copy the first

---

* Mr. Hall's appreciation of the moral merits of the onslaught on the faith of the Achill Catholics, sustained by English contributions of money, may be learned from the following passage of his "Tour through Ireland," p. 400. "It was impossible," says Mr. Hall, "not to appreciate the magnanimity of the poor, miserable, utterly destitute, and absolutely starving inhabitants of Achill, who were at the time of our visit enduring privations at which humanity shudders—and to know that by walking a couple of miles and *professing* to change their religion they would be instantly supplied with food, clothes, and lodging. Yet these hungry thousands—for it would scarcely be an exaggeration to say that nine-tenths of the population of the island were, in the month of July last, entirely without food—preferred patiently to endure their sufferings rather than submit to what they considered a degradation. Such fortitude we do believe to be without parallel in the history of any 'ignorant and unenlightened' people since the creation of the world."

and last paragraphs of this most characteristic document:

"The assassinations that are taking, and have taken place, almost daily, in our unhappy, but, alas! too notorious country, prove beyond a shadow of doubt that it is neither safe nor prudent for landlords to employ Roman Catholics as domestic or farm-servants, or to locate them on their lands as small farmers or stewards. To illustrate this statement by numerous examples would be to waste your time, and trifle with the most serious evil of the age in which we live."

The address goes on to urge, as the best means of preservation from Popish assassins, the employment of "Protestants only who are in favour of British connexion." Roman Catholics, indeed, may be employed; but only "in stations unaccompanied by risk and personal danger." They are to be shown a holy and edifying example, and to be taught to live "in the constant practice of godliness, industry, and every Christian virtue."

Having thus exhorted the Protestant employers to keep their dangerous neighbours at a prudent distance, the address concludes as follows: "This method of self-preservation would, we are convinced, be found a golden rule—a royal road to domestic safety, security, and protection, for Protestants individually and collectively. It would check the assassination and decimation of our gentry; and it would reflect its blessings on those who are not of our communion. It would elevate our class, edify the Church, receive the approval of the Most High, and attract the attention of the civilised and uncivilised inhabitants of Great Britain, of Europe, and of the World.

"Your very humble servant in Christ Jesus,

"THE SECRETARY,
"Employment and Aid Society for Protestants.

"July, 1863."

This address was intended for private circulation; but a copy of it accidentally reached the hands of Mr. A. M. Sullivan, the able and patriotic editor of the *Nation*, in which journal that gentleman published it on the 15th of August, 1863.

One mode of keeping up the sectarian excitement was by displaying anti-Catholic placards in the streets. This was for a long period constantly and offensively done. An English gentleman, one of the most illustrious of the Oxford converts, wrote to me from Dublin that if the Catholics were to retaliate with anti-Protestant placards, a state of things would be produced which would probably compel the Government to put a stop to that species of warfare. There were controversial handbills profusely scattered over the country—thrown upon the highways, flung into the fields, and pasted upon walls. The piers of my entrance-gate were thus decorated. Whether any of the handbills displayed talent, I am unable to say. The attempts at argument in those which I saw were the veriest sweepings of controversial rubbish. But they attacked "Popery," helped to exasperate the Catholics, and gave an appearance of activity in return for the large sums of money with which the managers of the affair were subsidised by credulous English fanatics.

Let me here observe, that, great as has been the evil resulting from religious bigotry, yet the presence of two rival creeds within the land has not been totally without its good. I have heretofore spoken of the Protestant Church with reference exclusively to its temporal Establishment.

I now speak of it as a religious system, and, as such, it has derived some moral advantage from the presence of antagonist Catholicity. The advantage has been mutual. Two rival Churches will watch and purify each other. Not that this is any justification of religious differences; not that such differences are necessary to preserve religion pure; but simply that where they happen to exist, God can educe good from the evil of disunion.

Contrast the morals of the Protestants of the present day with those of their fathers in the heyday of the penal laws, when Catholics were too insignificant to be their rivals—when Protestantism had everything its own way. Then were the golden days of duelling, of drunkenness, of profligate clubs in the metropolis—the Cherokee, the Hellfire, the Pinkers and Sweaters, whose orgies are still preserved in the local traditions of Dublin. Then were the days of gallant, jovial, hard-drinking parsons—

men who were paid by the State for talking every Sunday about religion, and who, accordingly, pronounced some cold and formal sentences to small congregations, who, on their part, conceived that they performed a meritorious duty in listening with grave faces to the solemn homilies. Catholicity, however, uprose in renovated strength, shook off its penal bandages, and assumed the attitude of spiritual rivalry. The State Church was alarmed. If the Protestant clergy and their flocks became more bigoted, they certainly became more virtuous. The majority of the parsons of our day are moral and pious. Apart from the drawbacks of anti-Irish prejudice and anti-Catholic slander (in which latter not one-twentieth part of them actively participate) they are in general personally virtuous and exemplary.

Would to God that Irishmen of all creeds could recognise and rejoice in each other's good qualities; that they could turn the rivalship of antagonist creeds to its legitimate account—the promotion of religion and morality; discard all unchristian acerbity, and unite with cordial, mutual trustfulness in the national cause!

CHAPTER XIII.

THE REPEAL CAMPAIGN OF 1832.

> 'Tis only to gather
>   Our strength and be ready,
> The son with the father,
>   The wild with the steady.
> In front of the danger,
>   To tramp all together;
> Defying the stranger
>   In hall or in heather.
>
> J. DE JEAN.

THE continued existence of the Union for thirty years had a powerful effect in benumbing nationality among those whose religious teachers had inspired them with a suspicion of their countrymen. They had become accustomed to be legislated for by England, and use had rendered them insensible to the degradation which had aroused in 1800 the Irish spirit of the very Orangemen. The Union had debased and degraded many of the generation who had grown up since its enactment. They sneered at the Repealers as visionaries, and—prejudging the whole matter in dispute—they flippantly asserted that there was nothing Ireland could gain from native legislation that she could not also obtain from the Imperial Parliament.

The Reform agitation of 1831 necessarily excited the English mind to a pitch of intensity. The Irish were busy with their own agitation; and when Reform had been carried, and some enlargement of the constituencies temporarily effected, the Repealers mustered their strength to send members to St. Stephen's who should represent their principles.

Many Irish agitators, with the prospect of Parliamentary distinction, were speedily in the field. Ere the senatorial vision had crossed their aspiring thoughts, some three or four had acquired more than ordinary notoriety by their agitation. Of these, one of the most conspicuous was Feargus O'Connor. Feargus was fourth son of Roger O'Connor, who, in 1798, resided at Connorville, near Dunmanway, in the County of Cork. Roger O'Connor was involved in the rebellion of which his brother Arthur was one of the principal leaders. Arthur wished, at the later period of his agitation, to make Ireland a republic on the French model of 1792. He was a thoroughly honest politician. Of his disinterestedness there is conclusive proof in the fact that he deliberately forfeited the splendid inheritance of his maternal uncle, Lord Longueville, who was childless, and who would have made him his heir on condition of his adopting his lordship's politics. Roger's views were monarchical; I believe he intended to exercise the sovereign authority himself.

Roger employed his military skill in fortifying Connorville to sustain an attack from the King's troops. He planned a trap for them also, of which I had a detailed description from a gentleman who was personally cognisant of the device.

There were two fronts to Connorville House. From the front that faced the public road the hall-door steps were removed, and the windows of the basement storey on that side of the house were strongly built up. No hostile entry could have been effected upon that front. The other front opened on a large courtyard, nearly surrounded with high buildings. From the eastern side of this courtyard ran a broad, straight avenue, some hundreds of yards in length, between two very lofty walls overgrown with ivy of extraordinary luxuriance. At the extremity of this avenue farthest from the house was a high and massive iron gate. The whole length of the avenue was commanded by cannon, which were placed in a shed in the courtyard, and managed by French artillerymen. The massive gate at the eastern end of the avenue was left constantly open, to invite the entrance of His Majesty's troops in the event of a hostile descent upon Connorville. There were men always stationed *perdu* in the huge ivy bushes at the top of the piers, to lock the gate the instant the military forces should have passed through.

The soldiers would thus be caught in a complete trap; hemmed in by the lofty walls that flanked the avenue, their retreat cut off by the iron gate behind them, and their position fully raked in front by the cannon in the courtyard.* The scheme seemed feasible enough, but it never was realised. The soldiers came to Connorville; they entered the avenue and courtyard; but whether the artillerymen had deserted their post, or whether Roger had not completed his intended preparations, certain it is that the redcoats scoured the premises without molestation, and Roger surveyed them from the friendly shade of a holly-tree in which he was ensconced, on a rocky eminence that overlooked the courtyard from the north. He escaped on that occasion; his capture did not occur for some months after. His subsequent imprisonment at Fort George in Scotland is well known. I possess, in his manuscript, a poetical "Invocation to Sleep," which he composed during his incarceration. It is manifestly an unfinished production; a few lines may serve as a sample of its merits:

> Far from my native land, far from my wife
> And all my little babes, on Moray Firth

---

* This account of Roger O'Connor's preparations was given me by my father. A lady, who professed to recollect Connorville at that period, had, I am told, asserted that the preparations were not actually made. It is, therefore, proper to say that my father may possibly have described to me a plan which Roger only devised, but did not bring to the point of preparation; but my impression of the communication I received is such as I have given it in the text.

Roger established at Dangan.

> Incag'd and barr'd with double bolts I drag
> My weary days and lengthened nights of pain.
> On Sleep, that dull and partial god, I call
> In vain! Unheard or slighted are my plaints.
> The constant tramp of feet, and watchful cry
> Of " Who comes there ? " the sentry's hollow cough
> Contracted from the midnight cold and damp,
> Assail my ear, still conscious of the sound ;
> The bell's loud voice, which speaks Old Time's decay,
> Is so familiar grown, I still conceit
> That I can tell his numbers by his note.
> O! for a cup of Lethe's pool to steep
> My weary senses in forgetfulness.

When Roger was released from Fort George, he was permitted to reside in England, but not for some time to return to Ireland. When at last this restriction was withdrawn, he returned to Ireland, and purchased the magnificent mansion and domain of Dangan Castle, in the County Meath, the family seat of the Wellesleys. Dangan was long supposed to have been the birthplace of the Duke of Wellington; but the minute researches of Sir Bernard Burke have conclusively established that His Grace was born in Mornington House, No. 24, Upper Merrion Street, Dublin, which mansion is at present occupied by the Commissioners of Church Temporalities and the Commissioners of the Land Court. The purchase money of Dangan was to remain for some time in Roger O'Connor's hands, bearing interest.

The following brief notice of Dangan occurs in Arthur Young's " Tour in Ireland," under date 28th of June, 1776 : "Went in the evening to Lord Mornington's at Dangan, who is making many improvements which he showed me. His plantations are extensive, and he has formed a large water having five or six islands much varied; and promontories of high land shoot so far into it as to form almost distant lakes; the effect pleasing. There are above 100 acres under water, and his lordship has planned a considerable addition to it."

The extensive plantations had grown up into lofty woods before Roger became their proprietor. His declared object in becoming the occupant of Dangan was, that he might possess a house fit for the reception of Bonaparte, as he professed a firm faith in the advent of the Emperor to Ireland. Wellington, however, was less hospitable, and effectually prevented the visit of Napoleon to his hereditary residence.

Feargus was born at Connorville in 1796. He resided a good deal with his father at Dangan until that mansion was consumed by a fire said to have been accidental. He had, however, been sent to two or three schools, at which he distinguished himself by a number of irregular pranks. At a school in Portarlington he fell desperately in love with the schoolmaster's fascinating daughter, and received a severe paternal admonition on the impropriety of sullying the glory of his illustrious lineage by such a *mésalliance*. He ran off from his family to England, and amused himself haymaking one summer in Wiltshire.` His father was eccentric and imaginative. Feargus early acquired a taste for an adventurous life, and politics naturally had a place in his ruminations. In 1822 he resided, with other members of his family, at Fortrobert, a spacious house—now a roofless ruin—on a hill adjoining the domain of Connorville. There he lived a jolly life, enjoying the society afforded by the neighbourhood, to which his entertaining conversation rendered him a welcome acquisition; playing whist, riding to foxhounds, outrivalling all his competitors iu desperate horsemanship; and giving occasional indications of the spirit within him by attacks on prominent local abuses. He published a pamphlet fiercely denouncing the oppressors of the peasantry—parsons, tithe-proctors, grinding middlemen, jobbing grand-jurors—with especial censure of all magistrates trafficking in justice.

As yet Feargus had not tried his rhetorical powers in public. But the exciting political transactions of 1831 and 1832 necessarily called forth so active and ardent a spirit. He first appeared at a Whig meeting held in Cork in December, 1831, for the purpose of forwarding Reform of Parliament. Messrs. Jephson, of Mallow; Nicholas Philpot Leader, then member for Kilkenny; Delacour, a banker; Stawell, of Kilbrittain; Baldwin, of Cork; with some youthful scions of the Shannon and Kingston families, and several other Whig notables of the county, were mustered in the old Court-house on the Grand Parade at an early hour. They all rehearsed the usual commonplaces of Reform; talked in a tone of aristocratic condescension of the claims of the democracy; announced that in order to establish a right to full citizenship it was not requisite that men should exhibit rent-rolls and pedigrees; with a great many equally respectable political truisms. Up to four o'clock the most amusing speaker was Leader, the member for Kilkenny. He was a stout, thick-set man, with a wild, ferocious eye; he shouted and bellowed, gesticulated like a harlequin, slapped his thighs, spun nearly round on tiptoe, emphasised remarkable hits by bobbing down his head within a couple of feet of the floor, roared, stamped, ranted, blustered, and perforce of a thundering expenditure of personal energy, elicited vociferous applause.

Late in the day Feargus came forward to the front of one of the galleries; distanced all the Whigs and Reformers by exclaiming that Repeal alone could save Ireland from ruin; and certainly so far as concerned the external matters of voice, action, and delivery, he made beyond comparison the best speech of the day.

Feargus now set himself to work in earnest to attain political leadership. He had not yet contemplated an attack on the representation of the county, for he had not yet seen to what extent the Reform Bill would popularise the constituency; but he dearly loved the greeting cheers of the multitude; he revelled in the consciousness of possessing unusual volubility; and he had a strong conviction that his popular talents would soon exalt him into a position of political command.

In the summer of 1832 the anti-tithe agitation extended all over the County of Cork. Feargus was ubiquitous; Macroom, Duumanway, Enniskean, and several other places, were visited in rapid succession. "Fargus," as the country folk familiarly called him, soon ingratiated himself into every one's favour; and by the frankness and ease of his address, and his great colloquial powers, disarmed the suspicious enmity of many in the middle ranks who had previously anathematised both himself and his cause.

He soon received the distinction of two or three public entertainments. At Macroom he got a dinner from about three hundred farmers and shopkeepers, at which he, for the first time, publicly announced himself a candidate for the representation. He declared, in accents of affecting pathos, that his advocacy of the people's rights had deprived him of the affections of his nearest relatives.

"Since I last," said he, "met my friends of Macroom, there has been no smile on my cheek, no comfort in my breast. My nearest relations have turned from me; it is true they recognise me privately, but in public they have wounded my feelings. I leave them to that awful moment when the sacred Monitor shall arouse them to reflection —when he shall tap here" (pointing to his breast), "and cry, Awake! be judged."

It behoved the people on whose behalf the sufferings in question were incurred, to apply the salve to the patriotic victim. It especially behoved the tradesmen of Macroom to indemnify him for his sorrows, inasmuch as he claimed the honour of membership with their fraternity in virtue of his having taken part in a meeting held in the large square in that town in the month of June previously.

The electors in the popular interest had been urged by the Catholic clergy to register their votes, and the shrewd ones began with confidence to augur a very large Liberal majority at the next general election. At the Macroom dinner, as we learn from the Cork *Southern Reporter* of that date, "the subject of the representation was freely discussed. Mr. O'Connor announced his attention of becoming a candidate for the County of Cork at the approaching election. He was received with great enthusiasm, and all present confirmed his pretensions by the highest eulogy of his claims and character. A general pledge was made by the company of their support and influence. At the suggestion of the chairman, a resolution was entered into for the formation of an Independent Club to organise the representative franchise in the county, the better to secure the return of Mr. O'Connor in conjunction with any other popular candidate who should present himself. The conditions laid down for the future candidates were a full support of the Repeal of the Union, total abolition of tithes, vote by ballot, and universal suffrage."

It was late at night when Feargus rose to announce his resolution to become a candidate for the county. The candles had nearly burned down to their sockets, and threw a dim and doubtful gleam upon the large apartment. A very prosy, windy speaker had occupied a great deal of time in delivering a speech which I cannot better describe than by saying that in matter and structure it resembled an interminable leading article in a tenth-rate country newspaper. Listeners got tired—Feargus was especially impatient; yet the orator not only prosed on, but seemed to regard his newly-found capacity for public speaking as a subject of particular congratulation. "This," he exclaimed, "is the first time that I ever made a speech, and I never thought I could have talked so long without stopping—it appears to me that I'm inspired;" and he continued to give the audience the benefit of his inspiration, either until he had exhausted the afflatus, or until the chairman checked him on the plea that the hour was now far advanced. The crowd had drawn close to the small daïs, or platform, on which were assembled the chairman, the guest, and two or three other country gentlemen. There was great exultation at the prospect of seeing the popular favourite returned to Parliament. When Feargus announced that he would stand for the county, a rapturous "hurrah!" testified the general delight. The candidate resumed his seat, much pleased with the sympathy of his friends, when a movement was discerned among the throng, as of some stalwart fellow elbowing his way to the front. Feargus rose, and recognised the person who was forcing himself forward; he was a broad-shouldered, red-haired, athletic Protestant farmer, named Whiting, who bore a strong personal resemblance to the burly candidate himself.

"Make room for Mr. Whiting," said Feargus in his blandest accents. Room was immediately made for his passage. "How are you, my worthy friend?" continued Feargus, courteously shaking hands with Whiting. "Would you wish to get on the platform? We've plenty of room for you."

Whiting accepted the invitation and was given a chair, on which he seated himself. He gazed for some moments at Feargus in mute ecstasy, and then broke forth: "O, Fargus! Fargus! is it not the murdher of the world to see you looking after the representation of a county in their English Parliament, instead of enjoying (as by right you ought) the royal crown of Ireland upon that honest red head, as was worn by your ancesthors in the ancient times of ould!"

Feargus, however, limited his ambition to a seat for the county, despite this stimulating burst of post-prandial enthusiasm. He smiled assuasively in return for Mr. Whiting's complimentary allusion to his ancestral honours. The scene was amusing, and its effect was heightened by the personal resemblance of the sturdy yeoman and the patriotic orator, who exchanged the most affectionate glances with each other.

Feargus lashed all jobbers, particularly jobbing

magistrates who made a profitable trade of their justice-ship; "they ate justice, drank justice, lay upon justice, rode justice, wore justice — aye, threadbare!"

He complimented the tradesmen of Macroom by whom he was surrounded: "Tradesmen we are all, in fact, from the monarch who fills the throne, and whose trade is that of cabinet-making, to the humble chimney-sweeper who loudly proclaims his calling from the house-tops. I am a tradesman of Macroom. I was bound apprentice in the great square on the 10th of June last" (alluding to the anti-tithe meeting held on that day); "and on my show-board shall be Peace, Industry, Union, and Freedom."

At the Enniskean anti-tithe meeting Feargus gallantly defied the Duke of Wellington. "I did hear that a military force was to have attended. If I saw that force under the command of the great Captain of the age, I would tell him he was in his dotage, and that the power of knowledge was greater than the power of cannon."

He defended himself from calumnious imputations: "Here I stand in the midst of thousands and tens of thousands to whom I have been known from my birth, and I fearlessly ask them if the breath of slander has ever dared to assail my character?" ("No, no!" and cheers.) "Have I ever oppressed the meanest individual among you?" ("No, no! hurrah!") "Have I not ever been your adviser and director?" ("Yes, yes! hurroo!")

He announced the religious object of his agitation at a dinner given him in Enniskean: "My object is to purify the religion I profess by lopping off its rotten and redundant temporalities"; and he fiercely inquired "whether the religion of the Almighty was to be set in blood?" alluding to the fatal tithe affrays.

At a dinner given in Cork to the late Bishop England, Feargus concluded a vehement speech in these words: "No! though our seabound dungeon were encompassed by the wooden walls of Old England—though the 300,000 promised Cossacks marched through the land with all the emblems of death, the rack, the scaffold, and the axe, yet I would suffer martyrdom ere I would throw up my hat and cry 'All hail' to him* who dragged my country's Liberator through the streets of the metropolis to answer a charge made crime by proclamation. No! though stretched upon the rack I would smile terror out of countenance, and die as I have lived—a pure lover of liberty!"

The critic in his closet who laughs at this fantastic bombast, will scarcely believe that when volubly thrown off, *rotundo ore*, and recommended by graceful and emphatic action, and an air of intense earnestness, it not only could pass for "fine speaking," but produce to some extent, upon a sympathetic audience, the effect of genuine eloquence. It seems to have found an admirer in the

---

* The Marquis of Anglesea.

reporter for the *Cork Mercantile Chronicle*, whose comment ran thus: "This splendid effusion of masculine eloquence created a most extraordinary sensation, coming, as it did, like a thunderclap on all. The talented speaker was long and loudly cheered on resuming his seat; and we will augur that it will be long before he is forgotten by the people of this city."

Feargus had now established his fame through the county as "a fine speaker." In the city of Cork he was generally called "the Rattler." Those who have not heard him in public in his best days, and who have only judged of his abilities by his printed effusions, have frequently done great injustice to his powers. He was remarkably ready and self-possessed. He was capable of producing extraordinary popular effect. He had very great declamatory talent. He had also great defects. As a stimulating orator in a popular assembly he was unexcelled. It is true he dealt largely in bombast, broken metaphor, and inflated language; but while you listened, those blemishes were lost in the infectious vehemence of his spirited manner; you were charmed with the melodious voice, the musical cadences, the astonishing volubility, the imposing self-confidence of the man, and the gallant air of bold defiance with which he assailed all oppression and tyranny. The difference between his spoken and printed harangues was surprisingly great.

He mingled the exciting qualities I have enumerated with a very small amount of argumentative power. He blended the facility of at first acquiring popular influence with a sad incapacity to retain it. He displayed an exhaustless fund of vituperative vigour in lashing all the parties disliked by the people; but he was sometimes betrayed, by want of reflection, into receiving and announcing as truths the most incredible exaggerations. For instance, he proclaimed to a numerous meeting in Bandon that certain portions of the parish of Timoleague paid tithe at the rate of £90 per acre; and that the fact of that extravagant tithe-charge had been confirmed upon oath before two magistrates.

During the agitating summer and autumn of 1832, scenes of a highly exciting and picturesque character were constantly exhibited. The meetings for Repeal and No Tithes were usually held on Sundays after mass. It was impossible to see without interest the rustic worshippers wending along the glen and down the hill-side, sauntering through "the lone vale of green bracken" beneath the brilliant morning sunshine; crowding to the Catholic church at the call of the bell; stragglers from the outskirts of the parish endeavouring to recover lost time by short cuts and increased speed, as they sprang with agility over the ditches. Then there was the muster of the hardy peasants in the churchyard; the more thoughtless occupying the interval before mass in inquiring the news of the day; the more devout kneeling apart before the altar rails, or under the rude pictures called the Stations of the Cross; or in some shaded spot without the sacred edifice, where, unmolested, they might recite a litany or a rosary beneath the shadow of an old hawthorn. Then came the last quick toll of the bell, announcing that divine service was just going to commence; then the hurried gathering into the church of a crowd that often overflowed its precincts; the Mass; the homely discourse in Irish; and after the " Ite, missa est," an announcement of the meeting of the day.

The meeting frequently comprised the inhabitants of many parishes. The dark multitudes streamed from the hills to one common centre—many on horseback, but the greater number on foot. There was a proud thrill in every man's breast; all felt the ennobling consciousness that a nation was peacefully mustering and banding together to assert and recover their rights. The Irish peasantry are not mere clodpoles. Many of them are imaginative and intellectual. They love their native land, and they are proud of it. They are susceptible of every external influence that can heighten the sentiment of patriotism; and as the multitudes traversed the grand scenery of the parishes on the sea-coast, doubtless many a foot was arrested on the heights which commanded a view of the bold mountain peaks, the magnificent expanse of ocean, the steep cliffs, and the rich green glens often winding from the shore among the hills; and many a heart felt to its centre that the freedom of such a glorious land was worth any struggle men could make—any peril men could encounter.

The meeting usually mustered in full strength at the appointed place about three o'clock in the afternoon. The chairman was often a Protestant, whose hatred of tithes was not less intense than that felt by the Catholic concourse around him. I only knew of one Protestant gentleman who was said to occupy his post with reluctance. He was a landlord of some hundreds a year. He was deemed a prize by his anti-tithist neighbours, who made many attempts to secure him for their chairman, which he always coquettishly evaded, until it was delicately hinted that in the event of his persisting in refusal, the requisitionists would develop to the Board of Customs certain smuggling transactions in which he had been engaged. The hint was sufficient. Mr. —— consented to preside, and he delivered a philippic against the Church temporalities, of which the pungent bitterness amply redeemed his previous apathy.

Feargus was quite in his element at all these public meetings. The first of them which he attended was, I think, a very large gathering held near Dunmanway on the 29th of June, 1832, at which my brother, Thomas Wilson Daunt, presided. Feargus delivered himself with a voluble energy which called down tumultuous cheers, and found so much favour with some of his hearers that they declared he was "finer than O'Connell." He hated the Union with cordial bitterness; he hated the tithes with equal intensity; and he had stories of ecclesiastical mismanagement at his fingers' ends much better authenticated than the legend of the ninety pounds per acre. He spoke of the parish in which his own residence, Fortrobert, was situated; told how the rector, Mr. Hamilton, had never set his foot within the parish for thirty-five years; exposed the vestry that had enlarged the clerk's salary because the clerk went to live at a distance from the parish, and required additional payment to remunerate him for the additional road to be travelled on Sundays to his church; and finally the orator denounced the jolly sexton who kept a house of ill-fame near the church gate.

Mr. Hamilton, the rector, resided in a remote part of the kingdom, and never visited the parish. I know nothing of his personal character or of his professional accomplishments, and am therefore unable to say whether his small Protestant flock were losers by his absence. Non-residence has often been stigmatised as a grievance. Certainly it withdraws the expenditure of the incumbent's income from the parish. But there have been, and perhaps still are, cases in which the incumbent, when inflamed with furious anti-Catholic bigotry, is so great a public nuisance that his absence would be a blessing; and it would, in such cases, be often worth the Catholics' while to subscribe some increase to his revenue on condition of his living elsewhere.

The people were enchanted with Feargus's scathing exposures of clerical, magisterial, and legislative iniquity; and "Fargus" was unanimously pronounced to be "the devil of a fellow." His manners were excessively conciliating; in private they were courteous and refined; in public they were hearty, rattling, and impulsive. He had frolicsome touches of mimicry, nickname, and claptrap; he now and then let off a telling pun. His courteous demeanour alternated with a certain indescribable swagger, which, however, was not in the least degree offensive, and merely indicated the excellent opinion which he entertained of himself, without disparagement to any one else. He was a capital *raconteur*. His talents as a mimic were considerable. His was not that mere parrot mimicry that imitates sounds only; he was a mimic of sentiment and feeling; he could take up the whole train of thought as well as the voice, and present you with an exquisitely ludicrous resemblance of mental as well as vocal characteristics. He also excelled in repartee. He had strong satirical powers, a formidable readiness in retort, and could pounce with merciless sarcasm on the weak or ludicrous points of an antagonist; so that whenever any incivility was attempted at his expense, he retaliated with a pungency that made his opponent repent the rash assault. But Feargus, when not attacked, was remarkable for suavity and excellent temper.

He was fond of puns, and sometimes made them tell. At a meeting which he attended, after having been for some time absent from the country, it chanced that there stood at his right hand a patriotic paper-maker named Kidney. Feargus assured his audience that his absence from home had not altered his politics. "Here I am," cried he "unchanged—the same pure lover of liberty you have ever known me, with the same honest heart, and the same stout *Kidney* too!" patting his worthy and stalwart neighbour on the shoulder amidst shouts of laughter.

Feargus's strongest point was his great physical energy. He was indefatigable in his agitation. In all the quarters of the compass, wherever a popular muster of sufficient magnitude was announced, there was usually to be seen the popular agitator with the brawny muscular figure, the big round shoulders, the red curly tresses overhanging the collar of his coat, the cajoling smirk, the insinuating manners, and the fluent tongue. His taste in eloquence was not rigorous; his language might, to borrow a Homeric phrase, be termed "poluphloisboios." He was fond of sounding and redundant sentences. He often declared, for example, that the people were "wrecked by disunion, torn by discord, revolutionised by faction." This description of talk rolled off his tongue in continuous torrents.

He considered it politic to assume towards the Catholic clergy an air of profound and affectionate reverence. He boasted that he had a larger number of clerical acquaintances than any other layman in

Ireland. He talked of convening an assembly of the Catholic clergy of the County Cork, at which he was to preside. Feargus's *concio ad clerum* would have been a curious deliverance.

The Whig and Tory squirearchy laughed to derision his prospects of success. They sneered at the rustic meetings, the public dinners got up among the village shopkeepers and farmers. "He had a genteel day of it!" writes one of them, who was scandalised at the overwhelming preponderance of the frieze coats at a public entertainment given to Feargus. Meanwhile, Feargus persevered with continually increasing activity. Some of the advertisements of his movements were headed with the appropriate words in huge types, "Up and doing!"

Whatever were the merits or defects of his public speaking, his manner and delivery were those of a gentleman. A clever writer remarks that in the earlier period of his agitation he addressed the people more in the style of a chieftain encouraging his gallant clansmen than of a commonplace agitator talking down to the level of an unenlightened auditory. The people appreciated his aristocratic demeanour, for the Irish democracy—(and this is a trait in the national character well worth the attention of politicians)—are eminently aristocratic in their prepossessions. They love ancient lineage; they can quickly discern, and they ardently relish the demeanour that should mark the far-descended gentleman. Those who in O'Connell's time, and still later in the time of Isaac Butt, feared that the Repeal of the Union would result in democratic anarchy, evinced by that fear their ignorance of the feelings, dispositions, and prejudices which then characterised the Irish nation. Writing of them many years ago, I said that there was not in the Empire a people more desirous to give practical efficacy to the theory of the British Constitution; to carry into practice the theoretic equipoise of Crown, Lords, and Commons. Loving the liberty of Ireland as their dearest earthly birthright, they rejoiced when they were led in the pursuit of it by men of high station and old lineage. Loyal to the Crown (but not to the Legislative Union), they honoured the coronet—those Irish worshippers of freedom. They merely desired to convert the aristocracy from oppressors into protectors.

But the aristocracy were hard to convert. At that time the State Church existed, offering a bribe of £700,000 per annum to the scions of the Protestant nobility and gentry to support the Legislative Union. There were large parochial incomes; great prizes in the wheel; bishoprics, archbishoprics, deaneries. The preservation of the State Church was especially provided for in the Act that destroyed the Irish Parliament. Then there was the spectre of Catholic ascendency; a spectre as unreal as Pepper's Ghost; yet held forth from pulpits and platforms to scare the Irish Protestants from nationality. There was also the elaborate ignorance of the facts of Irish history—ignorance in which the Irish Protestants were generally trained, by narratives that represented England as being always in the right, and Ireland always in the wrong.

Their attitude to their own country was hostile, and few of their number supported O'Connell in his noble efforts to recover the priceless possession of Home Legislation.

CHAPTER XIV.

ELECTIONEERING AGITATION IN 1832.

> My inmost heart is in your cause. I pray
> God speed your quarrel. Yet my hands are bound;
> There is a golden fetter that restrains
> The energies that should of right be yours.
> ANON.

REPEAL was now a topic of universal interest. The Rev. Charles Boyton, a Fellow of Trinity College, made several speeches at the Dublin Conservative Society, strongly impregnated with Irish nationality. In one of those speeches he ably dissected and exposed the fallacies which even then Mr. Spring Rice had begun to put forth, about the incalculable benefits produced to Ireland by the Union. Mr. Rice had been triumphant in the English House of Commons—that is to say, he had the votes, the majorities, the cheers, which in general await in that assembly the exploits of an Irishman who does the dirty work of England. It was easy to prove to the perfect satisfaction of an English audience that the subjugation of Ireland to England was an overflowing source of prosperity to the former country. His miles of figures, his tables of statistics, his carefully-contrived arithmetical legerdemain, made an imposing show in an assembly whose members cared nothing for the merits of the case, and cared everything for their own grasp on Irish resources.

But Mr. Rice's statistical jugglery did not prove so convincing to the Irish people. He did not find it so easy to persuade them that their starving population were comfortably fed; that their unemployed half-naked tradesmen were warmly clothed; that the manufactories crumbling into ruins in many parts of the country were hives of happy thriving industry; that the 14,000 silk-weavers just then stalking unemployed through Dublin were models of prosperity and comfort; that the crowded metropolitan mendicity demonstrated the brisk state of trade; that the insolvency of one-fourth of the number of houses in Dublin indicated the increasing opulence of the metropolis; that the Dublin people were greatly enriched by the removal to London of all the public boards; and that the drain of four millions of absentee rents out of Ireland, and the further drain of Irish public revenue, were a source of remunerative employment and national wealth to the Irish people.

All these brilliant paradoxes might easily be received as gospel-truths by a body of Englishmen interested only in keeping down Ireland, and wringing all the profit they could out of her poverty. But the suffering people themselves felt the poignant addition of insult to injury when they saw the great cause of their sorrows held forth to the world as the fountain of blessings to their country.

Boyton, despite his Conservatism, felt as an aggrieved Irishman would naturally feel, and in a speech which displayed full knowledge of the subject, he refuted with contemptuous sarcasm the fallacies of Mr. Rice. Boyton's mind and body were alike of athletic powers and proportions. He had the reputation of being an able pugilist, and, no doubt, in his reasoning there was many a knock-down blow. The man was in spirit, feeling, and conviction an Irish Nationalist, but he was bound up in the golden fetters of the State Church; his national vigour was therefore necessarily paralysed.

A gentleman on terms of intimacy with the leading members of the Repeal movement made (I believe at the instance of Mr. O'Connell) private overtures to Boyton for a junction between his party and the Repealers. Boyton's reply was in substance, and nearly in terms, as follows: "I would gladly acquiesce in your proposal if I thought there was the slightest probability of its being effectual. But, were I publicly to unite myself with the Repealers, I should only separate myself from my own party; I could not possibly carry them along with me. Sir, they hate you—their enmity is bitter, and cannot be mitigated. I trust

I need not say that I do not participate in it; but I know that any overture of mine to unite them with the O'Connellites would be perfectly fruitless, from the personal hatred they bear to your leader, and their bigoted horror of the great body of his followers."

The negotiation, of course, fell to the ground; but Boyton now and then continually made speeches savouring strongly of Repeal. One of his best was on the celebrated interview which took place in Cork between the Viceroy * and Dr. Baldwin, a highly respected advocate of national self-government. The Doctor beat the Viceroy hollow in the controversy; and the Viceroy threatened to blockade the Irish ports with four English gun-brigs, and to effect a total suspension of intercourse between England and Ireland.

"A total suspension of intercourse!" exclaimed the Rev. Charles Boyton; "and, supposing the intercourse was suspended, which of the parties would be the worse for it? England, whose exports are articles which derive their value from the great manufacturing skill exerted on materials of small intrinsic worth, or Ireland, whose exports chiefly consist of articles of food—the staff of human life? If the gallant Viceroy could suspend the intercourse between the countries and prevent our exporting Irish beef, butter, and corn to England, why, I really think that in so awful an extremity

---

* The Marquis of Anglesea.

we could manage to eat those commodities ourselves. Whereas, it would task the powers of even John Bull to masticate and digest a Sheffield whittle, a Worcester tea-cup, or a Kidderminster carpet."

Meanwhile, Feargus undertook to enlighten the Viceroy upon Irish affairs in "A Letter from Feargus O'Connor, Esq., Barrister-at-Law, to His Excellency the Marquis of Anglesea." Feargus had been threatened with a prosecution for his political misdeeds; and in the indictment were included James Ludlow Stawell, of Kilbrittain,* Francis Bernard M'Carthy, of Laurel Hill, with some others who had made themselves conspicuous by agitation. The principal subject of Feargus's Letter to Lord Anglesea was Feargus himself. He apprised the Viceroy that he (Feargus) was a barrister—a member of one of the most respectable families in the kingdom; that he possessed an

---

* I cannot cursorily mention James Ludlow Stawell without a passing tribute to his memory. He was a sincere Protestant; he was also a warm-hearted and enlightened Irishman. Descended from an ancient house, and possessed of an ample estate, he felt that he owed an account of his stewardship to the Providence who had bestowed on him the gifts of high birth and large fortune. He honestly and zealously laboured to render those advantages auxiliary to the freedom of his countrymen. He threw himself into their struggle; they revered and loved him. His useful and honourable career was cut short by sudden death. A feverish cold, of which the inflammatory symptoms were increased by the patient's anxiety about the prosecution, terminated fatally on the third or fourth day. He was deeply regretted by all parties. "Requiescat in pace."

unencumbered property beyond his wants; that when Lord Anglesea had been mobbed some time previously in Dublin, he (Feargus) followed him into Parliament Street and raised his arm in His Excellency's defence.

He also boasted of an exploit he had performed in 1822; the incident exemplifies the necessity of caution in accepting the assertions of habitual accusers of the Irish people.

"The parsons," said Feargus, "were then with the people, proclaiming that tithes had nothing to do with the disturbance, and that the cause was to be found in exorbitant rents. I convened a meeting of the neighbouring parishes in the Roman Catholic Chapel of Enniskean, at which nine or ten Protestant clergymen attended; they were principally rectors. They all spoke of the perfect tranquillity their respective parishes enjoyed, and unanimously signed the resolutions which strongly expressed that tranquillity, under the belief that they would not go farther. I, however, had a duty to perform. I published them in two of our provincial journals; and what will be your lordship's astonishment when I tell you that this publication was deemed by the clergy who attended the meeting a crime for which my head would scarcely have atoned! Because the declarations made by some of those reverend gentlemen at the meeting were diametrically opposite to those made by the same persons with respect to the state of their parishes but a day or two previously."

Feargus demanded from Lord Anglesea the publication of the informations on which he and his confederates had been charged as conspirators and dangerous persons.

The prosecution was abandoned by the Government. Stawell died after a few days' illness; and as his death was generally believed to have been accelerated by the harassing annoyance of the threatened proceedings, it is not improbable that the Government regarded it as a sufficient expiation of the political sins of the whole batch of offenders. But the fact of having been indicted was an additional feather in Feargus's cap. His having incurred the peril of martyrdom increased his popularity.

The summer and autumn passed away. The registries had been well worked, and in the month of December the general election took place. The second popular candidate for the County Cork was Mr. Garrett Standish Barry, of Lemlara, a Catholic gentleman of private worth, but not adapted for public business. He was brought in for the county under Feargus's wing, being, in truth, indebted for his success to the stirring agitation got up by his active and adventurous colleague.

The electors from the rural districts now poured into the city. Parties of the frieze coats, each detachment headed by the parish priest, came in for four successive days, the voters from the more remote parts of the county having generally travelled all night. I accompanied one of the nocturnal parties from the district around Dunmanway.

The night was cold, and the pace was slow. I occupied a seat in a gig belonging to the parish priest, who had called at my house after midnight. Our slow progress was rendered still slower by delays at various points, where accessions of voters from other districts were expected to swell our cavalcade from bohereens and by-roads. My reverend companion seemed insensible to the discomforts of a journey performed at a snail's pace under the darkness of a chill winter's night. His mind was engrossed by the coming struggle, and elated by the prospect of a triumph. On the first day of the election the rival candidates met upon the hustings. Lord Bernard (son of the Earl of Bandon) and the Hon. Robert Boyle (son of the Earl of Shannon) appeared on the Conservative side. The Hon. Robert King (afterwards Earl of Kingston) was a candidate in the Whig interest. Lord Bernard read a short speech from a paper which lay in the bottom of his hat, all about keeping up the tithes and the Union. Feargus made the audience laugh by remarking that if the noble lord had not spoken from his head, he had at any rate spoken from his hat. I do not recollect that Mr. Boyle made a speech. He had published an address to the electors in which he promised nothing—a promise which there was no doubt of his ability to redeem. Mr. King said that if returned he would vote for the discussion of Repeal. Garrett Standish Barry said that if the reformed Parliament in its first session should not give (what he called) justice to Ireland, he would vote for Repeal. He professed unqualified hostility to the tithes. Feargus made an eloquent declamatory speech for full, unqualified, unconditional, immediate Repeal.

The election terminated on the fifth day in the return of Feargus and Mr. Barry. The announcement of the victory was answered by a hurricane of cheering in the Court-house, which was echoed by the multitude without. Out of the eight seats for the city, the county, and its boroughs, the Tories only obtained one, namely, Bandon, for which the Hon. William Bernard was returned. The Tories were infuriate at the success of their opponents. Speaking of Feargus's triumph, the well-known Hedges-Eyre of Macroom swore deep oaths as he paced the Conservative club-room, that the county was lost, disgraced, destroyed for ever.

Whatever may have been Feargus's subsequent career, we must do justice to his really gallant achievement of wresting the County Cork from the families who had monopolised the representation prior to 1832. The task required indefatigable energy, a thorough contempt of all difficulties, a facility of rousing the despondent and nearly torpid population with fiery harangues, an undaunted audacity, and a superlative self-confidence. All these qualities Feargus enjoyed in perfection, and without them he never could have displaced the former parliamentary families. The people were fascinated, too, by the marked and respectful deference with which the Protestant agitator invariably treated the Catholic priesthood, to whom he never omitted an occasion of paying a well-turned compliment. He bragged loudly and constantly of his own aboriginal extraction; adverted frequently to the losses his family had sustained in the people's cause; and succeeded in producing a general conviction that the bold, dashing, voluble, swaggering champion of the people's rights was the *beau idéal* of a popular member of Parliament. Feargus's services were on that occasion very great. The truth is that no other man in Corkshire possessed the combination of qualities requisite to open the county at that period.

It is usual with the Tory, and often also with the Whig landlords, to accuse the Catholic clergy of unduly influencing the tenant-farmers in their exercise of the franchise. The charge is retorted. Of the multitude of tenants expelled from their holdings it is commonly believed that a large number have been punished by eviction for voting at elections against the will of their landlords, and that, previous to the enactment of the ballot, the tenure of many who still occupied their farms depended on their obedience to the landlord's political commands. The accusers of the priests assumed that if the tenant were uninfluenced by any party, and wholly left to his own free choice, he would by preference give his vote to the landlord's candidate. Those persons forget that the natural sympathies of the priest and of the Catholic tenant-farmer are the same, and consequently that when the priest exhorts the elector to support the advocate of tenant-right, or of Repeal, he only exhorts that elector to act upon his own principles, and to do that which his real inclinations would lead him to do. By investing the humble elector with a vote the Constitution plainly supposes him to have a political opinion. But those who assume that the landlord should be the master of that vote, suppose, on the contrary, that the humble elector has got no political opinion; or else that if he has one he should sacrifice it to the dictation of another man. If this were the real spirit of the Constitution it would have saved, before the introduction of the ballot, much trouble and much misery if the landlord, instead of driving his tenants to the hustings under terror of his wrath, had been empowered by law to tender, in his own person, as many votes as he had tenants on the roll of electors. Such a personage might have presented himself at the hustings, saying: "I give you twenty votes, or forty" (as the case might be), "for Mr. So-and-so." The tenants could have remained at home while their landlord did the voting for them; and they would have escaped the cruel alternative of being compelled to vote for some sturdy supporter of national wrongs, or of being exposed to the vengeance of, possibly, a spiteful and malignant tyrant.

It would be grievously unjust to the landlords of Ireland to deny that there are amongst them many excellent men, who have always respected the electoral liberty of their tenants. But landlords of the opposite stamp were unhappily plentiful. The system of the ballot has sheltered the tenants in most cases from the dangers to which they were exposed under the system of open voting. The protection, however, is incomplete. Some landlords, knowing, or strongly suspecting, that their tenants would vote for a candidate distasteful to the ruling caste, have prohibited them from voting at all, under the ancient penalty of landlord displeasure.

Looking back at the former system, it is interesting to recall the contrast between the English and Irish constituencies, as described a good many years ago in the House of Commons by the late Earl of Derby. He said that in England the rural tenants followed the command of their landlords with implicit submission; that they inquired for my lord's man, or the squire's man, and voted as their masters directed. In the towns venality was the dominant influence. In Ireland, however, notwithstanding the terrible and frequent exercise of landlord power, it was not so easy to drive electors like swine to the market. There was, and is, a much greater spirit of constitutional independence among the Irish electors than among their English brethren. They have more frequently voted, in proportion to their numbers, in accordance with their political preferences. Year after year they had seen before their eyes the bitter penalty of being politically honest; they had seen the old homesteads of their neighbours levelled to the earth and the miserable inmates turned adrift; they had seen that the crime of which this was the punishment, was the honest discharge of a trust committed to them by the Constitution, and yet great numbers of them persevered.

There is in this gallant defiance of local tyranny something grand and high-souled. It stamps the brave peasants with the ineffaceable character of political integrity. They were willing martyrs for their country's freedom. Men who could thus perseveringly and readily incur the bitterest persecution for the sake of principle, stand infinitely higher in the moral and intellectual scale, and are infinitely more capable of the duties of self-government than a people who surrender the Constitutional trust of the franchise at the dictation of another's will, or for the sordid and dishonest consideration of pelf. Of course there have been in Ireland, as elsewhere, many instances of corrupt voting, some of which are recorded in this volume. But the Irish electors, taken as a whole, have displayed true nobleness of character, and at no time more conspicuously than in the general election of 1826, when the forty-shilling freeholders defied the utmost wrath of anti-Catholic landlords and agents, and gave their support to the candidates who were pledged to sustain O'Connell in his struggle for Catholic Emancipation. For this honest and spirited discharge of their electoral duty they were disfranchised by Sir Robert Peel. At the present time the prevalence of electoral corruption in England has compelled the Government to introduce a Bill (46th and 47th Victoria) "for the better prevention of corrupt and illegal practices at Parliamentary elections." Instances of scandalous traffic in the franchise were elicited by commissions appointed in 1880 to inquire into the extent of the evil. Commenting on these revelations, the London *Spectator* said : "It is not too much to say that they (the Commissioners) have revealed the existence of constituencies in which the mass of the electors were mere hirelings, and the man who gives an honest vote is a noteworthy person. Even when this extreme has not been reached, and the open transfer of votes for money is still avoided, the evidence shows that the more indirect forms of bribery are practised upon a truly heroic scale."*

"There is no sign whatever," says the *Times*, "that Sandwich and Gloucester and Canterbury are shocked in any way at the exposure of their own demerits. Men come forward with a smile and a smirk to tell the Commissioners that they have taken bribes from both parties, or that they have put their votes up for sale and have given them to the highest bidders, or have promised them and had the money for them, and have not given them. Their belief seems to be that the common laws of morality

---

* Cited in the *Nation*, 23rd October, 1880.

are suspended while an election is going on, and that proceedings for which in ordinary times a man would be sent to prison are quite honest at election times. It is in vain that the Commissioners attempt to set up another standard. It is much if they can succeed in putting a damper on each joke as it arises. The next barefaced disclosure of fraud or corruption is taken for as good a joke as ever, and is as certainly and as heartily laughed over."*

In its issue of the 23rd of October, 1880, the *Nation* quotes some items of the evidence:

"At Macclesfield 'voting is frankly treated as a matter of business.' Prices ranged from 3s. 6d. to 15s. a vote. Out of £2,000 distributed by a prominent manager on one side, only £100 is admitted to have been legally spent, while another manager, on the other side, took each voter who came to him into a dark pantry and there made the best bargain he could. 'Out of every six voters, certainly four, and probably five, voted as they were paid.'"

I have referred to the late Lord Derby's assertion that in England the rural electors generally followed their landlords to the hustings. Apart from bribery, and with reference solely to the landlord influence over electors in England, it must, however, be admitted that the English voters have not the same reason for opposing their landlords that the Irish voters too often have. Whatever be the

---

* Cited in the *Nation*, 23rd October, 1880.

political party of the English candidate, the elector may be certain at the present day that he is zealous for the honour and power of England. Whig, Tory, or Radical, he will equally desire to uphold the glory of the British Lion.

But in Ireland the Nationalist elector has been frequently called on to vote for a candidate zealous only for the servitude and subjugation of his country; eager to revile and disparage her creed and her people; flippant to announce (as Lord Wicklow did in the days of O'Connell's agitation) that there is not in Ireland the material for self-legislation. He is called on to vote for some person whose political convictions originate in the false, degrading, calumnious, self-stultifying principle that the land of Swift, and Grattan, and Malone, and Flood, and Hussey Burgh, and Burke, and Sheridan, and Bushe, and Foster, and Plunket, and O'Connell, and many other men whose names shed lustre upon human intellect, is inhabited by a race incapable of making laws to govern themselves. The soul of the Irish peasant instinctively spurns the impudent libel on his country. There cannot be a cordial community of feeling between the peasantry and the landlord class until the owners of the soil learn to regard their native land with sentiments of just respect; until they learn to rejoice in Ireland's honour, to take pride in Ireland's fame, and to feel every insult to their country as an indignity inflicted on themselves.

CHAPTER XV.

NATIONAL COUNCIL CONVENED BY O'CONNELL IN 1833.

> Each voice should resound through our island;
> "You're my neighbour; but, BULL, this is *my* land;
> Nature's favourite spot,
> And I'd rather be shot
> Than surrender the rights of our Island."
> LYSAGHT'S *Anti-Union Song.*

O'CONNELL suggested, in December, 1832, to the members who were pledged to the Repeal of the Union, the expediency of meeting in Dublin to discuss various matters connected with Irish legislation. Between thirty and forty of them assembled in January, 1833, under the denomination of the National Council. The first meeting took place at Home's Hotel, in College Green, directly facing the principal front of our old House of Commons. The proximity was suggestive of some mournful recollections, associated, however, with some high resolves and hopes. The forms of a legislative assembly were strictly observed by the National Council. The first day was chiefly occupied in the examination of Michael Staunton, the able proprietor and editor of the *Dublin Register*, on the grievous fiscal wrongs which the Union enabled England to inflict upon this kingdom. On the subsequent days the members met in the Great Room of the Corn Exchange, Burgh Quay; there were a strangers' gallery and a bar, admission to which was charged the parliamentary price of two-and-sixpence. O'Connell's object in bringing together this embryo Parliament, was partly to present to the people of Ireland the spectacle of their own legislators deliberating on Irish affairs in the capital of their native land; to habituate the members to home service; and thereby to excite both the representatives and the represented to continuous energy in the great national enterprise.

"The cork," said the *Dublin Evening Post*, "was flying out of Feargus's high-bottled eloquence;" and at the National Council, as also upon some other public occasions in the capital, Feargus well sustained the reputation he had acquired in the South, of a ready, rattling speaker.

In Parliament he was not so successful. True, he talked away in the House with his customary fluency; but he failed to impress the public with any strong faith in his senatorial wisdom. He amused the Legislature with local anecdotes, sometimes extremely well told. He amused them also with occasional bursts of exaggerated energy; as, for example, when in the debate on the Coercion Bill, some foolish English member had blustered about opposing the Repeal *vi et armis*, Feargus resolved to outbluster him, which he did somewhat after the following fashion :

"The honourable gentleman," said the member for Cork County, "had declared that rather than consent to the Repeal of the Union he would submit to be pistoled and bayoneted. But he (Mr. Feargus O'Connor) would reply, that rather than submit to the oppression of Ireland, he would readily encounter swords, bayonets, guns, pistols, blunderbusses, muskets, and firearms of all sorts."

But to do Feargus justice, he often uttered very good Liberal principles, and he gave occasional expression to bold and spirited sentiments of liberty. He was deficient in logic. His speeches were what the French expressively term *inconséquent*.

In 1833 he made an effort to force forward the discussion of Repeal prematurely in the House of Commons. O'Connell was desirous to keep back the question until the organisation of the Irish Repealers should have become more effective and general. There had been undoubtedly a great deal of popular noise and excitement; but O'Connell did not deem that the people had been yet sufficiently organised to enable them to give to their representatives that steady and sustained support out of doors which was absolutely necessary to the success of the question in Parliament. O'Connell, in this cautious policy, could appeal to the authority of the venerable Henry Grattan, who, when in 1810 announcing to the people of Dublin his readiness to advocate Repeal, at the same time explicitly stated that it would be neither prudent nor possible to bring Repeal into the House of Commons until the question should be backed by the whole Irish nation. Feargus, however, overlooked all such considerations, and announced to the Repealers that if O'Connell should decline to lead them, he would himself become their leader.

Notwithstanding this intrepid announcement, he was fortunately induced to withdraw the notice he had given upon the subject, which, in truth, he was very ill qualified to discuss. He could declaim, indeed, about slavery and liberty, and give vehement utterance to popular feelings and sentiments; he could accumulate instances of local suffering, and denounce usurpation in sentences of thundering sound; but he knew nothing about the details of the financial swindle involved in the Union, nor could he reason with accuracy on its defects in a Constitutional point of view. He, however, had succeeded in exciting the popular impatience for a parliamentary discussion; so that O'Connell found it requisite to bring forward the question in the following session.* Feargus made a very long speech about Repeal in the debate. The sentiments of course were good, but the logic was *nil*, and the orator did not touch the marrow of the subject.

Parliament being dissolved in December, 1834, Feargus was again returned for the County of Cork.

---

* O'Connell's motion was made 22nd April, 1834.

Feargus becomes a Chartist.

In his address to the electors he declared his intention of excluding for the future the *new* families—namely, the Shannons, Kingstons, and Bandons—from the representation; and on the hustings he told Lord Bernard that the best blood in his lordship's veins was derived from "a Kerry strain," a connexion with the O'Connor family.

Feargus's majority was on this occasion large, but not so overwhelming as it had been at the previous election. The landlord persecution had already begun to work upon the county franchise. A petition against his return was briskly undertaken. He was unseated in June, 1835; and Mr. Longfield, of Longueville, near Mallow, slipped into the representation.

Feargus had evidently conceived the idea of supplanting O'Connell in the leadership of the Irish people; and in furtherance of this project he now published a pamphlet containing numerous allegations of political dishonesty against the Liberator. The pamphlet sold well among the Conservative party, but it necessarily alienated the Repealers of Ireland from its author.

Before long he formed a connection with a political society in London, of which the Rev. Doctor Wade, a Protestant clergyman, was a member. The principles of this society were those subsequently known as the five points of the charter, and its members assumed the designation of Chartists. He soon established in Leeds the *Northern Star*, a weekly newspaper, which was designed to propagate the principles of the society. He had talked the Chartist public into a belief that the new journal would work wonders; and showers of five-pound notes rained down on the projector to enable him to establish it.* Before long it acquired an enormous circulation. I have heard of 60,000 copies of a single publication being sold by the agent at Manchester; and it is said that —railway conveyance being then far from general —the Post Office authorities were in some cases obliged to hire carts or waggons for its transmission, as it occasionally overflowed the restricted accommodation of the mail coaches. It is long since defunct. While it lasted, many of the traits of the proprietor were amusingly chronicled in its columns.

One curious mode of extending his influence was by having the infant children of his followers christened by his name. A string of such baptisms was for a long time to be found in the columns of each successive *Star*, as for example: "On Monday, the 8th instant, the wife of Ichabod Jenkins, nailer, was delivered of a fine thriving boy, who was christened Feargus O'Connor Ichabod;" and so on for the best part of a column. Girls were also often christened after Feargus. A whole population of Feargus O'Connors, male and female, seemed rapidly springing up; and the lists of these baptisms were usually headed with the words: "More Young Patriots."

---

* So I was told by a person who, at that time, was employed in the office.

There was also a religious institution got up under the name of "The Chartist Christian Church;" and I presume that the Mr. Cooper who combines, in the following extract, the celebration of O'Connor's humility with the baptism of one of the young patriots was a minister of that society.

"We learn from the *Leicester Mercury* that Mr. Thomas Cooper, the leader of the O'Connorites in that borough, preached a sermon in the Amphitheatre on Sunday week, from Daniel ii. 34, 35. In the course of his address he said: 'The disciples of truth, and all great men, were humble, and did not like to have others depreciated for the purpose of exalting themselves;' and as instances he noticed Sir Isaac Newton, Haydn, Mozart, and Feargus O'Connor. After the sermon he announced that the tragedy of *Douglas* would be performed on the following Tuesday, and that *Hamlet* was in preparation. He then baptized a child, 'Feargus O'Connor Cooper Beedham.'"*

Ordinary agitators had for a long time adopted the system of banners at their public processions. The original genius of Chartism for once discarded such ensigns as stale, flat, and commonplace; and in lieu thereof startled the crowd at a meeting in Burnley with an infinitely grander conception: "The attention of the multitude was arrested by the ascent of a large balloon, with the words 'FEARGUS O'CONNOR' inscribed in large characters."

* *Dublin Evening Post*, 3rd January, 1843.

Banners, however, were admitted into other localities. On a banner at one of O'Connor's processions were inscribed the following stanzas:

> Lo! he comes! he comes!
>   Garlands for every shrine;
> Sound trumpets—strike the drums!
>   Strew roses—pour the wine!
>
> Swell, swell the Dorian flute,
>   Triumphal to the sky;
> Let the millions' shout salute,
>   For THE PATRIOT passes by.

Feargus now seemed to sweep through the world in the midst of a continuous triumph. Garlands, libations, Io Pæans. It was like the majestic advance of one of Homer's demigods. But Feargus was not exalted by these celestial honours above the old terrestrial mode of dealing with political questions *par voie du fait;* and accordingly, when confined at a subsequent period in York Castle for certain alleged misdemeanours, he published an "Appeal to the Working Men of Yorkshire" to obstruct by violence the proceedings of a meeting at which O'Connell was expected to be present at Leeds. The appeal was exceedingly vehement, and much of it was eloquently written. He inquired whether, if he were at large, would O'Connell dare to come to Leeds to meet him? And to this query he responded, "No! a million times no!" He then urged the great debt which he said the Yorkshire Chartists owed to himself, and declared that all would be cancelled—nay, infinitely overpaid—if they gave "O'Connor his day, and Dan his welcome." The conclusion of this eloquent incitement to a row is eminently characteristic:

"I live and reign," says Feargus, "in the hearts of millions who pant for an opportunity to prove their love, and who will embrace that which is now presented, to convince me of their approbation of my honest endeavours to serve the cause of universal freedom.

"I am, my friends and brothers, the Tyrant's Captive, the Oppressor's Dread! the Poor Man's Friend, and the people's Accepted Present,
"Feargus O'Connor."

The people did not respond to any great extent to the belligerent call of their Accepted Present. It was supposed, or promised, that 100,000 Chartists would assemble to oppose O'Connell; but the contemporary journals state that from two to three thousand at the utmost assembled upon Holbeck Moor.

Feargus, during the earlier part of his imprisonment in York Castle, was treated with atrocious severity. He published in the newspapers statements of the barbarous indignities inflicted upon him. In a letter to the *Times* he expressed a fear lest the prison discipline should abridge his existence; and desired that in the event of his death, his body should be opened by three surgeons whom he named; one residing at York, another at

Hammersmith, and the third in London. Before he had ended his epistle, however, he evidently thought that it would be better to live for future political squalls than to die in jail for a post-mortem examination. "Adieu, world," he exclaims, "for seventeen months: but, by heaven! I'll make a storm in you yet."

In jail he performed some eccentric exploits. On the first Sunday after his arrival he was conducted to the chapel of the prison, where he astonished the congregation and scandalised the parson by bellowing the responses of the service in stentorian tones. He was not again required to attend the chapel during his imprisonment.

He early acquired supremacy among the apostles of Chartism. Joining the Chartists as a volunteer, he speedily worked himself into the supreme command, although he had competitors of by no means contemptible ability. A Chartist gentleman once said to me, "He began with us as a disciple, but he soon distanced all of us."

In the *Evening Star*, a sort of adjunct to the *Northern Star*, and, like it, edited for a time by Feargus, an amusing writer published a series of sketches of the Chartist leaders, commencing with a portrait of the Chartist Chief. The writer, describing an interview with Feargus and a Scotch Chartist leader named MacDouall, acquaints us that the latter gentleman claimed a diabolical pedigree. "'Son of the Devil,' said the gallant little doctor, 'is the meaning of my surname.' 'And

I am a lineal descendant from Roderick O'Connor, the last King of All Ireland!' said Feargus, kindled into a momentary pride of ancestry by this flash of the untameable spirit in the brave Scot. 'There were five Kings of Ireland, all O'Connors, at the same time, but I am lineally descended from the Ardrigh, or High King. You see in me a specimen of what my countrymen of the true Milesian descent would all have been, had it not been for the dwarfing effects of bad living and ill-treatment.'"

It would seem that in thus offering himself as a specimen of the splendid proportions to which his countrymen might, if unpersecuted, have arrived, Feargus produced on the narrator an impression that he was, in truth, a being of mysterious and undefinable greatness.

"From that period," continues the writer, "I have never seen O'Connor without regarding myself as in the presence of a true representative of the ancient Celtic chieftains—beings who depicture themselves to us out of the mist of time as characterised by simple and unaffected majesty of form and deportment, without the adornments of civilisation—the frippery of jewels, crowns, and sceptres." The writer ends by remarking that "the reality of O'Connor's greatness, as a devotee of principle," overawed his enemies.

All this was doubtless very complimentary—not more so, however, than Feargus himself could be on an appropriate occasion. In Dublin lived a

Mr. Patrick O'Higgins, who got up a nibbling opposition to O'Connell, and devoted a room at the back of his house to the reception of a few discontented deserters from O'Connellism. Mr. O'Higgins professed himself an ally of Feargus, and promised to propagate Chartism in Dublin. Feargus acknowledged his merits in the *Star*, and ended an eloquent eulogium by exclaiming: " Rome had her Brutus —Ireland has her O'Higgins."

When Joseph Sturge, the Quaker, was candidate for Nottingham on the principles of moral-force Chartism, Feargus gave him active assistance in the preliminary agitation. An affray took place in the market square of Nottingham, in which Feargus displayed strength and valour befitting the descendant of the Ardrigh Roderick; for although beset by numbers upon every side, he knocked all down right and left. Next day twenty-one men swore that Feargus had severally knocked each of them down in the riot. The *Univers* translated the English accounts of the transaction into French, heading the narrative, "Mœurs Electorales Anglaises."

At one of the meetings for the Nottingham election Feargus exclaimed, "Hurrah for Sturge and Nottingham! or for the Devil, if he supports the Charter." I should like to have seen the quiet Quaker-face of honest Joseph Sturge on being thus hypothetically coupled with the Prince of Darkness by his reckless ally. Perhaps the hurrah for the Devil was intended as a compliment to Doctor

MacDouall, who asserted the diabolical derivation of his patronymic. When Charles Gavan Duffy heard that "Son of the Devil" was alleged by the Doctor to be the meaning of his name, he drily remarked, "It is a pedigree we see no reason to question."

The report of O'Connor's meetings and speeches in the *Star* are full of traits illustrating that wild energy which formed so marked a feature in his character. We are told how he sat down after a two hours' speech so exhausted that the perspiration oozed through his dress; how he said he would work the flesh off his bones or have the Charter; how he cheered his followers by declaring that he was "as strong as ten bulls;" how he described Lane End as the place "where the lads beat the cavalry and made them retreat," adding, "in this town all the people are born marksmen. I learn that a lad of fourteen or fifteen could kill a crow flying with a stone." He was resolved to lose nothing by unnecessary modesty. In one of his addresses to his followers he thus stated his achievements and his consequent responsibilities: "I have made the mind of England, and it is my duty now to guide it."

He was ambitious of the reputation of possessing classical and scientific knowledge, as appears by the following extract from the *Manchester Guardian*: "Mr. O'Connor next referred to the charge of the *Times*, that he did not know how to spell; and challenged any editor of that paper to be examined with him by any Fellow from one of the colleges in Greek, Latin, Hebrew, Geometry, Algebra, Arithmetic, etc., and if he (Mr. O'Connor) did not beat him, he would consent to be banished from the country for life."

In 1847 he was returned to Parliament for Nottingham, defeating Sir John Hobhouse by a majority of over six hundred. In 1848 an enormous Chartist demonstration, in which Feargus was of course the principal hero, took place in London. Serious disturbances were apprehended, and among the special constables then sworn in, it is said that Louis Napoleon, afterwards Emperor of the French, was enrolled.

Feargus had instituted a land scheme which elicited a vast number of five-pound subscriptions from members of the Chartist body who believed that the payment of that sum would entitle them to profitable settlements on four-acre allotments. The scheme broke down, and with it broke down its author's intellect. His insanity displayed itself in a number of strange freaks in the House of Commons and its immediate precincts. He was confined, by order of the House, in one of its apartments for some days. During that period the newspapers gave constant accounts of his condition and his actions. From one of those accounts I take the following: "He still indulges in rapid, rambling aberrations; reciting to his attendants snatches of what he states to be his own poetical compositions—uttering now and then an *éloge* on the late Sir Robert Peel, abruptly broken off to descant on the disasters of an old woman and her pig in the bogs of Ballinhassig—of a stud of some twenty long-tailed black horses his brother kept in Ireland—all whimsically interwoven with such canticles as are heard at the Coal-Hole, or by the recital of a litany, interlarded with tears, on the failure of the unfortunate land-scheme."

The exhibition was at once grotesque and melancholy. We discern among the shattered fragments of his once strong intellect, faint traces of the facetious humour which in his better days had rendered him an entertaining companion. He was removed to the asylum kept by Dr. Tuke, at Chiswick, and thence, in 1855, to lodgings at Notting Hill Terrace, where he died on the 31st of August in that year, in the sixtieth year of his age. The Chartists of London gave him a grand public funeral. He was buried at Kensal Green Cemetery. His admirers at Nottingham have erected a statue to his memory.

O'Connell preserved the Irish Repealers from the alliance with the Chartists which Feargus wanted to effect. O'Connell had no confidence in the leaders, and he condemned the unfair and intolerant policy repeatedly practised by their party, of violently obstructing all meetings held for any other political object than the attainment of the Charter.

CHAPTER XVI.

IRISH POLICY OF THE FIRST REFORMED PARLIAMENT.

> Justice hath done her unrelenting part,
> If she indeed *be* Justice, who drives on,
> Bloody and blind, the chariot-wheels of death.
> SOUTHEY.

WE have been constantly told to expect vast benefits for Ireland from the English Legislature, consequent on the extension of the Parliamentary franchise. We had been told, in like manner, to expect great benefits for Ireland from the Reform Bills of 1831. Our experience of that period does not encourage us to entertain sanguine hopes of any good from that source. The proceedings of the first reformed Parliament furnished a conclusive answer to those Irish Whig-Liberals who opposed Repeal on the plea that Reform in the English Legislature would supersede the necessity for domestic legislation for Ireland.

The Irish agitation in 1831-2 was not opposed by the Whig Government so long as it could be considered auxiliary to the English agitation for Reform. But as soon as the triumph of Reform was certain, and the Irish agitators were no longer required to subserve English purposes, prosecutions were threatened. Lord Anglesea proclaimed down meetings; and the Sailor-King was instructed by his Ministers in 1833 to express from the throne his "surprise" and "indignation" at the efforts of the Irish to obtain a restoration of their national Legislature, of which they had been deprived by a system of Machiavelian fraud and diabolic crime.

O'Connell denounced the King's speech as "a brutal and bloody speech—a declaration of war against Ireland." The address, echoing the speech, was of course carried by an enormous majority. The Coercion Bill, for restricting the people of Ireland from meeting to petition Parliament, was shortly afterwards introduced. There was a very full muster of Irish and English members on the night of its introduction. Expectation was strongly excited; it had been announced that disclosures of an appalling nature would be made to justify its enactment. Lord Althorp (afterwards Earl Spenser) opened the case for the Government. His delivery was heavy, hesitating, and unimpressive. He laboured under a disadvantage which, in an impartial assembly, would have been fatal—namely, that of requiring implicit belief in a tale of Irish outrages and horrors, in which the names of the informers were to a great extent suppressed. The House was called on to ground coercive legislation upon unauthenticated charges; and the pretext for withholding the authentication was, that to publish the names of the informers would expose them to personal outrage from their lawless neighbours.

The House was perfectly ready to ground coercive legislation for Ireland upon anonymous information. It was not nice as to pretexts. It was boldly alleged that prædial outrage was the result of political agitation, and that in order to put down the former the latter should be suppressed. Any other origin of prædial outrages than political agitation appeared to be ignored by the friends of coercion.

Lord Althorp's speech was a failure. O'Connell left the house immediately on its conclusion and remained for some time in the lobby, offering triumphant congratulations to all the anti-coercion members whom he met, on the wretched exhibition of his lordship. "Did you ever hear anything more miserable? Why, the Government have literally got no case at all. Bad as the House is, it will be impossible to get them to pass the Bill on such statements. Hurrah!" Thus did the Great Dan cheer the members of the Tail and his friends in general, expressing in the most sanguine terms his conviction that the Government must be defeated.

By-and-by Mr. Stanley (afterwards Lord Derby) rose. He enjoyed one great advantage—he had an audience strongly predisposed in his favour. But in other respects he laboured under difficulties. He had, in fact, to repair Lord Althorp's failure

He had to restate a series of allegations which had fallen, feeble and dull, from the incompetent lips of the blundering leader. And well did he perform his task. Before he had spoken for five minutes the attention of friend and foe alike was riveted in admiration of the orator's abilities. Clear, rapid, and animated, he scathed the Liberals with the fire of his sarcasm, and combated their arguments with his showy and plausible parliamentary logic. The natural graces of his unconstrained and easy action, the vivid glances of his eagle eye, the air of bold and well-sustained defiance which no one could better assume, greatly enhanced the effect of his eloquence. He had gathered up some of the unconsidered sayings of his Irish antagonists, and paraded them before the House with wicked ingenuity as indicative of seditious intentions. He closed with a ferocious invective against O'Connell personally, and sat down amidst thunders of Whig and Tory plaudits.

Well did he merit the cheers of his party. The rickety and misshapen bantling of Lord Althorp was moulded by the plastic powers of Mr. Stanley into showy proportions and apparent strength.

The Bill was obstinately contested. Mr. O'Connell led the opposition, and displayed all the qualities of a great parliamentary debater. An Irish Conservative exclaimed to me with astonishment as the House adjourned one night: "How stoutly Dan battles it out among these English!" O'Connell had, in the course of the evening, thus concluded a fiery invective against the Whigs: "You have brains of lead, and hearts of stone, and fangs of iron!" He displayed inimitable tact and dexterity in defence, promptitude and vigour in assault, and knocked about Whigs and Tories with an easy exercise of strength which astonished the members who had not previously witnessed such a brilliant display of his abilities.

Despite the opposition of the friends of Ireland, the Bill finally passed, and the Constitutional privileges that yet remained to the Irish people were temporarily invaded—ostensibly to check prædial disturbance, but in reality to thwart the agitation for Repeal. Mr. Stanley had boasted that he would make his Government feared before it should be loved. He did not make it either feared or loved; he only succeeded in making it hated.

The crime thus committed against Ireland was aggravated by the fact that it emanated from the English Reformers in the full flush and heyday of their triumph. The first use the friends of English liberty made of their great victory was to crush the Constitutional freedom of their Irish fellow-subjects. What a pregnant lesson to Irishmen! What a practical commentary on the doctrine of imperial identification! Lord Campbell, "who," says Sir Charles Gavan Duffy, "associated with Englishmen of every rank in succession during his slow ascent from the position of a writer of paragraphs for the daily papers to be Lord Chancellor of England," accounts for his party promoting the Coercion Bill without incurring unpopularity among the people of England in the following manner:

"They were probably tranquillised by recollecting how essentially Ireland is hated by the English nation, and what a lenient view is taken of any measure which tends to degrade the mass of the Irish population."*

Lord Campbell thus attests the contemporaneous existence of that inveterate anti-Irish sentiment among his countrymen, of which we in Ireland have had seven centuries' experience. Mr. Gladstone, in one of his speeches, expressed a desire to attach us to Great Britain "by the silken bonds of love." His past financial operations did not encourage Irish confidence in his friendship. He had greatly over-estimated our taxable capacity—he had mercilessly increased our taxation fifty-two per cent., and given a stimulant to the exodus by draining the country of the means that ought to circulate at home for the sustentation of our people. In fiscal affairs he has shown himself our unscrupulous foe; but he has given expression to the sentiment that Ireland, in all matters purely local, should be ruled in accordance with the feelings and principles of the Irish people.

He now seems to be sincerely desirous to atone for all past errors by restoring to the Irish nation their ancient possession of a resident Parliament. If he can succeed in this noble and statesmanlike

---

* "Life of Lord Campbell," vol. ii. p. 27; cited by Sir C. G. Duffy in "Four Years of Irish History," p. 51.

policy, and if his measure of Home Rule shall contain a just arrangement of the fiscal difficulty, he will have proved himself a real benefactor to Ireland, entitled to enduring national gratitude.

It may be observed that on the 18th of March, 1846, Sir James Graham made the following remarkable statement: "I think," said Sir James, "it is our bounden duty, in legislating for Ireland, not to legislate with regard to English feelings, English prejudices, and still less with reference to English law, which has long obtained the sanction of usage in this country. But we are bound to consult Irish feelings, Irish habits, Irish laws, as they have existed for centuries, though they may be at variance with the provisions found in the English statute book." *

Sir James spoke these words under the pressure of O'Connell's agitation. Mr. Gladstone now attempts to give practical effect to the principle they announced.

---

* Report in *Morning Chronicle*, 19th March, 1846.

CHAPTER XVII.

RESULTS OF THE COERCION ACT OF 1833.

> They came in the morning, scoffing and scorning,
> Saying: "Were you harassed—were you sore abused?"
> O! Orange haters, ye beat the traitors
> That betrayed our Saviour to the wicked Jews."
> Ruckite Song.

WHEN the Coercion Act was passed by the first Reformed Parliament, the Repealers were angry, but not depressed. If agitation was suspended for a season, its objects and purposes survived with undiminished vitality and vigour in the affections of the people. Affairs, however, wore a very dreary aspect. There was a cessation of the cheering, spirit-stirring activity which had enlivened the previous year, whilst the Catholic tenantry were, in many instances, mercilessly scourged for their anti-tithe and anti-union offences. Ejectments were served on non-voters as well as on voters by some of the more bigoted landlords of the Tory-evangelic school. I have two cleared districts at this moment before me—that is, districts from which the Catholic tenantry were swept out to make room for a docile Protestant colony. The town lands, respectively named Castletown and Kanavagh, are situated in the County of Cork, and in 1837 were part of the estate of a Union-Earl of high Tory politics and warm evangelic zeal. That noble lord is since dead; his political and evangelic mantle descended on his son, who is since also deceased, and who, whatever were his politics, was reputed, I doubt not deservedly, to possess an amiable disposition and a character of unimpeachable morality.

It is right to premise that in the instance now mentioned the landlord appeared to have acted from religious enthusiasm, not from political resentment; for the ejected occupiers had not registered their votes. But expulsion is the same, whether proceeding from the fanatical ardour or political vengeance. I have selected the townlands in question, because, from their proximity to my residence, I had access to the best information respecting them.

It may not be amiss to devote a few sentences to the past and present memoranda of these districts —the rather as the tale, with a few slight changes, is that of many a spot in Ireland. Instruction sometimes lurks in the simple annals of the poor.

Kinneigh, the parish in which Castletown is situated, is a wild, upland tract, rising into abrupt and rocky eminences abounding in furze and coarse herbage. The hills are savage without grandeur;

there is nothing picturesque in their outline, and none of them ascend to any considerable elevation. There has, some years since, been erected a handsome Protestant church, which replaces the former barn-like edifice, and in its immediate vicinity stands one of the inexplicable round towers, seventy feet high. This tower is the only thing in the parish worth looking at. A stern old monument it is of days so long gone by that man's memory retains no trace of their annals.

Having mentioned the church, I may as well waste a few words in commemoration of an ancient parson, now deceased, by whom the church-goers of Kinneigh were for a long time illuminated. This gentleman, the Reverend Gilbert Laird, dropped into the parish, no one could tell whence, about the beginning of this century, or perhaps a few years previously. All that the Protestant parishioners knew about the matter was, that a queer-looking little brown bunch of a man, whose appearance suggested the idea of an enlarged species of hedgehog, suddenly ascended the pulpit one day and delivered a discourse containing nothing about which anybody who heard it could predicate any quality in particular. The slight curiosity which was excited by the first appearance of the new parson died away when it was found that all inquiry as to his origin, birthplace, former associates, or habits, was fruitless. On all those matters he preserved to the end of his days an impenetrable silence. He bore with him due

credentials from the absentee rector, so that
his title to the curacy was undoubted and un-
questionable; and that, he conceived, was all
that his flock were entitled to know. He continued to officiate and to preach. I believe the
only effusion of his pulpit eloquence which survives
in the parochial memory was an exhortation to the
practice of industry, preached from the sixth chapter
of Proverbs: " Go to the ant, thou sluggard; consider her ways, and learn wisdom;" and illustrated
by a reference to the nursery fable of the " Idle
Grasshopper and the Industrious Ant," with appropriate amplifications from the preacher himself.
Feargus O'Connor, who was one of the Rev. Gilbert
Laird's congregation, excelled in his mimicry of this
sermon, and often delivered it with great comic
power for the amusement of his friends. No two
human faces could be more dissimilar in form and
feature than those of the clergyman and his imitator;
but this dissimilarity seemed to vanish, so exquisite
was Feargus's presentment of the voice, the manner,
and the expression of countenance proper to the
reverend original.

Mr. Laird became a sort of favourite with one
or two squires who played backgammon and lived
loose, rollicking lives. He rattled the dice with
more sociability than he had displayed in any other
occupation, and although personally free from vice,
he was not the man to annoy his patrons with
many troublesome moral remonstrances. By-and-
by the queer little man acquired a sort of small

popularity, probably because his absurdities furnished matter for mirth. Whimsical stories were told of him; people were amused with his odd habits, such as getting his bed thrashed with short flails every morning by the housemaids, and his sleeping with a bolster at the bed-foot in order to accommodate himself in the event of his choosing to reverse the relative positions of his head and feet during the night. His penurious style of living also supplied matter for irreverent jests. He existed on the smallest possible modicum of his salary as curate; and the residue he regularly invested in the purchase of a life-annuity. The whole income arising from these investments he invested again; so that if the insurance offices had given him ten thousand per cent., they would have still been gainers by their singular annuitant. Thus he went on—investing and reinvesting; and he flattered himself with the hope of enjoying the income thus created by the time it should reach £500 per annum.

He continued unmarried until about the age of eighty-seven. He then united himself with a lady who was some fifty years his junior. The union was not happy, for he bitterly reproached the bride with her deception in concealing the malformation of her left foot, which deformity he had not discovered until after the matrimonial knot was irrevocably fastened. He did not long survive the discovery, and he now reposes in one of the graveyards of the city of Cork. The old gentleman, although far from being a model clergyman, yet possessed the negative merit of doing no mischief.

Such was the pastor to whose care the souls of the Protestants of Kinneigh were for many years committed. While the spiritual interests of his small flock flourished under his tutelage, the temporal concerns of the Catholics were not in a very prosperous condition. It is indeed true that they enjoyed one important advantage—the rector was an absentee, who for many years never visited the parish. He had another benefice in a distant county where he always resided. The Kinneigh farmers were therefore relieved from the vexatious presence of a reverend spy, with his eye perpetually on the outlook for every agricultural production from which tithe could be extorted; and as the resident curate, Mr. Laird, was a quiet, harmless man, with a fixed salary, he had no interest in prompting his absent principal to harass the farmers by increasing his exactions. They were, however, harassed enough. They held the land from a middleman, named Gillman, who was the immediate tenant of the Earl of Bandon. Some of them eked out their rents from the proceeds of illicit distillation; and the necessary consequence of such a system was the demoralisation of the parish to a considerable extent. The falsehood and chicane indispensable to those who carry on a contraband trade are not the worst results of their illegal occupation. Men who live in defiance of the law become desperate, and blood has been shed in that unhappy district in defence of the pottheen stills. Undoubtedly the whole blame of these evils should not be cast upon the people. Those squires and squireens who encouraged their traffic by becoming their customers are to a great extent culpable.*

Let it not, however, be supposed that Castletown was an unmitigated pandemonium of pottheen desperadoes. There were many of the inhabitants who had nothing to do with the stills, and who were of very fair average characters.

The middleman from whom the people held their farms died, and their leases all expired with him. His term was for his own life; the townland at his death reverted to the Earl of Bandon. Here was a glorious opportunity to plant a Protestant colony. The noble Earl rejoiced with exceeding great joy at the facilities now presented of serving an ejectment on Idolatry and Wafer-worship, and inducting a colony of true believers into the evacuated district. The number of persons to be expelled, young and old, good, bad, and indifferent, was 247. The expulsion of such a multitude excited public interest. The Earl of

---

* An instance in point occurred not long since. A landlord at the quarter sessions of a southern town preferred a number of accusations against a tenant he was anxious to evict. Among the evil deeds imputed to the latter, he was charged by his landlord with keeping an illicit still. The accused turned round to his censor, and, amidst the laughter of the Court, exclaimed: "By virtue of your oath, didn't your honour often find a gallon of pottheen at your honour's hall door?" His honour was unable to deny the fact.

Mulgrave, then Lord-Lieutenant of Ireland, adverted to the circumstance in the House of Lords, and elicited the following reply from the noble proprietor:

"The Earl of Bandon felt, as the noble Earl had alluded to him in so pointed a manner, it was necessary that he should trouble their lordships with a very few words. The noble Earl had brought a charge against him founded on a newspaper report. He (the Earl of Bandon) was not in the habit of attending to newspaper reports, and he never condescended to answer them. He thought he had some reason to complain of the noble Earl for advancing so grave a charge against him, founded upon no more authentic information than that contained in a newspaper. He would not trouble their lordships by entering into a detail of his arrangements with respect to his own estate (hear, hear). He would only say that those whom he was accused, at that inclement season, of having turned adrift in the world, were, all of them, in their respective houses (laughter and cheers). Having made that statement he must repeat that he felt himself rather ill-used by having been called to defend himself from a charge founded on no better authority than that of a newspaper." *

Lord Bandon's virtuous indignation imposed

---

* Parliamentary Report in Cork *Southern Reporter* of 2nd December, 1837.

on Lord Mulgrave, who immediately withdrew the accusation. The natural inference from Lord Bandon's words was, that the tenants were not to be molested. It is true that he did not directly assert that they should not be disturbed, but his complaint of ill-usage at being accused of disturbing or expelling them, was calculated to convey that impression to his audience. The real fact was that the tenants had all received notice to quit, but the notices had not then yet taken effect. The time of ejectment soon arrived. The aboriginal occupants were turned out, and new tribes of Hosfords, Applebys, Swantons, Dawleys, and Burchells were introduced. Three of the former tenants were permitted to retain a portion of their holdings; of these a man named Hurley sought favour with the noble proprietor by promising to abjure Popery. The man accordingly went to the Protestant church, pursuant to his undertaking; but conceiving that a domestic calamity — the idiotcy of his son—was a mark of the Divine vengeance at his change of religion, he threatened (according to the information I was given at the time) to return to his former creed. Whether he did so I know not.

The whole machinery of proselytism was put in motion at Castletown and Shanavagh. Reverend personages exhorted; readers and teachers besieged the Catholics on highways and by-ways; schools were erected, to which some of the not yet extirpated Papists gave their trembling and reluctant attendance. The noble Earl's family occasionally visited these schools to watch the expansion of the nascent Gospel seed, and to accelerate the process of its ripening by the warmth and light of their countenances. They were, I doubt not, sincere enthusiasts; and when we consider the vast influence their station and fortune, if properly used, might invest them with, it was deplorable to witness the direction their zeal had taken; to contrast what they have been with what they might have been; to see them in the front rank of the anti-national interest, instead of being the honoured, cherished leaders of their countrymen to national independence. I cannot help remarking that there was a time when Francis Bernard, afterwards first Earl of Bandon, was associated with the people of Ireland in demanding the restoration of the Irish Constitution. On the 25th of March, 1782, at a meeting held in Bandon, he occupied the chair. There were three resolutions passed, of which the last affirmed:

"That no power on earth can make laws to bind Ireland, except the King, Lords, and Commons thereof.

(Signed) "G. STAWELL, Col., Bandon Cavalry.

"F. BERNARD, Col., Bandon Infantry."

Grattan had fired the mind of the nation, and the sacred flame ignited many persons who themselves, or whose descendants, have degenerated into anti-nationalists.

At Shanavagh, the politico-religious movement produced its natural results. A man named Hurley (a suspicious patronymic, it would seem, in these districts) attended the school with great assiduity, and after a due course of instruction, professed his willingness to attend the Protestant church. He accordingly became a church-going Protestant, and his new *confrères* thought that a valuable fish had been hooked. One day a tenant of mine met this convert on the road, and asked him wherefore he had quitted his earlier faith to adopt Protestantism.

"Musha, God help us!" responded the convert, "I have got a small family to support, and I thought by turning I could maybe get a lase of the ould ground from Lord Bandon."

"But you'd lose your poor sowl," remonstrated the other.

"Och, maybe not—maybe not. I expect God won't take me so short entirely but that I may quit them all and go back to mass once more afore I die."

The convert also told my informant, that, by way of an additional safeguard, he did not give attention to the preaching or prayers of the Protestant service, but rehearsed his own prayers mentally, while the parson performed the service.

Some time subsequently to the above conversation (which I took down from the lips of one of the parties), Mr. Hurley's duplex policy was curiously exhibited. He fell ill, and being afraid of death, despatched a messenger to bring the parish priest to administer the last rites of the Catholic Church. "But, hark ye!" added the politic invalid, "tell his Reverence not to come up till after dark, for fear any of the Protestants should see him and tell the minister."

Mr. Hurley had considered his alternative—death, then Popery and Father O'Sullivan; but if he should recover, then Protestantism and another attempt to conciliate his landlord's patronage. Father O'Sullivan (then priest of the parish) informed me that he refused to attend him, stating that his pertinacious duplicity at that awful period totally disqualified him from the profitable reception of the rites of the Church.* He recovered, and continued to attend the Protestant place of

---

* A reviewer, commenting on this narrative, said that it cut two ways, and that the priest must have left Hurley in a state of great ignorance. But Hurley was not ignorant that his conduct was criminal. He was plainly acting against conscience, and the priest had nothing to do with his conduct except to condemn it.

In 1845 public attention became excited by the case, tried at the Tralee Assizes, of the Rev. Charles Gayer, one of the leaders of a proselytising establishment at Dingle, County Kerry, *versus* Patrick Robert Byrne, proprietor of the *Kerry Examiner* newspaper. The defendant was convicted of what, in the rigid acceptation of the law, was deemed libel; but the organised system of rank bribery to proselytise the Catholics, which the evidence disclosed, must, I think, have received a salutary check from the publicity thus entailed upon it. TIMOTHY LYNCH, a witness and *ci-devant* convert, deposed that he got from Mr. Gayer the sum of £12 10s. and two half-crowns as the price of his adhesion. EDWARD HUSSEY, another witness, also deposed to having received money from Gayer in consideration of his becoming a Protestant. JOHN POWER, a fish-jolter, deposed to having received from Gayer " about £5 or £6 " for a similar consideration. THOMAS HOGAN deposed to having got from Gayer 17s. in two different sums, and two pecks of potatoes, and a house rent-free from another worship; but although he was permitted to remain in his farm, I am not aware that he obtained a lease of it. About the period referred to he sent an infant child to the priest to be christened; the child was smuggled in a covered basket to escape the observation of the Protestants.

It is but justice to say that the Protestant clergy then, and since, in the parish, have been men of irreproachable morals. They, in common with their brethren all over the kingdom, were startled at the march of nationality; they trembled for the stability, if not of their Zion, at least of its temporalities. Hence their itching and uneasy zeal

---

proselytiser named Moriarty, in consideration of which benefits he became a Protestant. JAMES KEARNEY, another convert, deposed that the considerations for which he conformed were plentiful employment and good wages from Gayer, and a house and garden rent-free; "he never paid a farthing rent; taxes and all are paid for him; has a garden behind the house the same way, and every one else has the same; none of them pay any rent." MAURICE POWER, a second fish-jolter, deposed to having bargained with Gayer to become a Protestant for the price of a horse to carry his fish. These statements were uncontradicted by Gayer, who was in court during the trial; and some of them (such as that of the houses being rent-free for converts) were of such a nature as, from the public notoriety of the facts, rendered denial in Kerry impossible.

It is difficult to resist a smile at the ludicrous character of the proselytising system, thus exhibited on the uncontradicted oaths of competent witnesses; but the horrible results of that system, the spiritual recklessness which it necessarily engenders, suggest solemn and mournful reflections. The total insensibility to real religious conviction of what nature soever, the organised hypocrisy resulting from the traffic of the people with the "Dingle Mission," appears in the following incident. A batch of Gayer's proselytes, finding their adhesion to the State Church less profitable than to make an inroad on the enemy's territories. I suppose Mr. Hurley's conversion has been chronicled in some exulting report of the progress of "the Gospel."

Well, Castletown was now peopled with a Protestant tenantry. Shanavagh also was pretty well dotted with the new settlers. A sort of miniature millennium was to be exhibited amidst the Kinneigh furze-brakes for the edification of the surrounding community. The noble landlord doubtless regarded his work with sentiments of self-applause. But—it is pleasant to be able to say it —the proselytising zeal of past years has died out at Shanavagh. The displacement of Catholics was not carried to the same extent as at Castletown. Among the tenants now residing on the land are

---

they had expected, turned off *en masse* to the Rev. Mr. M'Manus, Presbyterian minister at Miltown, and inquired what terms he would give them for becoming Presbyterians.

In Molière's *Bourgeois Gentilhomme*, Coviel denies that Monsieur Jourdain's father was a linendraper. He had, indeed, from disinterested benevolence, accommodated the public with linens ; and the public, from their grateful sense of his kindness, had gracefully and delicately presented him with certain monies. On both sides it was an elevated interchange of practical philanthropy—there was nothing of traffic in the transaction. Precisely thus did Messieurs Gayer and Company deny that they ever bribed "converts." True, some pauper Papists, from the force of sudden and simultaneous conviction, came rushing headlong into Protestantism—true, also, the Protestant agents gave money, and free houses, and employment to the converts ; but there was nothing of a *quid pro quo* in the transaction. On the one side it was conscientious adoption of religious truth ; on the other it was the most exalted benevolence and "mercy to the household of faith."

Catholics, not at present molested by their landlord, who, it is needless to say, cannot be considered responsible for transactions that occurred before he succeeded to the property.

The people in numerous parts of the kingdom feel the paramount necessity of efficient protection from the irritating persecution of which I have given a specimen. The best protection would be found in the principle of nationality. Were that principle well developed in Ireland, it would speedily absorb all wretched sectarian contentions. It would extinguish the pernicious desire to exalt any one sect or Church at the expense of any other. The doings I have briefly recorded are exploits of what is called the English interest in Ireland. The people can never be prosperous or happy until the magnates of the land cherish the Irish interest—which, if they did but know it, is their own true interest—as paramount to every other.

Every unprejudiced person will concede that the interests of real religion cannot be advanced by the system of evangelical bullyism. That much of the crime and insubordination of Ireland has arisen from the extermination—whether pious or profane —of the inhabitants, will be readily admitted, when it is remembered that in the five years from 1838 to 1842 inclusive, ejectment proceedings were taken against no less than 356,985 persons, as appears by the parliamentary papers to which the public attention was called in June, 1843, by the late Mr. Sharman Crawford, who then affirmed that the clearing process went on at an increasing ratio. And from that day to this, among the incidents most familiar to those who watch Irish events with anxious interest, are the evictions of the Irish tenantry, often under circumstances which show that the work of expulsion is prompted by political vengeance or sectarian bigotry.

It seems a curious and perverse fatality that the possession of the elective franchise, and also the want of it, have alike been fraught with bitter evils to the Irish peasantry. The exercise of the franchise in opposition to the landlord's will has drawn down extermination upon tens of thousands. That the want of the franchise in former days also caused the expulsion of the people from the soil, appears from a statement of John Keogh's in the published correspondence of Edmund Burke.

"It is a known fact," says Keogh in 1792, the year before the concession of the forty-shilling franchise, "that the Roman Catholics have been, and are every day turned out of very beneficial farms, deprived of the maintenance of themselves and their families, have lost their honest occupations, and the exercise (the most beneficial to the State) of their industry and capital, because they could not vote at an election, and to make room for those who could. *A fortiori* they have in multitudes of instances failed to obtain leases, nor can they ever obtain them on equal terms."*

---

* Burke's "Correspondence," vol. iv. p. 67.

It was natural that a peasantry thus trained to regard the franchise as conducive to their livelihood, should, on first acquiring it, have used it for several years with greater subserviency to landlord dictation than they have done in more recent times. When political corruption was at its greatest height, the landlords occasionally disposed of their electioneering interests to the candidates who bid the highest. The tenants saw that their votes were a subject of traffic by their landlords. An instance of impartial rascality is recorded of Mr. B—— F——. He sold the votes of all his tenants to two rival candidates, and pocketed the money of both. As he did not indicate to his tenantry the particular candidate for whose success he was desirous, one of the tenants, on behalf of the rest, asked his honour for which of the candidates they should vote?

"Faith, boys," answered Mr. F——, "you may take your choice. I have knocked the highest penny I could out of your votes already, so it would be unhandsome of me to hinder you from selling yourselves now to whoever will bid the best."

The tenants thanked his honour for his liberal permission, and proceeded as fast as they could to take his advice.

It is said that at a hotly contested election in the olden time, Denis D—— and his opponent ran so close to each other that the numbers were equal —a blacksmith only remaining unpolled. The blacksmith's horse was for sale. Denis bid twenty guineas; his rival bid thirty; so they went on bidding alternately, each bid being an advance of ten guineas, till at last Denis stopped, the horse being knocked down for two hundred guineas to his antagonist, who triumphantly cried to the blacksmith, "Come off and be polled." "Aye," whispered Denis to the blacksmith, *but remember who put up the horse to auction for you.*" The whisper was effectual—the artisan voted for Denis.

The expedients used to manufacture voters for an emergency were sometimes very curious. The well-known MacCoghlan, of the King's County, when hard pressed for a batch of electors to turn the scale in an approaching contest, granted freeholds to the requisite number of voters; the terms of the leases being for the life of one Jack Murphy. The voters were put in possession—the election came on—and MacCoghlan's friend, with the aid of the newly-made freeholders, carried the day. MacCoghlan, however, had not the least notion of allowing the new corps of voters to occupy his ground, now that their services were no longer necessary. He accordingly ended all their leases by shooting Jack Murphy, the common life in all. Be not horrified, good reader: Jack Murphy was an old spavined horse.

CHAPTER XVIII.

THE REPEAL DEBATE OF 1834.

> Ireland rests 'mid the rush of progression,
>   Like a frozen ship in a frozen sea;
> And the changeless stillness of life's stagnation
>   Is worse than the wildest waves could be,
>   Rending the rocks eternally.
>
> Trumpet-tongued to a people sleeping,
>   Who will speak with magic command,
> Bidding them rise—these dead men keeping
>   Watch by the dead in a silent land?
>
> SPERANZA.

O'CONNELL was at last obliged by the pressure of some members of the Tail, as well as by the remonstrances of the Repeal newspapers, to bring the question of Repeal before the foreign House of Commons on the 22nd April, 1834.

For some days previously Mr. Spring Rice, who was selected as the special champion of the Union, was observed to frisk about the purlieus of St. Stephen's with the smirking self-complacency of anticipated triumph. He knew that he should have an overwhelming majority against O'Connell's motion; he knew that whatever assertions he might make, however delusive, however contrary to truth, would be received with enthusiastic plaudits by that alien Parliament; and he had availed himself of his peculiar facilities of reference to official documents to prepare lengthy tabular statements illustrative of what he termed the giant-stride prosperity of Ireland under the Union. With these he expected to demolish O'Connell's allegations of Irish decay.

The 22nd arrived; the House was crowded with members, the gallery with strangers.

O'Connell's opening speech rehearsed the outrageous crimes committed by England against Ireland from the earliest date of their connexion. Having, by this historical retrospect, demonstrated the systematic enmity of England to this country, the speaker thence passed to the measure of the Union, dilated on the means by which it was carried, exhibited the falling off in national prosperity which had been its consequence, and concluded by moving for a select committee to inquire and report upon the means by which the destruction of the Irish Parliament was effected; of the effects of that measure upon Ireland, and upon the labourers in husbandry, and operatives in manufactures in England, and on the probable consequences of continuing the legislative Union between both countries.

O'Connell's able and comprehensive speech occupied five hours.

On the next day (the 23rd), Mr. Rice delivered his reply. He deprecated Mr. O'Connell's references to the English atrocities of former times, as being in their nature irritating, and irrelevant to the question before the House.

He alleged the danger of two independent Parliaments in one Empire, and inferred the likelihood of separation under such a system from the differences on the Regency Question in 1789. I shall not recapitulate his arguments here, as the subject will be examined in the Appendix to this work.

He alleged that the Irish Volunteers had tried to intimidate the Irish Parliament subsequently to 1782. Well had it been for Ireland if their interference had been potential. What the Volunteers sought was to procure a reform of the Irish House of Commons; of which measure the principle has been since recognised, and incorporated with the British Constitution by the English Legislature.

He alleged that the Irish Parliament had been notorious for bribery and corruption. Not more so, certainly, than the English Parliament. Lord Macaulay says that there was a time when the only way in which the Minister could manage the English Parliament was by corruption.* That the Irish Legislature was in this respect culpable only proves that it needed the reform which the Volunteers sought; not that it ought to be ex-

* "History of England."

tinguished. To urge the corruption of the unreformed Irish Parliament as a reason for putting an end to it, is extremely like saying that as death puts an end to disease, the best mode of treating a sick man is to kill him outright. Mr. Rice was amusingly impartial in his criticism. He censured the Irish Parliament on the score of its corruption; he also censured the Volunteers for trying to put an end to that corruption.

He next quoted Grattan to show that the Irish Parliament had not realised his expectations. But he took care not to quote Grattan's declaration that the Irish Parliament, with all its faults, had done more good for Ireland in fourteen years than the English Parliament had done for England in a century.

He denied that the rebellion of 1798 had been fomented in order to carry the Union.

He alleged the parental care of Ireland evinced by the Imperial Parliament; stating that no less than 175 Commissions on Irish affairs had been appointed by the House since the Union. He, however, forgot to state that the immense majority of those Commissions had ended abortively; and that the Committee of 1825, for which he claimed the merit of carrying Emancipation, was in fact the product of O'Connell's Irish agitation.

He claimed merit for England in admitting Irish corn and butter duty-free; as if it were a boon to Ireland to increase the supply of food to English customers and to ·cheapen its price for them. England has, since then, done the same for all the world; compelled by the exigencies of the English stomach to import as much food as she can get, and on the cheapest possible terms.

He inferred the giant-stride prosperity of Ireland from her largely increased exports of corn and cattle, omitting to notice that the producers of the corn and cattle were disabled by poverty from consuming the food of their own raising; and that much of the price received for the exports was again exported to England in the shape of absentee rents and absentee taxes.*

Mr. Rice stated some Acts of beneficial tendency which the United Parliament had passed for Ireland. But in claiming credit for the Union

---

* In truth, a table of exports and imports may afford no true test of a nation's prosperity. Let me borrow the following illustration from my able friend, Mr. Staunton (1844): "Fifty years ago we manufactured our own cloth; at present we get cloth from England. Fifty years ago £100 worth of corn sent from Tipperary to Dublin was consumed in Dublin, and was paid for with £100 worth of cloth made in Dublin. Here was a transaction which occasioned no exports or imports. Contrast this transaction with the present condition of affairs. The £100 worth of corn goes from Tipperary—not to Dublin, but to England; it is paid for with £100 worth of cloth made in England. An item is furnished to Spring Rice's table of exports and imports, and he cries out, 'Hurrah! I have got a triumphant proof of Irish prosperity.' But how stands the fact? In the former transaction, which exhibited no imports or exports, the Irish corn fed the Irishman, and paid for Irish manufactures. In the latter transaction, which exhibits both an import and an export, the Irish corn feeds the Englishman, and is paid for in English manufactures, while the Irish operative perishes for want of employment."

on this score he omitted to show that a reformed Irish Legislature would not have passed every one of the good laws in question, and many more into the bargain.

He produced multitudinous tables to demonstrate the improved condition and increased comforts of the Irish people generally after the Union. Cruel mockery! At the time when he spoke there was the evidence of the Railway Commissioners showing that 2,385,000 of the Irish people—being more than one-fourth of our then population—were destitute paupers for thirty weeks in every year.

He stated many grants made by the Imperial Parliament to Ireland from 1800 to 1834. But he did *not* state that the greater part of those grants had been made prior to 1821, in virtue of a stipulation at the time of the Union for their continuance for twenty-one years; nor did he state that the Imperial Parliament commenced the work of reduction as soon as the stipulated period had expired. And he did not state that the aggregate of the absentee rents and absentee taxes extorted from Ireland largely exceeded the whole of his boasted grants.

He stated that the consolidation of the Exchequers of England and Ireland in 1817 had been precipitated by the bankruptcy of Ireland. But he did not tell the House that Ireland had been made bankrupt by the fraudulent financial terms of the Union, which had forced her to contract for an expenditure she was totally unable to meet. The reader will find in the Appendix a paper in which the nature of the fiscal grievance is examined.

Mr. Rice quoted the amount of tonnage of the vessels clearing out from Irish ports, in proof of augmented commercial wealth; relying on his hearers' ignorance of the fact that tonnage is frequently a delusive index.*

He repeated the old fallacy that Irish agitation kept English capital out of the country. Just as if English capitalists were not constantly investing

---

* To illustrate this position I subjoin the following table of Dublin tonnage, which I obtained in 1842 from a well-informed source. It is close enough to accuracy to serve the purpose of the argument:

In 1832 there were about 130 vessels cleared outwards to foreign ports from Dublin. Of these 130 vessels,
        43 were in ballast (timber ships), and
        52 carried passengers. Thus,
95 out of 130 represented no profitable commerce.

Again, in 1833 there were about 180 vessels cleared out to foreign ports. Of these,
        90 were in ballast, and
        30 with passengers. Thus,
120 out of 180 represented no profitable commerce.

Again, in 1834 there were 150 vessels cleared out to foreign ports. Of these,
        64 were in ballast, and
        49 with passengers. Thus,
113 vessels out of 150 betokened no profitable commerce.

Before a table of tonnage, therefore, can be accepted as a test of commercial prosperity, it is necessary to ascertain the nature of the traffic which that tonnage represents. Of course a profitable export trade involves large tonnage; but on the other hand, large tonnage may exist without a profitable export trade.

their money in countries where real danger and real obstacles are encountered—in foreign lands, where a single hostile shot between the countries would destroy the security for repayment. "England," says Captain Marryat, "has now fifty-five millions sterling invested in American securities, which is a large sum; and the majority consider that a war will spunge out this debt."*

At a later period Lord George Bentinck gave the House of Commons a list of English investments in foreign speculations, both civil and military. He was urging an advance of money for Irish railways, and contrasting the reluctance of Parliament to give a farthing for that purpose with the lavish profusion displayed by Government as well as by private speculators in squandering English wealth on the objects he enumerated. "Send it abroad," said his lordship, "as you did some £70,000,000 for three years to foreign countries, to support their wars and to subsidise foreign nations. Send it abroad, as you did £10,000,000 or £12,000,000 in 1825; and invest £7,000,000 sterling in Peruvian mines, Mexican gold, and Mexican silver, as you did in 1825. . . . Sink your capital in no less than twenty-three foreign mining companies. . . . You also sent £13,000,000 to Portugal, and you sunk £22,000,000 in Spanish Actives, Spanish Passives, and Spanish

---

* Captain Marryat's "Diary in America," vol. ii. p. 118. London, 1839.

Timid Capitalists. 311

Deferred. To America in 1836 you sent millions. You got rid of £100,000,000 in this way."*

The English capitalist can scatter his investments broadcast all over the globe except in Ireland. Dangers of climate, dangers of war, perils of earth, air, or ocean deter him not. It seems there is only one scarecrow on the face of the earth that has terrors for his adventurous soul; and that scarecrow is Irish agitation. Mr. Spring Rice affirmed in 1834, with as much parliamentary gravity as if he expected a single human being to believe him, that the capitalists who were undeterred by the vast variety of real and substantial dangers that beset their undertakings in the most remote corners of the globe, were frightened out of Ireland by Irish agitation—that is to say, by the clack of our platform eloquence. Our subsequent experience teaches us a different lesson. There was, for a good many years after the famine, a cessation of what is called Irish agitation. We were nearly as quiet as the graves into which myriads of our countrymen had been precipitated by English misgovernment. Did English capital stream into the country, to reward our quiescence, and to verify the prophecies of Mr. Spring Rice? On the contrary, Mr. Gladstone seized the moment of our helpless prostration to add fifty-two per cent. to our previous taxes; which friendly achievement con-

---

* Speech of Lord George Bentinck in the House of Commons, 4th February, 1847.

stitutes, I presume, his claim to the enthusiastic confidence so warmly expressed by some of his Irish admirers.

The talk about English capital coming to Ireland is an impudent mockery. We should not want a shilling of English capital if England did not rob us of Irish capital. We are plundered of our own by a ceaseless process of abstraction, and then it is said to us, " Do but keep quiet, and suffer English capital to stream into your island."

Whatever other reasons may exist to prevent the investment of English capital amongst us, it is certain that the Union, by giving the English manufacturing capitalist the command of the Irish manufacture market, deprives him of at least one motive to expend his capital in establishing manufactures here. He has already got our market. What more does he require? From his mill or his factory in Yorkshire or Lancashire he can pour any amount of his fabrics into Irish circulation. Why, then, should he incur the needless risk and expense of establishing a factory in Tipperary or Roscommon?

Mr. Rice's oration occupied six hours and a half. At its close he was unable to find the amendment to which his long speech was a prelude. Some mirth was excited by his perplexity. The amendment was found on the following day, read by the Speaker, and seconded by Mr. Emerson Tennent in a speech which, pursuant to his invariable habit, he had carefully written out and got by heart. The only part of it worth extracting is the following ludicrous specimen of flippant nonsense:

"Ireland was, we were told, annihilated and extinguished by the Union, inasmuch as it then ceased to be a distinct kingdom. But on the same principle, Scotland must likewise have been annihilated when she, in 1707, ceased to be a distinct kingdom on being incorporated with England; and by a parity of reasoning, if the mere fact of incorporation, by destroying distinctness, involves extinction, England herself must have been extinguished when she became incorporated with the other two." (Loud cheers.) "So that, according to the doctrine of the Repealers, the whole Empire must at this moment be ideal, and exist, like the universe of Berkeley, only in the imagination of its inhabitants." (Renewed cheering.)

What an index to the discerning sagacity of the House is afforded by the plaudits elicited by Mr. Tennent! Here, now, are the facts:

Ireland lost two-thirds of her representation by the Union; England preserved her representation whole and intact.

Ireland lost the power of legislating for herself; England retained, unimpaired, the full power of self-legislation, and acquired, in addition, the power of legislating for Ireland.

Ireland lost the advantage of a resident Legislature and its consequent expenditure; England lost nothing, and acquired the residence not only of the Irish delegates, but of the largely augmented crop of Irish absentees whom the transfer of power to the London legislature attracted thither.

And yet a parrot-statesman is cheered by the collective wisdom when he glibly rehearses the absurd proposition that if the Union politically annihilated Ireland, which had lost much and gained nothing, it necessarily also annihilated England, which had gained much and lost nothing.

Richard Sheil made a brilliant speech in the debate. He had for some time after 1830 coquetted with Repeal. The Great Agitator had made many public appeals to him to join the movement; but vainly, until the general election of 1832 necessitated a decisive declaration on the subject. Sheil then declared himself a determined and unqualified Repealer. His accession was hailed with delight by O'Connell, who triumphantly exclaimed : "Richard's himself again." The important recruit proved a powerful ally in the parliamentary debate. Of his speech I shall quote one or two passages :

"At the time of the Union Ireland was charged with the contribution of two-seventeenths.* Was that fair ? Sir John Newport and Lord Plunket both asserted that it was most unfair ; but the fact was far better than the authority of either of them, for it turned out that Ireland was unable to pay

---

* Not two-seventeenths of the *whole* Imperial revenue, but two-seventeenths of that part of it which remained after the debt-charge of each country had been first provided for by separate taxes upon each.

it. It was necessary to make up her deficiency by a loan. Where was that loan borrowed? In England; and the revenue of Ireland was devoted to paying the interest on that loan to British capitalists."

Sheil produced great effect by his allusion to the case of Belgium:

"Now turn to Belgium. Does not the example bear us out? Hear an extract from the Declaration of Belgian Independence. After stating that the Union was obtained by fraud, the document goes on and states that 'an enormous debt and expenditure —the only dowry that Holland brought us at the time of our deplorable Union; taxes, overwhelming by their amount; laws, always voted by the Dutch *for* Holland only, and always *against* Belgium, represented so unequally in the States-General; the seat of all important establishments fixed in Holland; the most offensive partialities in the distribution of civil and military employments—in a word, Belgium treated as a conquered province, as a colony; everything rendered a revolution inevitable.'" (Loud cheers from the Repealers.) "You fear," continued Mr. Sheil, "separation may be the result of Repeal. What may not be the result of maintaining the Union? Let a few years go by; Catholic and Protestant will become reconciled (their divisions cannot last for ever); the popular power will augment; the feelings of the people will be extended to their representatives — the absentee drain will continue—the church system will still be maintained—the national mind will become one mass of heated and fiery emotion—the same disregard for the feelings and interests of Ireland will be displayed; and then (may God forfend that the event should befall!) if there be an outbreak of popular commotion here; if the prediction of the Conservatives should be fulfilled, and if your alliance with France, which is as unstable as its dynasty, should give way—then you may have cause to lament, but lament when it will be too late, that you did not give back her Parliament to Ireland."

Sir Robert Peel followed Sheil in a speech of great ability and eloquence, but which partook of the fallacious character necessarily attaching to all that was urged in defence of the Union. He treated the legislative Union as a measure whose necessity was an instinct of the British mind. "There are," he said, "truths which lie too deep for argument; truths to the establishment of which the evidence of the senses or the feelings of the heart have contributed more than the slow process of reasoning; which are graven in deeper characters than any that reasoning can either impress or efface."

This is undeniably true; and to this class of truths belongs the necessity to Ireland of self-legislation. Reason will enforce that necessity, but the slow process of reasoning is anticipated by the instinctive consciousness that an Irish Legislature, bound to Ireland by the very fact of residence, and the interests of whose members must generally run in the same groove with the interests of their country, is infinitely better qualified to promote Irish prosperity than a Parliament of strangers who inherit the traditionary British feelings towards Ireland of jealousy, hostility, or apathy, and whose idea of Union consists chiefly in taxing Ireland for British uses. All this is intuitively felt by our nation. Sir Robert's above-quoted words are indeed true, but they apply in a sense quite opposite to that which he intended. He went on to say:

"The conviction in favour of *the Union* springs from every source from which conviction in the human mind can arise. Consult your senses, consult your feelings, consult reason, history, and experience—they all concur in enforcing the same truth."

All true, provided that for "the Union" we substitute the words "self-government for Ireland."

He quoted Canning's smart saying, "Repeal the Union! Restore the Heptarchy!" but he omitted to state that the Repeal of the Union and the restoration of the Heptarchy had been instanced by Canning as absurdities analogous to a reform in Parliament. What Canning had said was, "Reform the Parliament! Repeal the Union! Restore the Heptarchy!"* Canning, in a debate in the

---

* So O'Connell told me. I have not seen the report of Canning's speech containing the passage cited. The speech next referred to I found in an old volume of the Debates of 1799.

British House of Commons on the Union in 1799, termed Catholic Emancipation "a wild and impracticable measure." These random expressions of statesmen are worth little or nothing. The supposition that the man who would give Ireland a Parliament is bound by his own principles to give separate Governments to Essex and Kent, was unworthy the intellect of Canning.

Sir Robert next urged that Repeal would be a dismemberment of the Empire.

He said that absenteeism was caused, not by the Union, but by "the cursed system of agitation."

He tried to terrify the Irish Protestants by predicting that they would have real dangers to encounter should Repeal be achieved. Since Sir Robert spoke, the Irish Protestants have had to endure a large share of the general poverty entailed by the Union, as the vast reduction of their numbers, the records of the Encumbered Estates Court, and other records also bear witness.

He manfully avowed the spirit of British usurpation by declaring that "he, for one, would never consent that to an Irish Parliament should be left the determination of the proportion of the amount that country should contribute in future to defray the general expenses of the State, and contribute to the diminution of the general public debt."

Considering that Ireland, by a system of barefaced fraud, had been swindled into an enormously disproportioned liability to that same public debt,

Sir Robert's cool avowal of the robber principle, "We will put our hands into your pockets whether you like it or not," was a miracle of impudence. It was just the thing to tell effectually with an English audience.

He denied, in defiance of O'Connell's proofs, that Pitt and Castlereagh had fomented the rebellion of 1798; alleging that those statesmen could not have afforded a rebellion at a time of foreign war, and when a mutiny broke out at the Nore. They could, however, afford to pour 137,000 troops into Ireland; and the forces thus left at their disposal well enabled them to afford a rebellion.

He defended the application to Ireland of the ruinous and infamous principle of *Divide et Impera;* alleging that this principle had protected the two parties from each other; and that he regarded it as the mediator by which, in all domestic quarrels, the fury of both sides had been allayed.

He quizzed Mr. Feargus O'Connor about the Irish King Roderick, quoting some ancient account of a barbarous ceremonial at the coronation of the kings of Ireland. Much laughter was excited by this sally.

He then wound up by a very eloquent allusion to the tremendous conflict which agitated Europe from 1803 to 1814, calling the attention of the House to the fact that among the bravest military leaders were the Irish Generals, Ponsonby and Packenham; that the British Army had been commanded by the Irish Wellington, "who, standing with his back to the sea on the rock of Lisbon, saw all Europe in dismay and her liberties jeopardised, but who never ceased from his glorious labours till he saw the whole Continent emancipated."

What the Union had to do with the valour of Ponsonby and Packenham, or with the glories of Wellington, it were difficult to tell. I presume that even if the Irish Parliament had continued to exist, England would have readily availed herself of Irish valour and Irish military genius.

"During that period," said Sir Robert (namely, from 1803 to 1814), "the reins of Government were placed in the hands of a Castlereagh and a Pitt,* and a Grattan was seen to join with a Fox in the deliberations of the Legislature of the country." It is political blasphemy to class the illustrious Grattan in the same category with the execrable patricide Castlereagh.

The conclusion of Sir Robert's speech was eloquent: "With the return of a separate Parliament, after the Catholic disabilities had been removed, what might not be expected from the triumphant rancour of religious hatred? It would amount to a complete disbanding of society. Who could set bounds, who could regulate the force of those antagonist powers? Who could so adjust the centrifugal force, if he might so term it, which

---

* Pitt died in 1806.

ought to keep Ireland within her proper orbit in the system of the empire, as to prevent her flying away into the chaos of lawless agitation, or a boundless sea of revolution? (Continued cheers.) To set such boundaries was beyond any power that man could possibly employ. To effect such a state of things required the might of that omniscient and omnipotent Power which in the material world had separated the light from the darkness (loud cheers), and prescribed the eternal laws by which the magnificent harmony of the planetary system was arranged and sustained."

Sir Robert sat down in the midst of a perfect tempest of applause, of which the enthusiasm was not diminished by the shameless libel on the Irish Catholics which he deemed it expedient to pronounce. "Triumphant rancour of religious hatred." The Protestant Parnell, in his "Historical Apology for the Irish Catholics," does their character justice in this respect: "The Irish Roman Catholics bigots!" he exclaims; "the Irish Roman Catholics are the only sect that ever resumed power without exercising vengeance." And another Protestant historian, William Cooke Taylor, LL.D., speaking of the Catholics of Ireland, says: "It is but justice to this maligned body to add, that on the three occasions of their obtaining the upper hand, they never injured a single person in life or limb for professing a religion different from their own."*

---

* Taylor's "History of the Civil Wars of Ireland," vol. i. p. 169.

In truth, one of the most prominent traits in the Irish Catholic character is the absence of religious bigotry. This trait is displayed in the fairness with which Catholic majorities in Corporations elect Protestant Mayors in due rotation. It is manifested in the fact that priests and people prefer Protestant candidates of popular principles to Catholic candidates of unpopular politics. The contests between the Protestant Spaight and the Catholic Ball, between the Protestant White and the Catholic Waldron, between the Presbyterian John Martin and the Catholic Preston, are instances in point. Our people are steadfastly faithful to the Catholic religion. But their politics are influenced, not by theological predilections, but by their desire for the success of some legitimate political object. It was stated in the debate of 1834, by Mr. Lambert of Wexford (an anti-Repealer), that the Catholic Bishop of Waterford was pelted with mud in the streets of that city because he was not a Repealer. No man of right feeling will approve such an outrage; but the fact shows that even among the lowest and most violent of the populace religious partisanship was absorbed in national prepossession. The Repealer was, with them, a character more sacred than the non-repealing prelate. The mitre was unable to protect its venerable wearer from the indignation of those who deemed their nationality outraged by his non-adhesion to their cause. "Triumphant rancour of religious hatred." Sir Robert, in this outrage upon truth, calculated that his words would influence that class of persons whom a blind, unreasoning hatred of Catholics and Catholicity diverts from the real interests of their country and of themselves. He calculated accurately.

After some further skirmishing among the smaller fry, the debate was closed by Mr. O'Connell in a speech remarkable for its vigour and vivacity. I extract from it the following passages:

"I have insisted on the incompetence of the Irish Parliament to create a new Legislature, and I am convinced I was right in that part of my argument. There was nothing to authorise the Parliament of Ireland to dispose of the Irish nation, any more than there was anything to authorise the British Parliament to dispose of the British nation to any other on the face of the globe. As to the fomenting of the rebellion in order to bring about the Union—upon that point I have been perfectly triumphant. 'But why,' said the right hon. baronet, 'should Mr. Pitt and Lord Castlereagh excite a rebellion in Ireland at a time when there was a mutiny at the Nore?' That mutiny had broken out suddenly and unexpectedly. What, therefore, had its existence to do with the fomentation of the rebellion? The English Ministry did not foresee the mutiny, though they might have conjectured the outbreak of the rebellion.* Could

---

* They might have more than conjectured it, seeing that it was designedly provoked by their intolerable tyranny.

the Union ever have been carried but for the rebellion? What answer could be given to the Report of the Secret Committee of the Irish House of Commons, from which it appeared that a person holding the rank of colonel of the United Irishmen, had given to the Government monthly reports of their secret meetings from March,* 1797? It was clear from this that the Government were cognisant of the plot, and had it in their power to put it down. But the right hon. gentleman said there were traitorous materials in Ireland. Undoubtedly there were; otherwise there could not have been a rebellion; but those materials were not of a formidable nature. They existed to a certain extent in Leinster and Ulster, and produced two skirmishes, in one of which Lord O'Neill was killed; but the only really formidable occurrence took place in Wexford. These matters were encouraged—not repressed; and the Union was brought about by fomenting the rebellion till it exploded."

Mr. O'Connell continued in a strain of great animation to reply to the arguments of several of his opponents seriatim.

The motion for the Repeal Committee was negatived by an enormous majority, the numbers being 525 against 40, including the tellers.

Mr. Stanley took no part in the debate. He was probably muzzled by Sir Robert Peel, who, with

---

* This should have been April.

characteristic policy and caution, contrived that the debate should sustain as little interruption as possible from the indecent shoutings and ferocious yells with which the Irish members had been assailed during the discussion of the Coercion Bills in the previous year. Mr. Stanley's silence was remarkable. His feelings against the Repeal were very strong; he had in 1833 declared he would "resist it to the death." That he did not now avail himself of the opportunity of renewing that declaration, is probably to be ascribed to the management of his more cautious leader, who naturally doubted his discretion.

The ministerial and English journals generally were loud in their glorifications. Spring Rice's speech they pronounced to be an unanswerable manual. No Repealer could in future dare to raise his voice against the demonstrations, clear as light, of the infinite benefits the Union had conferred upon Ireland. The question, they said, was finally set at rest; and they added much more to the same purpose.

Meanwhile, the result of the debate upon the Irish people was precisely what any man who knew the country and its inhabitants must have expected. They saw in the division a fresh proof of English hostility to their rights and of English indifference to their grievances. Mr. Rice's tabular dexterities—his "giant-stride prosperity" on paper, seemed a heartless and insolent mockery to a people of whom every fourth individual was a destitute pauper. The alacrity and fervour with which the House applauded the most hollow fallacies, afforded, to the minds of the Irish nation, fresh evidence of its total ignorance of their condition and its consequent incapacity to legislate for their advantage. Our people felt that the Constitution of Ireland was the indisputable property of the nation, and not of its Parliament, which, consequently, had no authority to sell it in 1800. Their resolve to struggle for the Repeal, to seize whatever opportunities God might send for its achievement, was thenceforth more firmly fixed than ever.

Both Houses had addressed the King, who replied in an echo of their joint address. The address and the reply contained a promise to uphold the Union; but at the same time a pledge " to remove all just causes of complaint, and to sanction all well-considered measures of improvement." The Irish people were not so foolish as to place the least faith in this pledge of King, Lords, and Commons; but they acquiesced in O'Connell's policy of testing their truth by the celebrated six years' experiment, at the end of which, as the pledges were demonstratively proved to have been mere delusions, the Repeal Association was established, and the agitation directed once more into its natural and legitimate channel. O'Connell was wrong, in my opinion, to have suspended for six years the national demand. It is scarcely conceivable that he believed the joint pledge of King, Lords, and Commons, " to remove all just causes of complaint." Moreover, the most important cause of just complaint was the refusal to restore the Irish Parliament; our greatest grievance was the Union; and this the King, Lords, and Commons declared they would uphold.

I shall pass over the six years of Whig ascendency, and the fruitless struggle for that chimera, Equality with England under the Union.*

There was, to do the Whigs justice, a fair administration of the law; and their legal appointments were excellent.

---

* In the *Anti-Union*—a most interesting periodical, commenced on the 27th December, 1798, and which reckoned Saurin among its contributors—I find, at page 63, the following: "It has been asserted that the powers of Irish representatives will be enlarged, and the rights of Irish electors improved, by Irish representatives having two shares in eleven in the direction of affairs relative to their own country only, instead of having the sole disposal of them in themselves alone."—The other nine shares being in the hands of a jealous rival! Such is the Union.

END OF VOL. I.

CHARLES DICKENS AND EVANS, CRYSTAL PALACE PRESS.

This book is a preservation facsimile.
It is made in compliance with copyright law
and produced on acid-free archival
60# book weight paper
which meets the requirements of
ANSI/NISO Z39.48-1992 (permanence of paper)

Preservation facsimile printing and binding
by
Acme Bookbinding
Charlestown, Massachusetts

2004

www.ingramcontent.com/pod-product-compliance
Lightning Source LLC
Chambersburg PA
CBHW030325240426
43673CB00040B/1279